School Effectiveness and School-based Management:
A Mechanism for Development

Yin Cheong Cheng

 The Falmer Press

(A member of the Taylor & Francis Group)
London • Washington, D.C.

UK   Falmer Press, 1 Gunpowder Square, London, EC4A 3DE
USA   Falmer Press, Taylor & Francis Inc., 1900 Frost Road, Suite 101, Bristol,
           PA 19007

First published in 1996

A catalogue record for this book is available from the British Library

Library of Congress Cataloging-in-Publication Data are available on request

ISBN 0 7507 0457 8 cased
ISBN 0 7507 0458 6 paper

Jacket design by Caroline Archer

Typeset in 10/12 pt Times by
Graphicraft Typesetters Ltd., Hong Kong

Printed in Great Britain by Biddles Ltd., Guildford and King's Lynn on paper which has a specified pH value on final paper manufacture of not less than 7.5 and is therefore 'acid free'.

School Effectiveness and
School-based Management

date shown below.

Student Outcomes and the Reform of Education

General Editor: Brian J. Caldwell, Professor of Education, Head, Department of Education Policy and Management, University of Melbourne, Australia

Student Outcomes and the Reform of Education series is concerned with the reform of public policy-makers, practitioners, researchers and scholars for much of the 1990s, with every indication of more to come with the approach of the new millenium. This series reports research and describes strategies that deal with the outcomes of reform. Without sacrificing a critical perspective the intention is to provide a guide to good practice and strong scholarship within the new arrangements that are likely to provide the framework for public education in the foreseeable future.

Contents

List of Figures and Tables

Figures

Tables

Acknowledgments

This book is developed from my keynote speech presented at the International Congress for School Effectiveness and Improvement held in Melbourne, Australia in January 1994. I would like to acknowledge the organizing committee of the Congress, particularly Professor Brian Caldwell and Professor Tony Townsend for giving me the opportunity to write the speech and this book. I am indebted to my doctoral students for their contribution to my thinking. Part of the book is based on the materials in some of our published papers. Particularly, Mr Wing Ming Cheung, Mr Bong Yiu Yuen, Mr Wai Ming Tam, and Mr Kwok Hung Ng have contributed to Chapters 5, 7, 8, and 10 respectively.

I am grateful for permission of the *International Journal of Education Management Journal, School Effectiveness and School Improvement, Education Journal, Educational Research Journal,* and *Journal of Primary Education* to use the materials in my articles published in their journals to develop this book. I also thank my research assistant Miss Winnie Leung for drawing the figures for my manuscript. Special thanks to the editors of the Falmer Press for their serious professional support.

Introduction

Currently, numerous education reforms and school restructuring movements work towards educational effectiveness and school development, not only in the West such as Canada, USA, and UK, but also in the Asia-Pacific regions such as Australia, New Zealand, Mainland China, and Hong Kong. The search of effective schools, the shift to school-based management, the emphasis on development planning in school, the ensurance of school education quality, and the implementation of various school restructuring programs are typical examples of efforts on reform movements. From these reforms, several trends can be observed:

- *From improvement to development*: There is a shift of emphasis from school improvement to school development. In the school improvement tradition, it is often assumed that school goals are clear and static and schools should be improved if they cannot achieve these goals successfully. But nowadays, educational environments are changing very quickly and school goals are not so clear and unchanging anymore. In order to adapt to the changing environments, there is a strong need to continuously develop nearly every important aspect of the school, including school goals, staff, organizational structure, school process, and technology in management, teaching and learning. Continuous school development is necessary for long-term school effectiveness. Conceptually, school improvement is a narrow, short-term and remedial concept. On the contrary, school development is a comprehensive, long-term, and formative concept;
- *From quantity to quality*: A clear shift can be seen from education quantity to education quality. People are not satisfied only with the quantity of educational service provided in the school. They are more concerned about the quality. Whether the quality of school education can meet the high and diverse expectations of school constituencies, and how it can be enhanced and assured become key issues in most of the current educational reforms;
- *From maintenance to effectiveness*: Traditionally, people are more concerned about problems happening in schools, and they make great efforts to avoid troubles and maintain normal school functioning. They often ignore whether or not schools are effective. But now, there is a shift of emphasis from school maintenance to school effectiveness. Maintaining daily functioning is not sufficient to satisfy the need for high quality school education. The present school reforms aim at maximizing school effectiveness to serve diverse educational needs;

- *From external control to school-based management*: The shift in school management from the external control mode to the self-management mode or school-based management is evident. The traditional centralized management often ignores school-based needs; it is found to be ineffective and too rigid to develop school-based initiative and meet changing school-based needs. In current school reforms, decentralization of power from the central authority to the school level, school autonomy and self-management, and participation of school constituencies are strongly encouraged to facilitate the school-based initiative for school development and effectiveness; and
- *From simplistic techniques to sophisticated technology*: In present school reforms, a clear shift of emphasis from using simplistic techniques to applying sophisticated technology in school management or planning can be observed. Traditionally, it is often assumed that school goals are obvious, static, standard and given by the central education authority. Schools are all under external control and are dependent on the management of the central authority. Therefore, there is no strong need to use any sophisticated management technology to deal with impacts from the changing environments. But now, following shifts in reforms, the use of sophisticated technologies such as the technology of strategic management, development planning, participative management, and quality assurance is strongly emphasized and promoted in schools.

Responding to these trends and developments in educational reforms and school changes, there have been considerable advances in knowledge, research, practice and policy particularly in the areas of school effectiveness and school-based management. But compared with the huge scale of the ongoing education reforms involving numerous schools, staff, and students, these advances seem to be too small to support the implementation of reforms. It is not surprising that many reforms with good will have experienced failure and frustration. There is a strong need for more empirical research and theory building to support the ongoing educational reforms and school restructuring movements. Particularly, at the current stage, how to integrate the different developments in school effectiveness research, school-based management and school strategic management into a coherent framework and to establish a mechanism for the continuous pursuit of school development and effectiveness should be a critical question to be answered if we hope to make any breakthrough to the ongoing reform movements.

This book is developed from my keynote speech presented at the International Congress for School Effectiveness and Improvement held in Melbourne, Australia in January 1994. In this book, I propose an integrative and dynamic view to understanding the complex nature of school effectiveness and school-based management, and develop a theory for establishing a school-based management mechanism for the pursuit of school development and effectiveness. There are three parts in the book. The first part focuses on the basic issues, ideas and theories of school functions and school effectiveness. The second part explains the theory of school-based management and multi-level self-management, and develops a school-based management mechanism for school development. The third part describes the practice of the school-based management mechanism in terms of leadership, staff development, curriculum change, and school-based change.

School effectiveness is a very vague concept even though it is frequently used in research and practice. Without discussing school functions, it is difficult to understand the concept of school effectiveness. In Chapter 1, school functions are classified as technical/economic functions, human/social functions, political functions, cultural functions and educational functions at the individual, institutional, community, society and international levels. According to the nature of school function, there may be as many as twenty-five categories of school effectiveness. From this classification, we can see that the traditional conception of school effectiveness is over-simplistic, making wrong assumptions about the complicated relationship between categories of school effectiveness. New directions should be proposed for studying school effectiveness. In Chapter 2, eight models are introduced to explain and assess school effectiveness from an organizational perspective. They are the goal model, resource-input model, process model, satisfaction model, legitimacy model, organizational model, ineffectiveness model, and total management model. How these models are related to the categories of school effectiveness, and how school effectiveness can be maximized on the multiple criteria are important questions in research and practice. These issues are discussed in the light of a dynamic perspective proposed in Chapter 3. According to this perspective, a school may be assumed effective if it can adapt to the changing internal and external environments and achieve the multiple goals of its multiple constituencies in the long run.

The rise of school-based management is closely related to the pursuit of school effectiveness. The theory and characteristics of school-based management are introduced in Chapter 4 to explain how school-based management can be developed as the necessary condition that facilitates schools to pursue school development and dynamic effectiveness. Also, the advantages of school-based management can be further developed and reinforced by the integration of the concepts of strategic management and self management at multi-levels in the school (Chapter 5).

In addition to the theory of school-based management and multi-level self-management, school process characteristics should be taken into consideration if we want to establish a school-based mechanism for pursuing school development and dynamic effectiveness. In Chapter 6, through generalizing the matrix conception of the school process, a new concept called *layer management* is introduced and used to construct a comprehensive unit for management. Matrix conceptions of school technology and school culture are developed to facilitate the understanding of internal school functioning. A principle of congruence is proposed to explain the effectiveness of the internal school process and direct the activities of management, teaching and learning. Finally, based on the school-based management theory, the multi-level self-management concept, the layer management concept, the matrices of school technology and school culture, and the principle of congruence, an effective school-based management mechanism is proposed for practice in school (Chapter 6).

The concept of the mechanism is new even though it is based on the integration of recent developments in theory and practice. Its theory is considerably different from traditional thinking and therefore its practice is correspondingly different from what people are now doing in schools. Leadership is the driving force for developing, establishing, and implementing this mechanism. Its nature and functions should be reconceptualized in the light of the theory of the mechanism. New concepts of *strategic leadership* and *layer leadership* are proposed and explained in Chapter 7.

Staff development and curriculum change are the key elements of current educational reforms. Whether they can be successfully implemented or not often directly influences the development and long-term effectiveness of the school. Based on the new ideas of the school-based management mechanism, the management of school-based staff development and school-based curriculum change should be different from the traditional practice. Chapters 8 and 9 introduce the alternative management models.

School changes can be divided into externally imposed school changes and school-based changes. The school-based management mechanism provides a framework for facilitating continuous school-based changes in the direction of long-term school development. In Chapter 10, the theory and strategies of managing school-based changes are developed with insights from the new mechanism.

Since the theories and ideas proposed in the above chapters are different from the traditional thinking about school effectiveness and school-based management, a new set of implications can be drawn for research, policy, and development for the ongoing or future educational reforms and school restructuring movements.

I hope researchers, educators, teachers, educational administrators, policy-makers, reform consultants, and all those involved in school reforms would have opportunities to reflect on current developments and develop their schools successfully from a more comprehensive perspective. I believe this book can make a contribution to creating such an opportunity and can benefit the ongoing and future efforts on school development and effectiveness in different parts of the world.

Part I

School Effectiveness

Chapter 1

School Functions and School Effectiveness

School effectiveness is still a very vague concept even though it is often used in the literature of school management and improvement. To different people, the definition of school effectiveness may be very different. Also, school effectiveness is often confused with *school efficiency*. The critical elements of effectiveness conceptualization such as *what criteria, whose criteria, effective for whom, who to define, how to evaluate, when to evaluate,* and *under what environmental constraints* are often problematic because there seem no standard elements accepted by all concerned constituencies for evaluation. A school is an organization in a changing and complicated social context, bounded with limited resources and involving multiple constituencies such as education authorities, school administrators, teachers, students, parents, taxpayers, educators, and the public (Cheng, 1993j). In such a social context, understanding school effectiveness is quite difficult without discussing school functions. Schools may have different performance and effectiveness for different functions or goals. For example, some schools may be good at helping students' personal development, whereas some may be excellent in producing competent technicians for the needs of the community. Therefore, it is necessary to clarify the aims and functions of schools before we can discuss what *is* school effectiveness.

School Functions at Multi-levels

Twenty years ago, when reviewing school effectiveness in the USA, Averch, *et al.* said that 'most of this century, public schools in the United States have been viewed as carrying out five important functions: *socialization*, a unifying and disciplinary force in a society of diverse origins; *sorting*, identifying people's future socioeconomic roles; *custody*, the childsitting function; *knowledge and skills training*, developing a literate popular, with at least a minimum of job-related skills and encouragement of such *individual attributes as creativity and self-reliance*' (1974: 3). In 1989, the President of USA convened the Education Summit with the nation's Governors and they embarked on a historic venture to change the national educational emphasis. They initiated six national education goals as a framework for action:

1   By the year 2000, all children in America will start school ready to learn;
2   By the year 2000, the high school graduation rate will increase to at least 90 per cent;

3   By the year 2000, American students will leave grades four, eight, and twelve having demonstrated competency in challenging subject matter, including English, mathematics, science, history, and geography; and every school in America will ensure that all students learn to use their minds well, so they may be prepared for responsible citizenship, further learning, and productive employment in our modern economy;

4   By the year 2000, US students will be first in the world in science and mathematics achievement;

5   By the year 2000, every adult American will be literate and will possess the knowledge and skills necessary to compete in a global economy and exercise the rights and responsibilities of citizenship; and

6   By the year 2000, every school in America will be free of drugs and violence and will offer a disciplined environment conducive to learning (The National Education Goals Panel, 1992: 4–5).

From these goals, the functions of US schools should offer a disciplined environment, help American children or students be ready to learn, graduate successfully, acquire competency in academic subjects, particularly mathematics and science, and be prepared for responsible citizenship, further learning, and productive employment in a modern global economy. In drafting these goals, the National Panel emphasized the contribution of the education system to the nation's strength and international economic competition (1992: 2).

For the case of Hong Kong, the fundamental aim of school education service is to 'develop the potential of every child, so that our students become independent-minded and socially-aware adults, equipped with the knowledge, skills and attitudes which help them to lead a full life as individuals and play a positive role in the life of the community' (Education and Manpower Branch, 1993: 8) and therefore the schools and their support services should aim to deliver the following services (pp. 14–22):

1   To the individual, 'every school should help all its students, whatever their ability, and including those with special educational needs, to develop their potential as fully as possible in both academic and non-academic directions' (p. 14), including literacy, numeracy, learning skills, practical and technical skills, social, political and civic awareness, personal growth, physical development, and aesthetic and cultural development; and

2   To the community, 'school education should aim to meet the community's need for people who can contribute to Hong Kong's social and economic development' (p. 14).

In addition to the above formal goals related to education of students, schools also serve other implicit or explicit functions at different levels in the society according to both Functionalism or the Conflict Theory in sociology (Blackledge and Hunt, 1985; Cheng, 1991a). For example, Functionalism suggests that school education can facilitate social mobility and social change but the Conflict Theory argues that school education reproduces class structure and maintains class inequality at the society level. In the light of commonly espoused education goals and organizational studies and development studies (for example, Bolman and Deal, 1991a; Kazamias and Schwartz, 1977; Townsend, 1994), we may classify the potential school functions into five types: technical/economic functions, human/social functions, political functions, cultural functions, and educational functions, as shown in Table 1.1.

Technical/economic functions refer to the contribution of schools to the technical or economic developments and needs of the individual, the institution, the local community, the society and the international community. At the individual level, schools can help students to acquire knowledge and skills necessary to survive and compete in a modern society or a competitive economy, and provide staff job training and opportunity. At the institutional level, schools are service organizations providing quality service; also they serve as a life-place or workplace in society for clients, employers and all those concerned. At the community and society levels, schools serve the economic or instrumental needs of the local community, supply quality labor forces to the economic system, modify or shape economic behaviors of students (future customers and citizens) (McMahon, 1987) and contribute to the development and stability of the manpower structure of the economy (Hinchliffe, 1987). At the international level, school education supplies the high quality forces necessary in international competitions, economic cooperation, earth protection, and technology and information exchange.

Human/social functions refer to the contribution of schools to human developments and social relationships at different levels of the society. As indicated in nearly all formal education goals, at the individual level schools help students to develop themselves psychologically, socially and physically, and help them develop their potential as fully as possible. At the institutional level, a school is a social entity or social system composed of different human relationships. The quality of social climate and relationships in it often determines the quality of work life and learning life for teachers and students. At the community and society levels, according to the perspective of Functionalism, schools serve the social needs or functions of the local community, support social integration of multiple and diverse constituencies of society, facilitate social mobility within the existing class structure, reinforce social equality for all people of different backgrounds, select and allocate competent people to appropriate roles and positions, and contribute to social change and development in the long run (Cheng, 1991a). From the alternative view of the Conflict Theory, it is possible that schools reproduce the existing social class structure and perpetuate social inequality (Blackledge and Hunt, 1985). Due to the growing global consciousness (Beare and Slaughter, 1993), schools are expected to play an important role in preparing students for international harmony, social cooperation, global human relationship, and elimination of national, regional, racial, and gender biases at the international level such that both the local community and the international community can benefit in the long run.

Table 1.1: *School functions at multi-levels*

	Technical/Economic Functions	Human/Social Functions	Political Functions	Cultural Functions	Educational Functions
Individual (students, staff, etc.)	• Knowledge and skills training • Career training • Job for staff	• Psychological developments • Social developments • Potential developments	• Development of civic attitudes and skills	• Acculturation • Socialization with values, norms, and beliefs	• Learning how to learn and develop • Learning how to teach and help • Professional development
Institutional	• As a life place • As a work place • As a service organization	• As a social entity/system • As a human relationship	• As a place for political socialization • As a political coalition • As a place for political discourse or criticism	• As a center for cultural transmission and reproduction • As a place for cultural revitalization and integration	• As a place for learning and teaching • As a center for disseminating knowledge • As a center for educational changes and developments
Community	• Serving the economic or instrumental needs of the community	• Serving the social needs of the community	• Serving the political needs of the community	• Serving the cultural needs of the community	• Serving the educational needs of the community
Society	• Provision of quality labor forces • Modification of economic behavior • Contribution to the manpower structure	• Social integration • Social mobility/social class perpetuation • Social equality • Selection and allocation of human resources • Social development and change	• Political legitimization • Political structure maintenance and continuity • Democracy promotion • Facilitating political developments and reforms	• Cultural integration and continuity • Cultural reproduction • Production of cultural capital • Cultural revitalization	• Development of the education professions • Development of education structures • Dissemination of knowledge and information • Learning society
International	• International competition • Economic cooperation • International trade • Technology exchange • Earth protection • Sharing information	• Global village • International friendship • Social cooperation • International exchanges • Elimination of national/regional/racial/gender biases	• International coalition • International understanding • Peace/against war • Common interests • Elimination of conflicts	• Appreciation of cultural diversity • Cultural acceptance across countries/regions • Development of global culture	• Development of global education • International education exchanges and cooperation • Education for the whole world

Political functions refer to the contribution of schools to the political developments at different levels of society. At the individual level, schools help students to develop positive civic attitudes and skills to exercise the rights and responsibilities of citizenship. At the institutional level, schools act as a place for systematically socializing students into a set of political norms, values and beliefs, or for critically discussing and reflecting on the existing political events. Schools often become a political coalition of teachers, parents, and students that can contribute to the stability of the political power structure. At the community and society levels, schools play an important role to serve the political needs of the local community, legitimize the authority of the existing government, maintain the stability of political structure, promote awareness and movement of democracy, and facilitate the planned political developments and changes (Thomas, 1983). The growing awareness of international dependence reinforces the need for the contribution of school education to international understanding, global common interest, international coalitions, peace movements against war, and elimination of conflicts between regions and nations. It seems that the political functions of schools should also be important at the international level for the long term benefit of the world.

Cultural functions refer to the contribution of schools to the cultural transmission and development at different levels of society. At the individual level, schools help students to develop their creativity and aesthetic awareness and to be socialized with the successful norms, values and beliefs of society. At the institutional level, schools act as a place for systematic cultural transmission to and reproduction of the next generation, cultural integration among the multiple and diverse constituencies, and cultural revitalization from the outdated traditions. At the community and society levels, schools often serve as a cultural unit carrying the explicit norms and expectations of the local community, transmit all the important values and artifacts of the society to students, integrate the diverse subcultures from different backgrounds, and revitalize the strengths of the existing culture such that the society or the nation can reduce internal conflicts and wastage and build up a unifying force for national benefits. Of course, the Conflict Theory provides an alternative view that for different classes of the society, schools socialize students with different sets of values and beliefs — different cultural capital such that some people may benefit more from the prestige cultural capital but some suffer from the poor culture (Apple, 1982; Cheng, 1991a; Collins, 1971; Giroux, 1981). In other words, schools reproduce and perpetuate cultural inequality within the society. Obviously, Functionalism and Conflict Theory have different views on the cultural functions of schools at the society level. At the international level, schools can encourage appreciation of cultural diversity and acceptance of different norms, traditions, values and beliefs in different countries and regions, and finally contribute to the development of global culture through integration of different cultures.

Education functions of schools refer to the contribution of schools to the development and maintenance of education at the different levels of society. Traditionally, education is often perceived as only a means for achieving the economic, social, political, and cultural values and goals. Due to the rapid development and change in nearly every aspect of the world, people begin to accept education in itself as an important value or goal. Education represents learning and development. Like economics, politics, culture, and social relationship, education becomes a necessary component of our life particularly in an era of great change and transformation. The content, system, and structure of education need to be developed and maintained. At the individual level, it is important for schools to help students to learn how to learn and help teachers to learn how to teach. Also, facilitating teachers' professional development is one of the key education functions at this level. At the institutional level, schools serve as a place for systematic learning, teaching, and disseminating knowledge, and as a center for systematically experimenting and implementing educational changes and developments. At the community and society levels, schools provide service for different educational needs of the local community, facilitate developments of education professions and education structures, disseminate knowledge and information to the next generation, and contribute to the formation of a learning society. In order to encourage mutual understanding among nations and build up a global family for the younger generation, schools can contribute to the development of global education and international education exchange and co-operation. At the international level, schools can make an important contribution to education for the whole world.

As shown in Table 1.1, there may be 25 categories of school functions in a typology composed of five types of functions at five different levels. Taking the time span into consideration, school functions may be further divided into two types: *long-term functions* and *short-term functions*. Long-term functions refer to the contributions or effects of schools that happen and continue in a long time (more than a few years). These functions are often very important even though they may not be so obvious to people's perception. Short-term functions refer to those contributions or effects of schools that occur explicitly in a short time (a few months or less than a few years). In general, for each type of the technical/economic, human/social, political, cultural or educational functions, there may exist both long-term and short-term functions even though short-term functions may be often more easily identified at the individual level or the institutional level.

To different people or constituencies, the expectations of school functions are often different. Some people may be more concerned with the technical and economic functions but others with the political functions. Some people may pay attention to the functions at the individual levels, but others may focus more on the functions at the community level or society level. Even though in the past years school functions at the international level might not attract much attention, there seems to be a growing concern about it in recent years (Beare and Slaughter, 1993).

To different academic disciplines, the emphasis on types and levels of school functions may be different too. For example, school functions at the individual level may receive more attention in educational psychology. For the sociology of education, school functions at the society level, particularly those related to social mobility, equality and class stratification, may attract more concern. Obviously, economics of education often focuses on the economic functions of schools at different levels. In the field of school management or organizational behavior, school functions at the institutional level are inevitably the major topic of study.

Based on different beliefs and emphases on the types of school functions, different strategies or policies are usually proposed for school management and improvement. Traditionally, people often focus narrowly on a few categories of school functions, such as technical functions and social functions at the individual levels, and ignore the other categories. The ignorance of a wide spectrum of school functions inevitably sets a tight limit to policymaking and management effort for school improvement. Therefore, it is not a surprise that an educational reform policy mainly based on the beliefs about technical functions at the individual level cannot improve the cultural or social functions at the individual level or other levels.

Categories of School Effectiveness

From the conception of school functions, we may define *school effectiveness* as the capacity of the school to maximize school functions or the degree to which the school can perform school functions, when given a fixed amount of school input. Since there are five types of school functions, school effectiveness may be further classified into five types: technical/economic effectiveness, human/social effectiveness, political effectiveness, cultural effectiveness and educational effectiveness. For example, technical/economic effectiveness represents the capacity of the school to maximize technical/economic school functions. Furthermore, since there are five levels of school functions, school effectiveness may be classified into five levels: school effectiveness at the individual level, at the institutional level, at the community level, at the society level, and at the international level. By the combination of 5 types and 5 levels, there are 25 categories of school effectiveness in a typology as shown in Table 1.2.

From an input–output perspective, school effectiveness is often assumed as a combination of or a comparison (or even a ratio, if in a quantitative sense) between what a school can produce (i.e., school output or function) and what has been put into the school (i.e., school input). Assuming that this preliminary idea of school effectiveness is acceptable, we adapt Lockheed's (1988) ideas to school organizations and use them to differentiate school effectiveness from school efficiency in the following way:

- School effectiveness — If the discussion is mainly in terms of non-monetary inputs or processes (number of textbooks, classroom organization, professional training of teachers, teaching strategy, learning arrangements, etc.), then the comparison of output function to non-monetary input (or process) may be called school effectiveness.
- School efficiency — If the discussion is mainly in terms of monetary input (for example, $1000 input per student, cost of books, salary, opportunity cost, etc.), then the comparison between school output function and monetary

Table 1.2: Categories of school effectiveness

Levels	Technical/Economic Effectiveness (TE)	Human/Social Effectiveness (SE)	Political Effectiveness (PE)	Cultural Effectiveness (CE)	Educational Effectiveness (EE)
School Effectiveness at Individual Level	TE at Individual	SE at Individual	PE at Individual	CE at Individual	EE at Individual
School Effectiveness at Institutional Level	TE at Institutional	SE at Institutional	PE at Institutional	CE at Institutional	EE at Institutional
School Effectiveness at Community Level	TE at Community	SE at Community	PE at Community	CE at Community	EE at Community
School Effectiveness at Society Level	TE at Society	SE at Society	PE at Society	CE at Society	EE at Society
School Effectiveness at International Level	TE at International	SE at International	PE at International	CE at International	EE at International

input may be called school efficiency. With the consideration of the five types of school functions at five levels, school efficiency may be similarly classified into twenty-five categories including technical/economic efficiency, human/social efficiency, political efficiency, cultural efficiency, and educational efficiency at the individual, institutional, community, society and international levels.

The above classification of school effectiveness (or efficiency) into twenty-five categories can help us to clarify what kind of school effectiveness is under discussion. The term *school effectiveness* is used broadly in past studies but it may have different meanings. Some studies are interested in the school's social effectiveness but the others are interested in cultural effectiveness or economic effectiveness. It is important to point out that the relationship between the five types of school effectiveness, between the five levels of school effectiveness, and even between effectiveness and efficiency may be very complicated, and not necessarily positive. A school's high technical effectiveness at the individual level does not necessarily promise high technical effectiveness or social effectiveness at the society level, although people often assume the existence of such a positive relationship (Grosin, 1994). For example, the success of some technical training in school does not imply high productivity for the society if these skills learned in school are found to be outdated (or useless) in students' later career life. Furthermore, numerous studies from radical perspectives challenge the traditional belief of schools' positive functions, such as social mobility for the society (Blackledge and Hunt, 1985; Cheng, 1991a). To a great extent, the relationship between technical effectiveness and social effectiveness or cultural effectiveness is very controversial in the field of sociology of education. Also, the relationship between technical effectiveness and technical efficiency may not be simple. It is often the hot topic for study in the field of economics of education (Cheng and Ng, 1992; Psacharopoulos, 1987).

In general, a school high in a few of the twenty-five categories of effectiveness may not be high in the other categories. Furthermore, enhancement of one type of school effectiveness does not necessarily promise increase in the other four types. Similarly, increasing school effectiveness at one level does not necessarily result in improvement of effectiveness at the other levels. We should be careful in the discussion of school effectiveness. From the above conception of school effectiveness for multi-functions at multi-levels, some new directions can be proposed for consideration in future research, policy-making and practice, as contrasted with the old traditions in Table 1.3.

Traditionally, the discussion of school effectiveness is often based on the simplistic conception of school functions, particularly on technical and social functions at the individual or institutional levels only. This sets a great limitation to generate significant implications for effective school improvement and development. Therefore, we should be more aware of its multiplicity and complexity in nature. If possible, a wider spectrum of school effectiveness with both short-term and long-term time frames should be taken into consideration.

Table 1.3: New directions and old traditions in studying school effectiveness

	New Directions	**Old Traditions**
Nature of School Effectiveness	• Based on multiple conception of school functions: technical, social, political, cultural and educational • Conception at five levels: individual, institutional, community, society and international • Both short-term and long-term considerations	• Biased on simplistic conception of school functions, particularly on technical and social functions only • Conception only at one to two levels, particularly at the individual or institutional levels • Mainly short-term consideration
Expectation of School Effectiveness	• To different constituencies, different types of school effectiveness are expected • Dilemmas exist	• Emphasizing mainly technical or social effectiveness, assuming no big differences in expectations • Dilemmas are ignored
Assumption about Relationships	• Complicated relationship between types • Complicated relationship between levels • Complicated relationship between effectiveness and efficiency • Between-relationships not necessarily positive, need to be studied and managed	• Positive relationship between types • Positive relationship between levels • Positive relationship between effectiveness and efficiency • No strong need to study and manage between-relationships
Disciplines for Investigation	• Interdisciplinary cooperation and efforts are needed	• Mainly single discipline is used; separate efforts are made
Focus of Study and Discussion	• Multi-types of effectiveness • Multi-levels of effectiveness • Relationship between types • Relationship between levels • Relationship between effectiveness and efficiency	• Separate/single type of effectiveness • Separate/single level of effectiveness
Implications for Management and Policy	• To maximize effectiveness in multi-types at multi-levels • To maximize efficiency in multi-types at multi-levels • Need to ensure congruence between types and between levels • Need to ensure congruence between effectiveness and efficiency	• Mainly to maximize effectiveness in separate type at single level • Mainly to maximize efficiency in separate type at single level • No need to ensure congruence between types and levels • No need to ensure congruence between effectiveness and efficiency

In traditional discussion, people usually emphasize mainly the technical/economic or human/social effectiveness and assume no big difference in expectations of different constituencies at different levels, such as parents, students, teachers, administrators, community, economic sector, social service sector, policy-makers, the public, etc. They may ignore the potential dilemmas from differences in the constituencies' expectations on school effectiveness. If we agree that there are multi-functions of schools and diverse expectations of the constituencies at different levels, inevitably dilemmas do exist in any management efforts for school effectiveness. The study and management of these dilemmas should be one of the key focuses in current movements of school effectiveness.

Based on the simplistic conception of school effectiveness, there is a strong traditional belief that the relationship of school effectiveness between types, between levels, or between effectiveness and efficiency is often positive and we do not need to study and manage these between-relationships. As discussed previously, this belief is very problematic. The between-relationships may be very complicated, not necessarily positive. The increase in one type of school effectiveness does not promise the other. Therefore, there is a strong need for us to study these between-relationships if we want to make sensible efforts for school effectiveness. Traditionally, school effectiveness studies may involve mainly one single discipline, for example, educational psychology, or depend on separate efforts. Obviously, it is not sufficient for studying the complexity of school effectiveness. We should encourage inter-disciplinary cooperation, such as involving educational psychology, economics of education, sociology of education, anthropology, organizational theories, etc., and efforts to investigate school effectiveness. The focus should include multi-types of effectiveness at multi-levels, relationship between types, relationship between levels, and relationship between effectiveness and efficiency. Also, there is urgent need to develop a comprehensive theory to explain these between-relationships and direct actions for enhancement of school effectiveness.

Traditionally, people often focus on maximizing school effectiveness or efficiency of separate types at one or two levels without considering the other categories of effectiveness and efficiency. No measure is implemented to ensure the congruence between types of school function or effectiveness, between levels, and between effectiveness and efficiency. It is not surprising that most of the policy efforts or management initiatives may not be so successful for a wide spectrum of effectiveness and efficiency in schools, if not resulting in failure. Taking the multiplicity of school effectiveness into consideration, the future direction for policy and management should aim to maximize school effectiveness and efficiency in multi-types at multi-levels. Of course, how to ensure congruence between types, between levels, and between effectiveness and efficiency, how to enhance not only one but all the five types of school effectiveness at the five levels, and how to solve the dilemmas from the different expectations of various constituencies should be critical questions to be considered in the current movements of educational reforms.

Chapter 2

Models of School Effectiveness

In Chapter 1, we discussed the different categories of school functions and school effectiveness. Without a theoretical model as a guide to further interpret school effectiveness and select criteria to assess it, it is still very difficult, if not impossible, to determine whether one school is effective or not. The school is a kind of organization, and therefore school effectiveness may be discussed in the light of organizational literature. In this chapter, I will discuss the models that can be used to explain and assess school effectiveness from an organizational perspective.

Cameron (1984) and Cameron and Whetten (1983) had made a comprehensive review of the literature on organizational effectiveness. Cameron (1984) suggested seven major models that can be used to study effectiveness of organizations in general, including the goal model, system-resource model, internal process model, strategic-constituencies model, competing-values model, legitimacy model and ineffectiveness model. To a great extent, the competing-values model is a submodel of the strategic constituencies model, both emphasizing constituencies' needs, preferences, and satisfaction. My previous papers, Cheng (1990b) and Cheng (1993i), adapted their ideas to school organizations by combining these two models and adding the organizational learning model into the classification. Recently, the development and emphasis of total quality management in education indicates a new conception of school effectiveness that should be included. Therefore, with the reference of Cameron (1984) and my previous papers, I will classify in this chapter the conceptions of school effectiveness into eight models including the goal model, resource-input model, process model, satisfaction model, legitimacy model, organizational model, ineffectiveness model, and total management model. The basic characteristics of the models are summarized in Table 2.1.

The Goal Model

The goal model is very often used in evaluating school performance or studying school effectiveness. Many people believe that the formally stated goals should be the basic requirements for schools to fulfill, and therefore they should be used to assess school effectiveness. The model assumes that there are clearly stated and generally accepted goals for measuring school effectiveness, and that a school is effective if it can accomplish its stated goals with given inputs. This model is useful if the school outcomes are clear and the effectiveness criteria commonly accepted by all involved constituencies are available.

Table 2.1: Models of school effectiveness

	Conception of School Effectiveness	Conditions for Model Usefulness	Evaluation Indicators/Key Areas
Goal Model	• Achievement of stated goals	• Goals are clear, consensual, time-bound and measurable; Resources are sufficient	• Objectives listed in the school/program plans, e.g., achievements
Resource-Input Model	• Achievement of needed resources and inputs	• There is a clear relationship between inputs and outputs; Resources are scarce	• Resources procured, e.g., quality of student intake, facilities, financial support, etc.
Process Model	• Smooth and 'healthy' internal process	• There is a clear relationship between process and outcome	• Leadership, communication, participation, coordination, social interaction, etc.
Satisfaction Model	• Satisfaction of all powerful constituencies	• The demands of the constituencies are compatible and cannot be ignored	• Satisfaction of Education Authorities, management board, administrators, teachers, parents, students, etc.
Legitimacy Model	• Successful legitimate or marketing activities for school survival	• The survival and demise among schools must be assessed	• Public relations, marketing, public image, reputation, status in the community, accountability, etc.
Ineffectiveness Model	• Absence of characteristics of ineffectiveness in school	• There is no consensual criteria of effectiveness; but strategies for school improvement are needed	• Existing conflicts, dysfunctions, difficulties, defects, weaknesses, etc.
Organizational Learning Model	• Adaptation to environmental changes and internal barriers	• Schools are new or changing; the environmental changes cannot be ignored	• Awareness of external needs and changes, internal process monitoring, program evaluation, development planning
Total Quality Management Model	• Total management of internal people and process to meet strategic constituencies' needs	• The constituencies' needs are compatible; the technology and resources are available for total management	• Leadership, people management, strategic planning, process management, quality results, constituencies' satisfaction, impact on society, etc.

The indicators of school effectiveness are often objectives listed in school plans and program plans, particularly those related to quality of learning and teaching environment, and academic achievements in the public examinations, etc. The usefulness of the model is often limited because it depends on the clear, measurable, time-bound, and all accepted goals that are often impossible. For example, teachers may be more concerned with students' development of character and personality, but parents more concerned with students' examination achievements. Employers may emphasize those job-related attitudes and skills of students and policymakers may be more concerned with school contribution to political stability or economic growth. Even though there is diversity in school goals expected by different constituencies, in many countries in the Asia–Pacific area, student achievement in public examinations is frequently used as the major goal outcomes in measuring school effectiveness. The ignorance of other educational effects on the school's educational processes may yield adverse effects to assess the success of a school.

According to the five types of school functions at five levels, there are technical/economic goals, human/social goals, political goals, cultural goals, and educational goals at the individual, institutional, community, society, and international levels for schools to achieve in different timeframes. Within each category of school goals, there may also be a number of objectives. It would be important to include a comprehensive set of school goals and objectives when the goal model is used to assess school effectiveness. But given the limited resources, it is often very difficult for schools to achieve multiple goals in a short time (Cameron, 1978; Hall, 1987). Inevitably, dilemmas exist in maximizing effectiveness on the multiple goals with limited resources.

The Resource-Input Model

Due to the existing pressure of different expectations of multiple powerful constituencies, schools often need to pursue multiple but often inconsistent goals. Resources become the critical element in school functioning. The resource-input model assumes that more scarce and valued resources input are needed for schools to be more effective. A school is effective if it can acquire its needed resources. Therefore, inputs and acquisition of resources become the primary criteria of effectiveness (Etzioni, 1969; Yuchtman and Seashore, 1967). Quality of student intake, facilities, resources, and financial support procured from the central education authority, alumni, parents, sponsoring body or any outside agents are important indicators of effectiveness.

This model is useful if the connections between inputs and outputs are clear (Cameron, 1984) and the resources are very limited for the school to achieve goals. In some Asian countries and cities, for example, Hong Kong, quality student input is often assumed as an important indicator of a school's success. Attraction of high quality student input seems to be a necessary condition for some schools to become effective or achieve high academic performance in public examinations. On the other hand, in the inner city schools of some Western societies, students from low socioeconomic status families often bring with them a lot of behavioral and criminal problems from their community that seriously hinder normal educational processes in school. In order to help problem students, more resources are needed if not reallocated from other school purposes. Capacity of acquiring resources represents the potential of a school's becoming effective, particularly in a context of great resource competition. To some extent, the model redresses the limitation of the goal model, linking effectiveness to the environmental context and resources input.

Obviously, this model has its defects because its overemphasis on acquisition of inputs may reduce the school's effort put to educational processes and outputs. The acquired resources may become wastage if they cannot be used efficiently to serve school functions. Taking the five types of school functions at five levels into consideration, the contribution of resource-effective schools may be indirect and limited mainly at the institutional level, depending on whether the resources can be used to support a wide range of school functions.

The Process Model

From a system perspective, school inputs are converted into school performance and output through a transformational process in school. The nature and quality of school process often determine the quality of output and the degree to which the school goals can be achieved. Particularly in education, experience in the school process is often taken as a form of educational aims and outcomes. Therefore, the process model assumes that a school is effective if its internal functioning is smooth and healthy. It further argues that to view effectiveness in terms of a process instead of an end state is a solution that at least minimizes many of the obstacles to effectiveness (Steers, 1977). Therefore, internal activities or practices in school are taken as the important criteria of school effectiveness (e.g. Cheng, 1986b; 1993h; 1994d). Leadership, communication channels, participation, coordination, adaptability, planning, decision making, social interactions, school climate, teaching methods, classroom management and learning strategies are often used as indicators of effectiveness. School process in general includes management process, teaching process and learning process. Thus the selection of indicators may be based on these processes, classified as management effectiveness indicators (for example, leadership, decision making), teaching effectiveness indicators (for example, teaching efficacy, teaching methods), and learning effectiveness indicators (for example, learning attitudes, attendance rate).

If there is a clear relationship between school process and educational outcomes, this model should be useful. For example, democratic education is strongly emphasized in schools. If we believe that democratic management process and democratic teaching process in school are the necessary conditions for implementing democratic education (Cheng, 1987b; 1987c), then the indicators of democratic process in school such as participation in decision making and partnership in teaching and learning may be chosen as criteria for evaluating school effectiveness in implementing democratic education. To a certain extent, the current emphasis on leadership and school culture to school effectiveness may reflect the importance of the process model (Caldwell and Spinks, 1992; Cheng, 1994d; Sergiovanni, 1984).

The process model has its limitations, such as difficulty in monitoring processes and gathering related data and the focus on means instead of ends (Cameron, 1978). If we assume that schools need to perform the five types of school functions such as technical/economic functions, human/social functions, political functions, and educational functions at the individual, institutional, community, society and international levels, the usefulness of the process model depends on the knowledge of the relationship of the school process to these functions. If we know the relationship well, we may predict school effectiveness from the characteristics of the school process. But unfortunately, up to now there still lacks systematic and comprehensive knowledge about this relationship that can direct the design of school process for various types of school effectiveness, even though we know some aspects and have made a lot of positive assumptions about some important factors such as leadership, participative decision making and school culture, etc.

The Satisfaction Model

School effectiveness may be a relative concept, depending on the expectations of concerned constituencies or parties. If expected school goals are high and diverse, it will be difficult for schools to achieve them and meet the needs and expectations of multiple constituencies. If expected school goals are low and simple, it will be easier for schools to achieve them and satisfy the expectations of constituencies such that schools may be more easily perceived as effective. Furthermore, the objective measurement of goal achievement is often technically difficult and conceptually controversial. Therefore, satisfaction of powerful and strategic constituencies instead of some objective criteria is often used as the critical element to assess school effectiveness. Recently, there is a strong emphasis on quality in school education. The concept of quality is, in fact, closely related to the satisfaction of clients' (or customers', constituencies') needs or the conformance to clients' requirements and expectations (Crosby, 1979; Tenner and Detoro, 1992). From this point, the recent demands for education quality reinforce the use of constituencies' satisfaction in explaining and assessing school effectiveness.

The satisfaction model defines that a school is effective if all of its strategic constituencies are at least minimally satisfied. It assumes that the functioning and survival of a school are under the influence of its strategic constituencies, for example, principal, teachers, school management board, education authority, parents, students and the public, and school actions are mainly reactive to the demands of the strategic constituencies. Therefore, satisfaction of these demands is the basic criterion for school effectiveness (Keeley, 1984; Zammuto, 1982; 1984).

If the demands of all the powerful constituencies are compatible and the school has to respond to these demands, this model may be useful in studying school effectiveness. The indicators of effectiveness are often the satisfaction of students, teachers, parents, administrators, education authority, school management committee, or alumni, etc. In some Eastern societies such as Hong Kong and Tai-wan, the school management board of a school has a dominant influence on the school. Comparatively, the influence of parents, students, teachers and the public is not so strong. Therefore, the satisfaction of the school management board is often the most important indicator of school effectiveness. If the school management board demands high achievement in academic and athletic activities, the school is effective only if it can satisfy these demands.

If the demands of powerful constituencies conflict and cannot be satisfied at the same time, the model may not be appropriate. Recently, due to the drastic society developments and serious international competition, more people become the strategic constituencies of schools, and more parties have different interests in school functions. Previously, people may be concerned with only school functions at the individual level or the institutional level. Parents, students, teachers and management board members may be the only powerful constituencies. But now, the economic sector, the public and the central government have also very strong expectations of the school functions at the community level, the society level and the international level, and they tend to cast more influence on schools and often become the 'hidden or overt strategic constituencies' of schools. Inevitably, schools have more powerful constituencies than before. The expectations of these multiple powerful constituencies are often high, diverse and even inconsistent. It is obviously difficult for schools to satisfy all these needs and expectations in a short time when the resources available for schools are so limited.

The Legitimacy Model

In the past decades, the educational environment changed slowly and the external challenges to school were relatively very small. There might not be any big problem to threaten the survival of schools, particularly when the traditional respect for school education was still valid and the resources for education were not competitive. But now, under the impacts of rapid changes and developments in the local com-munity as well as in the global context, the educational environment for schools becomes more challenging and competitive. On one hand, schools have to compete seriously for resources and overcome internal barriers and on other hand they have to face the external challenges and demands for accountability and 'value for money' (Education and Manpower Branch and Education Department, 1991; Education Commission, 1994). It is nearly impossible for schools to continue or survive without the legitimacy in the community or the public. In order to gain the legitimacy for resources and survival, schools have to show evidence of accountability, satisfy the requirements of the community and win the support of important constituencies.

Along this line of thinking, the legitimate model suggests that a school is effective if it can survive as a result of engaging in legitimate or marketing activ-ities. It assumes that schools 'strive for legitimacy with the external public in order to enhance their longevity and avoid being selected out of the environment' (Cameron, 1984: 278). Therefore, the indicators of effectiveness are often related to the activities and achievements of public relations and marketing, accountability, school public image, reputation or status in the community, etc. The model is useful when the survival and demise among schools must be assessed in a changing environment. For example, in some old districts, the primary student population reduces quickly and some primary schools have to be closed if no sufficient number of parents are willing to send their children to them. Among the schools at risk, only those successfully striving for legitimacy or better public relations with the community can survive. From the viewpoint of this model, the schools are effective if they can survive in a competing environment. On the other hand, due to the expansion of secondary education in some districts, a strong demand for secondary schools may reduce the competition but increase the legitimacy for survival among secondary schools in these districts. Therefore, the application of the model to conceptualize effectiveness in this context may not be so relevant as that in the context for primary schools.

The current emphasis on parental choice and accountability in educational reforms in both Western and Eastern societies seem to support the importance of the legitimacy model in assessing school effectiveness. Increase in parental choice of schools may create a competitive market environment for schools to compete and try their best to provide high quality educational services for the needs of parents. Also, the implementation of accountability systems or quality assurance systems provides a formal mechanism for schools to gain the necessary legitimacy for survival. This can explain why so many schools are now paying more attention to public relations, marketing activities and building up school-based accountability systems or quality assurance systems.

The contribution of this model to the technical/economic functions, human/ social functions, political functions, cultural functions and educational functions of schools at different levels depends on whether the competitive environment and the legitimacy process can encourage or direct the schools' attention, energy and action towards a wide spectrum of school functions at the individual, institutional, community, society and international levels. If the environment is very competitive and the legitimacy process is too tight, in terms of supervision and control, schools may tend to focus on short-term survival through achievement of short-term functions at the individual level, the institutional level or the community level. They tend to fulfill the overt, specific, measurable, short-term requirements, such as attendance rate, examination results, etc., of the accountability system but ignore the hidden long-term functions, particularly at the society level or the international level. Even though there is strong interest in using market mechanism and accountability system to enhance school effectiveness in current worldwide education reforms, the knowledge of their relationship to the full spectrum of school functions and effectiveness is still underdeveloped. Therefore, we should pay attention to the potential limitations of this legitimacy model when using it in educational reforms.

The Ineffectiveness Model

As Cameron (1984) explained, the difficulty of identifying appropriate criteria is often the single most important problem in organizational effectiveness research in general and in school effectiveness study in particular. One of the important difficulties is to identify the indicators of success. It seems much easier to identify the weaknesses and defects, such as indicators of ineffectiveness, than the strengths of an organization, such as indicators of effectiveness. It has been found that 'organizational change and development is motivated more by knowledge of problems than by knowledge of success' (Cameron, 1984: 246). Therefore, Cameron suggested that 'an approach to assessing organizational ineffectiveness instead of effectiveness may help expand our understanding of the construct of organizational effectiveness' (p. 247). Borrowing his idea, the ineffectiveness model describes school effectiveness from a negative side and defines that a school is basically effective if there is an absence of characteristics of ineffectiveness in the school.

The model assumes that it is easier for the concerned school constituencies to identify and agree on criteria of school ineffectiveness than criteria of school effectiveness. Also identifying strategies for improving school effectiveness can be more precisely done by analyzing school ineffectiveness as opposed to school effectiveness. Therefore, this model is useful particularly when the criteria of school effectiveness are really unclear but the strategies for school improvement are needed. The indicators of ineffectiveness may include existing conflicts, problems, difficulties, defects, weaknesses and poor performance. In general, many schools, particularly those new schools, are more concerned with overcoming obstacles to basic school effectiveness than pursuing excellent school performance. This model may be appropriate to them. For those practitioners such as school administrators and teachers, the ineffectiveness model may be more basic than the other models. It seems that 'no ineffectiveness' may be the basic requirement for effectiveness. But if people are more interested in high school performance, this model is not sufficient.

Since the ineffectiveness model focuses mainly on operational weaknesses and defects of the school's internal process, it may contribute to the technical functions at the individual level or the institutional level. But the contribution of this model to the wide spectrum of school functions at the community level, the society level or the international level may be very limited if there is no sufficient knowledge about how the operational ineffectiveness at the lower levels is related to the ineffectiveness in social functions, political functions, cultural functions and educational functions at the higher levels.

The Organizational Learning Model

As discussed above, the changing education environment is producing great impacts on nearly every aspect of school functioning. From the points of view of the satisfaction model and the legitimacy model, satisfying strategic constituencies' needs and fulfilling requirements of legitimacy in the community are critical to the survival of schools in a competitive and accountability-demanding environment. From the perspective of the process model, continuously improving school process is necessary for effective performance and achievement of school goals in a rapidly changing context. There seems no static factor or single practice that contributes to school effectiveness forever. Therefore, how to deal with the environmental impacts and internal process problems is the key question in determining a school's effectiveness.

The organizational learning model assumes that the impact of environmental changes and the existence of internal barriers to school functioning are inevitable and therefore, a school is effective if it can learn how to make improvement and adaptation to its environment. Whether the school and its members (particularly, the administrators and teachers) can learn to deal with the change and reduce the internal hindrance is very important (Argyris, 1982; Argyris and Schön, 1978; Levitt and March, 1988; Louis, 1994; Lundberg, 1989).

To some extent, this model is similar to the process model. The difference is that this model emphasizes the importance of learning behavior to effective school performance, and whether or not the internal process is currently smooth is not so critical. The line of thinking supports the current emphasis of strategic management and development planning in school (Dempster, *et al.*, 1993; Hargreaves and Hopkins, 1991). The model is particularly useful when schools are developing or involved in educational reform particularly in a changing external environment. The indicators of school effectiveness may include awareness of community needs and changes, internal process monitoring, program evaluation, environmental analysis, and development planning, etc.

In developing countries or areas, there are many new secondary schools due to the expansion of secondary education. The new schools have to face many problems in establishing organizational structures, educational processes, dealing with poor quality students, developing staff, and struggling against the adverse influence from the community (Cheng, 1985). Also, the changes in economic and political environment demand effective adaptation of the school system in terms of curriculum change, management change and technology change (Cheng, 1995b). In such a background, this organizational learning model may be appropriate for studying school effectiveness. Obviously, the usefulness of this model will be limited if the connection between organizational learning process and school outcomes is not clear. For example, some old schools have a tradition of prestige that can attract high quality student input. Even though they may lack organizational learning, they can still win relatively high student achievement and high school status.

Comparatively, this model has high potential to contribute to the technical/ economic functions, human/social functions, political functions, cultural functions, and educational functions at different levels. With the awareness of external changes and needs and the commitment to internal improvement, schools may be more sensitive to the existence of multiple functions and goals at the five levels and develop appropriate strategies to achieve them. The organizational learning process can promise a dynamic view to maximize effectiveness on multiple school goals. The detail will be discussed in Chapter 3.

The Total Quality Management Model

Recently there is a rapidly growing emphasis on education quality (Cheng, 1995a; Education Commission, 1994; Hughes, 1988). The concepts and practices of total quality management in schools are believed to be a powerful tool to enhance education quality and increase school effectiveness (Bradley, 1993; Cuttance, 1994; Greenwood and Gaunt, 1994; Murgatroyd and Colin, 1993).

Due to the recent development of management theory and practice in different organizations, people begin to believe that improvement of some aspects of the management process is not sufficient to achieve excellence or total quality in performance. For long-term success, quality performance or effectiveness, total management of the internal environment and process to meet the customers' (or clients', strategic constituencies') *needs* is the key. The critical elements of total quality management in school include strategic constituencies' (for example, parents, students, etc.) focus, continuous process improvement, and total involvement and empowerment of school members (Tenner and Detoro, 1992). According to the total management model, a school is effective if it can involve and empower all its members in school functioning, conduct continuous improvement in different aspects of the school process, and satisfy the requirements, needs, and expectations of the school's external and internal powerful constituencies even in a changing environment.

To a great extent, the total quality management model of school effectiveness is an integration of the above models, particularly the organizational learning model, the satisfaction model and the process model. According to the famous Malcolm Baldrige Award framework or the European Quality Award framework for total quality management, the key areas for assessing school effectiveness may include leadership, people management, process management, information and analysis, strategic quality planning, internal constituencies' satisfaction, external constituencies' satisfaction, operational results, students' educational results and impacts on society (Fisher, 1994; George, 1992).

Compared with other models, the total quality management model provides a more holistic or comprehensive perspective to understanding and managing school effectiveness. If the strategic constituencies' needs and expectations are compatible and the technology and resources are available for such a full span of management in school, this model should be appropriate.

Since this model is more comprehensive than the other models, its contribution to the different types of school functions at different levels may be more promising. Similar to the organizational learning model, the constituencies' focus, continuous process improvement, and total involvement and empowerment of members emphasized in this model can help schools to maximize effectiveness dynamically on multiple school functions. The main concern is whether the technical/economic functions, human/social functions, political functions, cultural functions and educational functions of schools can be reflected in the expectations of strategic constituencies at different levels, and whether schools can be provided with the necessary knowledge, technology and resources to initiate total management of their internal environment and process responsive to the expectations of constituencies for multiple school functions.

As discussed above, each of the eight models has its own strengths and limitations. In different situations and different time frames, different models may be useful for studying school effectiveness. Comparatively, the organizational learning model and the total quality management model seem to be more promising for achievement of multiple school functions at different levels. In the next chapter, I will further discuss the relationship between models of school effectiveness and types of school functions, and propose a dynamic perspective to interpret how to maximize effectiveness on multiple functions and goals.

Chapter 3

A Dynamic Perspective of School Effectiveness

Types and models of school effectiveness have been introduced in Chapters 1 and 2. It would be interesting to discuss further how the classification of effectiveness models and effectiveness types can contribute to research and practice of enhancing school effectiveness. In this chapter, I will discuss this issue from a dynamic perspective.

Matrix of School Effectiveness

When the eight models are compared with the five levels of school effectiveness or the five types of school effectiveness, two matrices of school effectiveness can be formed as shown in Tables 3.1 and 3.2. These matrices can be used to facilitate our thinking about maximizing school effectiveness. In them, column one represents the eight different models of school effectiveness, helping us to conceptualize how to measure and manage school effectiveness. Columns 2–5 represents the five different levels or types of school effectiveness, helping us to identify the categories of effectiveness to be evaluated. For each case of research or practice in school effectiveness, we may ask which models should be used and which categories of effectiveness should be chosen or emphasized. Of course, it is often that the selected model may affect the choice of categories of school effectiveness.

For example, in the *goal model*, the choice of categories of effectiveness may depend mainly on which type and level of goals have been listed in the school plan and program plans. If the planned goals are related only to technical learning at the student level, then only technical effectiveness or efficiency at the individual level, but not other types of functions (for example, social effectiveness, cultural effectiveness or political effectiveness) at the higher levels, would be in focus. For another example, in the *satisfaction model*, the emphasis on the categories of school effectiveness may be different among various strategic constituencies. Parents and students tend to be more concerned with the effectiveness at the individual level or the institutional level. But policymakers are concerned with not only the effectiveness at the lower levels but also the effectiveness and efficiency at the higher levels.

In general, different models may have different focuses on the level of school effectiveness. As shown in Table 3.1, the focus of the *goal model* may vary from only one level to all the five levels, depending on the nature of goals and mission

Table 3.1: Models of school effectiveness and levels of school effectiveness

	Internal Effectiveness/Efficiency		External Effectiveness/Efficiency		
	Individual Level	Institutional Level	Community Level	Society Level	International Level
Goal Model	X	X	X	X	X
Resource-Input Model	X	X			
Process Model	X	X			
Satisfaction Model	X	X	X	X	X
Legitimacy Model			X	X	X
Ineffectiveness Model	X	X			
Organizational Learning Model	X	X	X	X	X
Total Quality Management Model	X	X	X	X	X

Note: X represents the potential focus of the model.

formulated in the school plan. The *resource-input model* has focused on resource acquisition, so it relates mainly to the internal effectiveness at the institutional level or the individual level. Clearly, the *process model* may be concerned mainly with the internal effectiveness or efficiency at the individual or institutional levels. Depending on the demands of the strategic constituencies, the focus of the satisfaction model may range from one to all the five levels. Since the *legitimacy model* emphasizes the school's survival in a competing and accountability-demanding environment, inevitably the effectiveness and efficiency particularly at the community, society and international levels become the critical concern. As the *ineffectiveness model* pays attention mainly to the internal problems and defects, its concern tends to be the internal effectiveness and efficiency at the individual and institutional levels. Both the *organizational learning model* and the *total quality management model* have their theme on learning to deal with changing environmental demands and internal barriers, and meeting the needs of strategic constituencies at different levels. Therefore they may cover all the five levels of school effectiveness. In sum, the *goal model*, the *organizational learning model*, and the *total quality management model* may have greater potential to relate to school effectiveness or efficiency at all the five levels. The *resource-input model*, the *process model*, and the *ineffectiveness model* tend to focus on internal effectiveness and efficiency (i.e., at the individual level or institutional level). The *legitimate model* is more likely to focus on external effectiveness and efficiency (i.e., at the community level, the society level, and the international level).

The relationship of the models to the types of school effectiveness is not so

Table 3.2: *Models of school effectiveness and types of school effectiveness*

	Technical/Economic Effectiveness	Human/Social Effectiveness	Political Effectiveness	Cultural Effectiveness	Educational Effectiveness
Goal Model	• The contribution depends on the types of goals covered in the school plan. • The coverage is often incomplete or even ignored.				
Resource-Input Model	• The contribution depends on how the resources are used on the types of school functions. • The knowledge is unclear and the use is often biased towards the overt functions.				
Process Model	• The contribution depends on how the internal process is related to the types of school functions. • The knowledge is underdeveloped.				
Satisfaction Model	• The contribution depends on how the strategic constituencies' expectations are related to the types of school functions. • The relevance is unknown and some constituencies are ignored.				
Legitimacy Model	• The contribution depends on the relevance of the legitimacy process and marketing activities to the types of school functions. • The relevance is unclear and indirect.				
Ineffectiveness Model	• The contribution depends on how operational defects and weaknesses are related to the types of school functions. • The relevance is unclear and the knowledge is often biased on the overt functions.				
Organizational Learning Model	• The contribution depends on how schools can have the knowledge of the types of school functions. • The knowledge is earned by the learning process.				
Total Quality Management Model	• The contribution depends on how the total quality management process is related to the types of school functions. • The relevance is strengthened and the knowledge is earned in the total quality management process.				

clear. For all eight models, their contributions to the different types of school effectiveness are limited by their own characteristics, as discussed in Chapter 2. Table 3.2 has summarized these contributions and their limitations. For the *goal model*, the contribution depends on the types of goals covered in the school plan. If there is a balance in the emphasis on the five school functions, it may ensure opportunity for the school to achieve all of them. But in general, the coverage of school functions is often incomplete or even ignored by school members, such that school effectiveness can be successful in part, if it succeeds at all.

The contribution of applying the *resource-input model* is affected by the use of procured resources to achieve the different types of school functions. Decision making on the allocation and use of resources is very important. But knowledge about decision making is often unclear as to how the resources relate to each type of school function. Therefore, the use of this model is often biased in overt or short-term functions, such as technical functions, but not in hidden or long-term functions, for example, cultural or educational functions.

The contribution of using the process model depends on how the internal process is related to the types of school functions. If a clear path from the school process activities to each type of school functions exists, it is more likely for the improvement of school process to result in high school effectiveness of different types. But unfortunately, the knowledge about the path is underdeveloped and not sufficient to make any reliable suggestions. This may reflect why a strong tradition of school effectiveness research has focused on identifying how the instructional process or learning environment is related to student outcomes (Cheng, 1994a; 1994j; Creemers, 1994; Fraser, 1992; Fraser and Walberg, 1991; Wang and Walberg, 1991).

For the *satisfaction model*, the contribution depends on how strategic constituencies' expectations are related to the types of school functions. If all the internal and external strategic constituencies have equal opportunity to express their expectations and exercise their power on the school, a greater possibility for achieving balanced types of school functions may exist. But it is often the fact that the expectation of certain strategic constituencies dominates the school direction and focuses only on some limited types of school functions — academic achievements or social satisfactions. Of course, it is also possible that the expectations of strategic constituencies, for example, the personal interest of the school manager, may not be so relevant to the types of school functions.

The contribution of using the *legitimacy model* depends on the relevance of the legitimacy process and marketing activities to the types of school functions. For example, if the external quality assurance system or the accountability system can be designed with careful consideration of all the five types of school functions, it will ensure a greater tendency for schools to pursue the full spectrum of effectiveness. Therefore, how to clarify the direct relevance of the legitimacy process or marketing activities to all five types of school effectiveness should be an important issue in current educational reforms with emphasis on 'market mechanism' and 'accountability system'.

In using the *ineffectiveness model*, the contribution relies on how the operational defects and weaknesses in the school process are related to the types of school functions. We may have some limited knowledge about these defects and weaknesses in relationship to some overt technical functions, but unfortunately we still have no sufficient knowledge to confirm their relationship to the human/social functions, political functions, cultural functions and educational functions. Therefore, the usefulness of this model is somewhat limited.

The contribution of using the *organizational learning model* depends on how schools can have the knowledge of all five types of school functions. If schools can learn the importance of these types of school functions, they can develop appropriate strategies to achieve them. Even though they have no sufficient knowledge and technology for school performance, they can earn them in the process of organizational learning. The major concern is how to develop a learning mechanism and maintain it in school.

Integrating the strength of the organizational learning model, the contribution of the *total quality management model* depends on how the total quality management process is related to the types of school functions. Since this model emphasizes internal and external constituencies' focus, continuous process improvement, and total involvement and empowerment of members, its total management process may provide a good opportunity to learn the importance of the five types of school functions and how to achieve them. Also, the relevance of total quality management to effectiveness can be strengthened, and the related knowledge and technology can be earned in the total quality management process. Comparatively, this model may have a larger contribution to the development and achievement of multiple school functions.

The Congruence Concept

According to the concept of congruence in the system (Cheng, 1987c; Cheng, in press (d); Nadler and Tushman, 1983), there are two kinds of congruence that can contribute to the discussion of maximizing school effectiveness. One is the *category congruence*, indicating the extent to which categories of school effectiveness are consistent. High category congruence indicates that the higher the effectiveness in one category, the higher the effectiveness in the other categories; or, the lower the effectiveness in one category, the lower the effectiveness in the other categories. Low category congruence represents a negligible relationship among the categories of school effectiveness. It means that high effectiveness in one category does not necessarily mean high effectiveness in the other categories. Furthermore, category incongruence indicates an existing reverse relationship between categories. The higher the effectiveness in one category, the lower the effectiveness in the other categories. In general, we are interested in maximizing both effectiveness and efficiency on the five functions not only at the individual level and institutional level, but also at the community level, societal level and international level. If it is true, then category congruence may be important in thinking about maximizing school effectiveness.

The other kind of congruence is the *model congruence*, referring to the extent to which the conceptions of school effectiveness in models are consistent or compatible. High model congruence indicates that the criteria and indicators of effectiveness developed from the models are similar, consistent, compatible, or at least not conflicting in nature. On the other hand, model incongruence represents the potential conflict between conceptions or indicators of school effectiveness developed from different models. To different people who have different concerns, different models may be used to define and measure school effectiveness. If the chosen models are congruent, then these models can be integrated and provide a complete and consistent assessment of school effectiveness from different perspectives. If the chosen models are incongruent, then the evaluation of school effectiveness and ways for maximizing school effectiveness may become very controversial, since the criteria and indicators of effectiveness developed from the models may conflict and cannot be maximized at the same time.

For each case of maximizing or studying school effectiveness, we would like to know whether the models used to conceptualize school effectiveness are congruent and whether the categories of school effectiveness are congruent. If both category congruence and model congruence can be ensured, then evaluating or maximizing school effectiveness would be less problematic. How to ensure these two kinds of congruence when studying school effectiveness in different contexts still needs further exploration.

Assuming that model congruence exists between models, some investigators tried to integrate several models and proposed multiple criteria models to define and measure effectiveness (see Cheng, 1986b; 1993h; Hackman, 1987; Hackman and Walton, 1986; Hoy and Miskel, 1991; Miskel, McDonald and Bloom, 1983). For example, from Hackman and Walton's (1986) idea, school effectiveness may be defined by the following three dimensions:

1 The degree to which the school's productive output (that is, its product or service) meets the standards of quantity, quality, and timeliness of the people who receive, review, and/or use that output;

2 The degree to which the process of carrying out the work enhances the capability of school members to work together interdependently in the future; and

3 The degree to which the school experience contributes to the growth and personal well-being of school members.

This conception comprises some important elements of the *goal model*, the *process model*, the *satisfaction model*, the *organizational learning model*, and the *total quality management model*. For another example, based on a social-function approach, Hoy and Miskel (1991) developed an integrated model for exploring the organizational effectiveness of schools. They used the four necessary functions of social systems (i.e. adaptation, goal achievement, integration, and latency) as guidelines to select specific criteria of school effectiveness. They proposed that school effectiveness is a multidimensional concept and therefore many process and outcome variables can be used as indicators of effectiveness. Basically, both Hackman and Walton (1986) and Hoy and Miskel (1991) assume the existence of congruence across the different effectiveness models, and hence the different effectiveness criteria or categories. But we should pay attention to a basic dilemma, that maximizing school effectiveness in multiple criteria at the same time is often impossible (Hall, 1987). For example, when a school is very academically productive through very tense working pressure, this pressure may frustrate teachers' personal satisfaction and growth and also increase the conflict between school members. Since the resources available for a school are always limited, it is very difficult, if not impossible, to maximize effectiveness on all the criteria, or to achieve the goals of all the constituencies in a short time. Inevitably, there are conflicts and contradictions in schools.

Hall (1987) proposed a contradiction perspective to describe the conflicting characteristics inherent in every organization. According to this perspective, no school is always effective because of the existence of multiple and conflicting environmental constraints, goals, constituencies and time frames. Or instead, schools can be viewed as effective (or ineffective) to some degree only in terms of some specific criteria based on certain effectiveness models.

Along this line of thinking, ensuring congruence across all models or categories of school effectiveness as well as maximizing effectiveness at all criteria seems very difficult, at least in a short time. In current educational reforms, we emphasize maximizing school effectiveness. What should we do when facing this dilemma or limitation?

It seems that from an organizational perspective, the conception of school effectiveness is complex and problematic, and raises many debates over model selection and level of analysis among investigators (Cameron, 1984; Cameron and Whetten, 1981). Some researchers even argued that the concept of organizational effectiveness in general, or school effectiveness in particular is futile and has no inherent meaning in 'scientific analysis of comparative organizational effectiveness' (Hannan and Freeman, 1977: 131).

A Dynamic Perspective

A dynamic perspective can be used to ensure model congruence and maximizing school effectiveness on multiple criteria. This perspective is explained as follows (Cheng, 1990b):

A school often pursues multiple goals because it has multiple environmental constraints and constituencies. It may try to be effective on multiple criteria for its survival. Since the available resources are often limited, it is very difficult for a school to maximize the effectiveness on all criteria and achieve all the goals at the same time. In order to solve this dilemma of effectiveness, acquisition of more scarce resources becomes one of the necessary activities for a school's survival.

A school may experience different pressures from the multiple and conflicting environmental constraints and constituencies in the process of pursuing multiple

(an illustrative example)

Driven by Unbalanced Pressures

Priority	Criteria	Criteria	Criteria	Criteria
Top	A	A	D	E
	B	C	A	B
	C	D	E	A
	D	B	B	D
Low	E	E	C	C
Time	t1	t2	t3	t4

A,B,C,D and E are multiple effectiveness criteria. For example, they may be Production, Social Relationship, Personal Growth, Job Satisfaction or Organizational Development. The priorities for these effectiveness criteria are varied with time. For example, E is at the bottom priority at time t1 but at top priority at time t4.
(Adapted from Y.C. Cheng (1990b)).

Figure 3.1: *Varying priority for pursuing school effectiveness on multiple criteria*

goals. According to the strengths of these pressures, it develops different priorities for goals to be pursued and effectiveness criteria to be maximized. The importance and priority of goals and criteria may vary with time and across circumstances, as shown in Figure 3.1. But when some specific goals are strongly emphasized (for example, academic achievement in public examinations), and more resources and efforts are allocated to them, the school will experience higher pressure from in-effectiveness of achieving other goals — school organizational development or staff personal growth and satisfaction. Therefore, unbalanced pressure on a school may be inevitable at any given instant.

Following this thinking, a school may be assumed effective if it is aware of the unbalanced situation and can show adaptability and flexibility to set up a new priority for goals to be pursued in the coming time. It pursues dynamic equilibrium among the multiple and conflicting pressures. Even though it cannot maximize the effectiveness on all criteria at the same time, it can in the long run. The dynamic process for a school to struggle for effectiveness on multiple criteria may be illustrated by an imaginary diagram. As shown in Figure 3.2, a school becomes effective if it can pass along a spiral path to maximize the effectiveness on multiple criteria (A,B,C,D and E) in a time frame (t1 to t2) in a multi-criteria space. Specifically, the average achievement in the multiple criteria in the time interval t3–t4 is bigger than in the early time interval t1–t2.

How can a school be driven along the spiral path for effectiveness? According to the current emphasis on leadership and strategic management or development planning in school management reforms (Caldwell and Spinks, 1992; Cheng and Ng, 1994; Cheung and Cheng, in press; Dempster, *et al.*, 1993; Hargreaves and Hopkins, 1991; Sergiovanni, 1984; 1992; Silins, 1992; 1993), the driving forces for

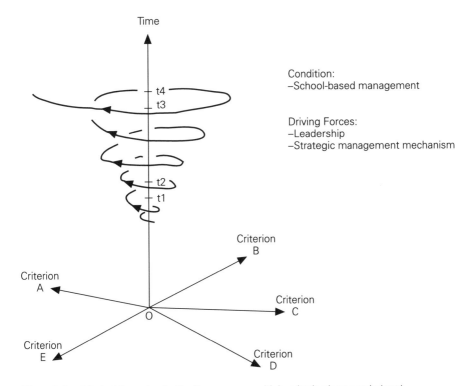

Figure 3.2:   Maximizing school effectiveness on multiple criteria along a spiral path

a school passing along the spiral path can be a leadership and development planning mechanism. The relationship of the dynamic perspective with strategic management, development planning and school-based management will be elaborated in later chapters.

In a short period, due to the limited availability of resources, the multiple goals to be pursued may conflict and therefore, maximizing effectiveness on some criteria may offset effectiveness in others. But in a long period, the achievement of some goals may reinforce or at least not offset the effectiveness for achieving the others if a school can carry out the dynamic process of maximizing the effectiveness on all criteria through appropriate development planning. For example, according to the literature of staff development, the increase in teacher personal growth and professional development may result in later enhancement of educational quality in school (Cheng and Tam, 1994; Lieberman, 1988; Oldroyd and Hall, 1991). Also it is possible that the success in school educational outcomes may win more opportunities and resources from the community for teachers' personal growth and professional development in the school.

According to Quinn (1988) and Quinn and Cameron (1983), at different stages of its organizational life cycle (such as entrepreneurial stage, collectivity stage, formalization stage, and elaboration of structure stage), a successful school may pursue different sets of goals or values and therefore try to maximize effectiveness on different criteria. The shift of effectiveness criteria may be due to the internal demands in the transition of the school life cycle stages as well as its response to the pressures from the external environment.

From the above dynamic perspective, school effectiveness can be conceptualized as the extent to which a school can adapt to the internal and external constraints and achieve the multiple goals of its multiple constituencies in the long run. This conceptualization is based on a dynamic long-term consideration and multiple criteria. For short term, a school may be effective on some criteria but ineffective on others, and it may be effective at a certain period but not at another. If school effectiveness is conceptualized and assessed only from a short-term consideration, its meaning may be very restricted and biased, if not meaningless. It is difficult to provide useful information for long term school development.

The eight models of school effectiveness put the emphasis respectively on the different aspects of the dynamic process of a school struggling for survival and effectiveness:

- The goal model — It reflects the importance and priorities of goals of some powerful constituencies to be satisfied in the dynamic process in a given period;
- The resource-input model — The limitation of resources available for a school restricts its ability to maximize its effectiveness on multiple goals. Acquisition of more resources can enhance a school's potential to pursue multiple goals. Therefore, the resource-input model reflects the importance of the acquisition of resources in the process of becoming effective. This model measures the potential school effectiveness;
- The process model — The internal constituencies are also multiple, generating different pressures on the school's process of achieving multiple goals. The internal process model reflects the interactions among internal constituencies and also the importance of internal interaction process to school effectiveness;
- The satisfaction model — Pressures from different strategic constituencies influence the survival of a school and also the priorities of goals to be pursued. The model reflects the impact of powerful constituencies on the dynamic process of maximizing effectiveness on multiple criteria. It measures the relative achievement of multiple goals in terms of constituencies' satisfaction;
- The legitimacy model — Environmental constraints set limits to the school's process of struggling for survival. Whether a school can eliminate these limits reflects its effectiveness. The legitimacy model emphasizes the importance of environmental constraints to the school's survival in terms of legitimacy with the external public. It measures a school's effectiveness in dealing with legitimate activities through marketing and public relations;
- The ineffectiveness model — The ineffectiveness model provides a baseline

for a school to identify the 'obvious' unbalanced situation in the process of achieving multiple goals;
- The organizational learning model — In the dynamic process, the awareness of unbalanced pressures from environmental constraints and multiple constituencies and the dynamic adaptation to the unbalanced situation are critical for long term effectiveness;
- The total management model — As discussed in Chapter 2, to a great extent, this model is an integration of the above models, particularly the organizational learning model, the satisfaction model, and the process model. In other words, the model emphasizes a holistic perspective of the dynamic process of struggling for school effectiveness.

Multiple models are needed if we want to know how well a school performs in different aspects of the dynamic process. From the dynamic perspective, the models of school effectiveness may be congruent in pursuing effectiveness in the long run even if not in the short run. In other words, model congruence should be taken in a long-term consideration if it cannot be achieved in a given short period. As discussed above (Table 3.1), different models are associated with different categories of school effectiveness. If multiple models are used and they are congruent in a dynamic process, then all the categories of effectiveness tend to be congruent too and can be maximized in a long term consideration.

What conditions and management mechanism can help schools to pursue effectiveness and development along a spiral path dynamically? This question will be discussed in the following chapters.

Part II

School-based Management

Chapter 4

The Theory of School-based Management

In this chapter, I will explain how school-based management can be developed as the necessary condition that facilitates schools to pursue dynamic effectiveness on multiple categories of school effectiveness in the long run.

The Rise of School-based Management

In the 1960s and 1970s, numerous innovations and efforts were made to promote new curricula and new teaching approaches but the results often seemed unsatisfactory. It was not until the eighties when there was successful development of modern management in industrial and commercial organizations, that people began to believe that to improve education quality, it is necessary to jump from the *classroom teaching level* to *school organization level*, and reform the structural system and management style of schools. Various school reform movements followed. Those emphasizing improvement of certain school internal functioning such as interpersonal relationship and instructional leadership introduced different kinds of school improvement programs. The *effective school* movement looked for and promoted the characteristics of effective schools. The *self-budgeting school* movement emphasized the autonomy of using school resources. Those focusing on decentralization of authority from central education offices introduced school-based activities such as *School-based curriculum development, School-based staff development* and *School-based student counseling*, etc. However, some people argued that decentralization of central power to school level could not guarantee that schools would use power effectively to enhance education quality. Therefore, both school responsibility bearers and education service receivers should share the decision making power at the school level. Thus followed the emergence of the shared decision making movement in school management reform. Undoubtedly in the late 1980s, different forms of school-based management soon became the central topics and strategies in educational reform in different parts of the world (Caldwell, 1990; Caldwell and Spinks, 1988; David, 1989; Dimmock, 1993; Mohrman and Wohlstetter, 1994).

To a certain extent, the education reform in Hong Kong has followed this pattern. In the 1970s and 1980s, much effort was put to increase school vacancies and expand education systems, and educational reform was confined to input of resources and improvement of teaching or learning facilities such as remedial teaching, student counseling and some teacher refresher training programs (Education

Commission, 1988; 1990). However, the effort was not enough for successful school improvement (Cheng, 1992e; 1995b). Knowing that 'the success of individual quality improvement measures will be limited if schools are not able to draw effectively on the skills, energy, and commitment of every member of the school community' (Education and Manpower Branch and Education Department, 1991: 1), the policy-makers of Hong Kong planned to set a framework for enhancing quality in schools by issuing a new school management reform policy entitled, The School Manage-ment Initiative (SMI). This policy tried to change to a great extent the centralized management model, giving the schools greater autonomy on management and finance at the site-level.

Some researchers have illustrated the diverse forms of school-based manage-ment and their implementation (Brown, 1990; Chapman, 1990), but very few have explained the conception and theory of school-based management and map its characteristics of school functioning from an organizational perspective. Caldwell and Spinks (1988; 1992) and Mohrman and Wohlstetter *et al.* (1994) are two of the few.

The Theory of School-based Management

David (1989) summarized school-based management from the ongoing reforms into two basic characteristics:

- School as the major decision making unit — decision should be made at the frontier of school functioning, therefore school autonomy on finance and management should be increased and control from the central office should be reduced;
- Ownership as the major requirement of school reform — effective reform does not rely on external procedure but it needs mainly the participation of members concerned to share decision making. In addition to these two characteristics, we may further conceptualize school-based management as follows:

  School-based management means that the school management tasks are set according to the characteristics and needs of the school itself and therefore school members (including board of directors, supervisor, principal, teach-ers, parents and students, etc.) have a much greater autonomy and respons-ibility for the use of resources to solve problems and carry out effective education activities, for the long-term development of the school.

On the contrary, traditional school management is often a type of *external control management* characterized by external tight control from the central office of the school system. In external control management, the school management tasks are performed under instruction of the external central authority, often not in accordance with school characteristics and needs, and school members do not have much autonomy and commitment.

Table 4.1: Theory of school-based management vs theory of external control management

	School-based Management	External Control Management
Assumptions about Education	• Multiplicity of educational goals • Complex and changing educational environment • Need for educational reforms • Effectiveness and adaptation oriented • Pursuit of quality	• Unification of educational goals • Simple and nearly static educational environment • No need for educational reforms • Standardization and stability oriented • Pursuit of quantity
Theories used to Manage Schools	*Principle of equifinality:* • Many different ways to achieve goals • Emphasizes flexibility *Principle of decentralization:* • Problems are inevitable, should be solved at where they happen in time • Looks for efficiency and problem-solving *Principle of self-managing system:* • Self-managing • Actively exploitative • Responsible *Principle of human initiative:* • Develops internal human resources • Wide participation of school members	*Principle of standard structure:* • Standard methods and procedures to achieve goals • Emphasizes generalizability *Principle of centralization:* • Things big or small are carefully controlled to avoid problems • Pursues procedural control *Principle of implementing system:* • Externally controlled • Passively receptive • Not accountable *Principle of structural control:* • Enforces external supervision • Expansion of bureaucratic system

Adapted from Y.C. Cheng (1993i).

School-based management and external control management are different in school functioning and performance, reflecting different management theories used by the central authority to manage the school system. The major differences in assumptions about education and management theories are summarized in Table 4.1 and illustrated as follows:

Difference in Assumptions about Education

In the tradition of external control management, educational goals are often assumed to be simple and unified and the educational environment is seen as nearly static. Therefore, there is no strong need to conduct any educational reforms to adapt to the environment and the management tends to emphasize standardization and stability and pursue educational quantity. But in school-based management, educational goals are assumed as multiple, based on the expectations of multiple-school constituencies, and the educational environment is believed to be complex and changing. Therefore, educational reforms or changes in school are inevitably needed to adapt to the changing environment, to enhance effectiveness, achieve educational goals and pursue educational quality.

Principle of Equifinality vs Principle of Standard Structure

Based on classical theories such as scientific management approach (Taylor, 1947; Urwick, 1947) and the theory of bureaucracy (Weber, 1947), the traditional management of school systems emphasizes the function of organizational structure and standard procedure. In external control management, it is assumed that there should be standard methods and procedures to achieve management goals, and they are suitable for all schools. Therefore, the major means of managing schools is only the inspection from outside on the extent to which the standard structures have been operated.

On the contrary, school-based management is based on the *principle of equifinality*, a modern management theory (Hackman and Walton, 1986; Katz and Kahn, 1978) assuming that there may be different ways to achieve goals. Flexibility is emphasized and schools should be managed by themselves according to their own conditions. Due to the complexity of current educational work and the big differences among schools (for example, student academic level and community situation), it is impractical to manage schools with a standard structure. Therefore, the principle of equifinality encourages decentralization of power to let schools have ample space to move, develop and work out their unique strategies to teach and manage their schools effectively.

Principle of Decentralization vs Principle of Centralization

Decentralization and centralization represent two entirely different principles of management. Centralization is consistent with the principle of standard structure, both looking for controlling procedures to avoid creating problems in schools. Being carefully controlled by the central authority, schools have little power for decision making and have to consult the central authority on nearly everything. As a result, the problems and crises a school runs into could not be solved or attended to as soon as possible. This management style tends to be more ineffective as educational tasks have become more complicated and changeable. (See the Education and Manpower Branch and Education Department of Hong Kong (1991) analysis which detailed the disadvantages of centralization in school management.)

Decentralization is an important phenomenon of modern school management reform (Brown, 1990; Caldwell and Spinks, 1988; Hill and Bonan, 1991) which is consistent with the principle of equifinality. It brings about school-based management, of which the basic theory is that school management and teaching activities inevitably have difficulties and problems, that, therefore, schools should be given the power and responsibility to solve problems effectively where the problems happen as soon as possible (Provenzo, 1989). In other words, it aims at efficiency and problem-solving, not avoiding problems. Therefore school-based management should be able to discover problems, solve them in time, and make a greater contribution to the effectiveness of teaching and learning activities.

Principle of Self-managing System vs Principle of Implementing System

In the whole education system, schools are often regarded as a tool to achieve educational policy goals or as a passive implementing system which needs careful external control. The role of the school is to receive orders from the central authority passively, and no initiative power and accountability are explicitly assigned to them. School-based management does not deny that schools need to achieve policy goals, but there should be many different ways to achieve them (i.e., principle of equi-finality). Therefore, it is necessary to let schools become a self-managing system under some major policies and structures, possessing considerable autonomy to develop teaching objectives and management strategies, distributing manpower and resources, solving problems and accomplishing goals according to their own conditions. As the schools are self-managing, they are more likely to take the initiative for their own responsibility.

The current school-based management movement can be regarded as the shift of school management from a *passive implementing system* to a *self-managing system*.

Principle of Human Initiative vs Principle of Structural Control

School-based management and external control management represent the past experiences of two different ideologies of management. What is more important, human factor or structure? As long as the goals and tasks of the organization are clear and well-defined, the structural factors of organization may be emphasized, and an ideal organizational structure or a precise system may be designed to make people work effectively. But if the functioning is not sound or if it creates any problem, something must be wrong with the structure or with the external control (Bolman and Deal, 1991a). From this perspective, there is always a tendency to enforce supervision on schools and increase ordinances for controlling them. Naturally the result is the expansion of the bureaucratic system of the central authority. A possible ecological phenomenon would be that the more the external control is enforced, the more the school members depend on the central authority and the lower their initiative. As a result, as a response to the ineffectiveness and dependence of schools, the central authority needs to put more resources on supervision and control when it tries to enhance education quality. This is obviously inefficient. The current school management issues and dilemmas in Hong Kong represent a typical case of such phenomenon (Education and Manpower Branch and Education Department, 1991).

In accordance with the development of the human relations movement and behavioral science movement of modern management, people have begun to pay serious attention to the critical influence of human factors on organizational effectiveness. The human resource perspective emphasizes that people are a precious resource of an organization, and so the main point of management is to develop the human resources within a school to give play to initiative (Bolman and Deal, 1991a). Based on this perspective, school-based management aims at building up a suitable environment for school members to participate widely and develop their potential. Thus, enhancement of education quality comes mainly from the improvement of internal process, particularly on the human aspect. A number of existing studies have already demonstrated that school performance often depends on whether the school organizational environment can motivate school members (Beare, Caldwell and Millikan 1989; Cheng, 1986b; 1991c; Likert, 1967; Tam and Cheng, in press (a); in press (b). Therefore, it is necessary for the school management to change from the external control model to the school-based model step-by-step. In fact, this change does not mean that structure should be abandoned. Without organizational structure, people may lose their direction and it may be difficult to make evaluation and ensure accountability. But due to the existing multiplicity and complexity of education work, it is impossible to enhance education quality without the initiative and creativity of school members.

The dilemma between human and structure in organization has always been the core problem of management (Bolman and Deal, 1991a), and no precise solution has yet been found. Some scholars proposed the idea called 'simultaneous loose – tight properties' which might be worth considering (Peters and Waterman, 1982; Sergiovanni, 1984). In managing schools, clear structural systems and ordinances should be set and the role and responsibility of people concerned should be explicitly defined according to the main policies and goals. But for the actual management functioning within a school, ample space should be given to encourage school members to take initiatives of giving full play to their specialties. The School Management Initiative policy in Hong Kong has adopted this idea (Education and Manpower Branch and Education Department, 1991). On the aspect of tight property, the role and responsibility of people concerned in the education system should be explicitly stated, and clear constitution of the school management, complete and specific school plan, school profile and teacher appraisal system should be set up for ensuring accountability. On the aspect of loose property, the power of allocating and using school resources is enlarged at the school-level, encouraging the participation of parents, teachers, students, and alumni in decision making.

The Characteristics of School-based Management

Based on different theories of management, many aspects of the school's internal functioning may be different between school-based management and external control management. In contrast to external control management, the characteristics of school-based management may be mapped in terms of school mission, management strategies, nature of activities, use of resources, role of school members, interpersonal relationship, quality of administrators, and indicators of effectiveness, as shown in Table 4.2.

School Mission

Although almost every school seems to have a mission, many are abstract and impractical such as 'to develop the five virtues of a person', 'to foster human ability for the society', 'to educate people to become talented', etc. All these cannot be used as guidelines for the managing and teaching activities of a school. From the viewpoint of external control management, the school is only a tool implementing the standard education mission given by the central authority with well organized supervision on teaching. Unified public examinations are often used to lead the aims of teaching activities, such that the ideal of a school itself seems to be un-important or vague and the ideal of guiding teaching activities has in fact been externally molded or given. No development of or commitment to school mission is needed for school members. If we believe that the ideal or mission of a school is representing its organizational culture, then schools under external control man-agement probably lack vivid and strong organizational culture to motivate school members to be hard-working and fully involved in the school (Beare, *et al.*, 1989; Peters and Waterman, 1982; Schein, 1992).

For schools under school-based management, the ideal of running a school represents a group of shared expectations, beliefs and values of the school, guiding school members in educational activities and the direction of work. This is organ-izational culture which greatly affects the functioning and effectiveness of a school (Beare, *et al.*, 1989; Cheng, 1993h; Sergiovanni, 1984). Vivid and strong school organizational culture should be developed and shared by school members so that they are willing to share responsibility, work hard and be fully involved in school work for achieving their shared ideal. Strong school culture also socializes new members to commit to the school mission and at the same time reinforces old members to cooperate continuously to carry on their mission even when they face difficulties and challenges (Deal and Kennedy, 1982; Schein, 1992).

The missions of school-based management and external control management represent two different kinds of school organizational culture. There are big differ-ences in the school performance between them. If we want our schools to take the initiative to provide high quality services to meet our multiple and complicated educational needs, then a strong organizational culture should be developed by school members for their own schools.

Nature of School Activities

According to management styles, the school process may be differentiated into either school-based or non school-based activities. The nature of school-based activities means a school conducts its educational activities according to the

Table 4.2: *Profiles of school-based management and external control management*

Characteristics of Internal Functioning	School-based Management	External Control Management
School Mission	• Mission clear, shared, developed and willingly actualized by members • Emphasize participation in developing educational mission • Strong and unique organizational culture exists	• Mission unclear, given by outside, not developed and accepted by members • Emphasize keeping and implementing external mission • Weak and vague organizational culture exists
Nature of School Activities	• School-based activities: managing and educating according to characteristics and needs of a school	• Non school-based activities: content and style of education and management determined by external authority
Management Strategies Concept of Human Nature	• Theory Y • Complex Man • Participation and development regarded as important	• Theory X • Rational Economic Man • Supervision and control regarded as important
Concept of School Organization	• School is a place students, teachers and administrators live, everybody has the right for development	• School is a tool, teacher is employee, kept when needed, out when not needed
Style of Decision Making	• Decentralization • Participation of teachers, parents and even students	• Centralization • Administrators make decisions
Leadership Style	• Multi-level leadership: symbolic, cultural and educational leadership in addition to technical and human leadership	• Low level leadership: mainly technical and human leadership
Use of Power	• Mainly expert and reference power	• Mainly legitimate, reward and coercive power
Managing Techniques	• Sophisticated scientific techniques	• Simple techniques or experiences
Use of Resources	• Autonomy; self-budgeting • According to school needs • In time to solve problems • Tend to broaden sources of education resources	• Tightly restricted by the central • According to external rules • Apply and wait for permission • Tend to avoid troublesome procedures for more resources

Table 4.2: (Cont.)

Characteristics of Internal Functioning	School-based Management	External Control Management
Role Differences Role of School	• Active-developing style: exploit all possibilities for development of the school, teachers, and students • Problem-solving	• Passive-receptive style: implement centralized mission, follow administration procedure • Avoid making mistakes
Role of Central Authority	• Supporter and advisor	• Strict supervisor and controller
Role of Administrator	• Goal developer and leader • Manpower starter and coordinator • Resources developer	• Watcher of static goals • Personnel supervisor • Resources controller
Role of Teacher	• Partner • Decision maker • Developer • Implementer	• Employee • Follower • Order receiver • Implementer
Role of Parent	• Receiver of quality services • Partner: positive participation and cooperation • School supporter	• Receiver of quantity services • Outsider: not eligible for participation and cooperation
Human Relations	• Partnership • Team spirit, open and cooperative • Shared commitment • Organizational climate: commitment style	• Hierarchical • Superior — subordinates, closed and defensive • Conflict of interest • Organizational climate: headless disengagement, or control style
Quality of Administrator	• Possess knowledge/ techniques of modern management • Continue to learn and grow, discover and solve problems • Open-minded	• Possess considerable administrative experience • Work according to ordinances and rules, avoid problems • Familiar with current ordinances
Index of Effectiveness	• Multi-leveled and multiple, including input, process and output; academic achievement being only one of them • Evaluation is a learning process for school improvement	• Pay much attention to academic achievement or a few final outcomes, neglect the process and development • Evaluation is a means of administrative supervision

Adapted from Y.C. Cheng (1993i).

characteristics, needs and situation of the school while the nature of non school-based activities means a school lets external factors (especially the central authorities) decide its educational activities.

When a school is externally controlled, it only implements the assigned tasks according to the policy of the central authority. The content and method of teaching and examinations tend to have unified standards and the facilities, personnel organization, teaching and managing of the school are all carefully controlled by the external central authority and therefore the activities of the school is non school-based. For example, the teaching curriculum of Hong Kong schools is standardized, directed and controlled by the central authority. Although school-based curriculum design has been advocated recently, it is confined to changes in teaching methods and teaching aids. Undoubtedly, when school management remains externally controlled, it is difficult for school activities to become really school-based.

Given that external control management fails to meet the practical needs and motivate the initiative of school members to solve problems and carry out activities with flexibility, different forms of school-based reforms have been proposed to raise the effectiveness of school activities. For the last decade, school-based activities have been widely accepted and carried out all over the world (Caldwell and Spinks, 1988; Chapman, 1990; Provenzo, 1989). Recently there are also activities like school-based curriculum design, school-based remedial teaching, school-based counseling, and school-based staff development carried out in Hong Kong (Education Commission, 1990).

Having discussed some aspects of school activities, it has been shown that a school-based nature is important in enhancing the quality of education. It indirectly promotes the change of school management from the external control model to the school-based model. However, the effectiveness of any individual school-based activity, such as school-based staff development, always depends on to what extent the school is in a mode of school-based management. Therefore, it is not difficult to understand why school-based curriculum development activities often cannot be effectively carried out in external control schools.

Management Strategies

The change along the direction from external control management to school-based management can be reflected in the following aspects of management strategies: concept of human nature, concept of school organization, decision making style, leadership style, use of power, and management skills (Cheng, 1990d).

Assumptions about human nature. Holding different assumptions about the human nature of teachers and students, school administrators may develop different means of school management. According to McGregor (1960), there are two different assumptions about human nature in management: Theory X and Theory Y. The former assumes that humans are born lazy and irresponsible, close supervision is the managing method and punishment for controlling is inevitable. The latter assumes that humans do not have an innate dislike for work. Under suitable conditions, a human is willing to serve for his/her shared goals without being pushed, not only to bear responsibility, but also to look for more responsibilities to take up. Theory Y suggests that democratic participation, professional development, and work–life improvement are important to motivate teachers and students. According to Maslow (1943) and Alderfer (1972), teachers and students may have different levels of needs, apart from economic gains. They pursue social interaction and affiliation, self-actualization and development opportunities. In order to satisfy higher level needs, they are willing to accept challenges and work harder. Schein (1980) further classified human nature into four categories: the rational-economic man, social man, self-actualizing man and complex man. Different managing methods are often based on different assumptions about human nature. External control management with Theory X assumptions tends to use close supervision to manage teachers and students. But if we believe that the human is complex and changeable and every school member has different needs and abilities, it is more suitable to use Theory Y. School-based management can provide more flexibility and opportunities to satisfy the needs of teachers and students and give play to their talents.

Concept of school organization. In the external control management model, school managers always regard that the goals of the school are clear and simple and the school is only a means to achieve the goals. The teachers in a school are only employees and their value is instrumental. Suitable teachers are kept while unsuitable ones are out. Obviously this concept of school organization may not be appropriate in modern management. Now, whether in business organizations or public service organizations, the concept of organization has changed. People believe that an organization is a place for life and development, not only a tool for achieving certain static goals, for example, quantity of product (Likert, 1967; McGregor, 1960). The school as an organization should not only be a place for the preparation for the future of children, but also a place for students, teachers and even administrators to live, to grow and to pursue development. Without professional development and enthusiastic involvement of teachers and administrators, a school cannot be developed and improved continuously, and students cannot have a rich learning life. Therefore, a school-based managing school is not only a place to foster student growth, but also a place to foster the development of teachers and administrators. This is also the reason why school-based staff development is important to school effectiveness (Cheng and Tam, 1994).

Decision making style. Under the tight control of the central authority, the decision making of traditional schools is usually done by administrators or the central authority and then the decided tasks are carried out by teachers. Teachers' participation in decision making is often very little or treated as unnecessary. However, as education work and external environment have become more complicated day-by-day, school managements should change from the decision making style at the school level to *power-sharing* or *participation* for the following reasons:

- The goal of a school is often unclear and changeable. The participation of teachers, parents, students, and even alumni can help to develop goals which will be more able to reflect the present situation and future needs;
- The goals of a school are multiple and the mission of a school is complicated; they need the intelligence, imagination and effort of more people to accomplish. The participation or involvement of teachers, parents and students in decision making is an important contribution to the school;
- Participation in decision making provides opportunities for members and even administrators to learn and develop, and also to understand and manage the school;
- Participation in decision making is the process for encouraging teachers, parents and students to be involved in the school.

These reasons also explain why school-based management should be better than external control management in decision making.

Leadership style. According to Sergiovanni (1984), there are five levels of leadership of a principal (from low to high): technical leadership; human leadership; educational leadership; symbolic leadership; and cultural leadership. The leadership style of external control management may stay at the lower levels where techniques and human relationship are regarded as being more important in achieving the school goals and complete the tasks assigned by the external authority. This style may neglect the symbolic and cultural aspects of leadership. If we believe that school work is becoming more uncertain, complicated and difficult, and the background, thought and talent of school members are more diverse than before, then the symbolic and cultural aspects of the principal's leadership should be emphasized. The principal should set a good example to help school members to understand and appreciate the underlying meaning of various school activities, unify the diversity among members, clarify the uncertainty and ambiguity, develop the unique culture and mission of the school, and motivate everybody to work for a better future. In short, responding to the change to school-based management, the principal's leadership style may be changed from the lower levels to multi-levels of leadership, including not only technical leadership and human leadership but also educational, symbolic and cultural leadership.

Use of power. Management cannot avoid the use of power. Based on the different sources of power, French and Raven (1968) classified power into five categories: *reward, coercive, legitimate, reference and expert* power. The frequently used power in externally controlled schools may be *legitimate, coercive, reward* power, but *reference* power and *expert* power are often neglected. Using this unbalanced power to manage education organization may bring about bad results that influence the performance and satisfaction of school members (Bachman, *et al.*, 1968). Therefore, the traditional style in the use of power should be changed. Since school-based management intends to develop human resources and encourage members' commitment and initiative, administrators are recommended to use mainly *expert* and *reference* power, and pay attention to teachers' professional growth, become professional leader of teachers, and inspire teachers and students to work enthusiastically with their noble personality.

Management skills.   Following the rapid development of studies in the behavioral science and organization theory, many important management skills have been developed and widely applied to various organizations. For example, there are many scientific methods for decision analysis, various skills for conflict management, and effective strategies for organizational change and development. In external control management, schools implement only orders from the central authority and they are closely supervised. In this way the central authority is bearing most of the internal managing responsibility of the school and thus the managing work and skills required for school administrators are comparatively more simple. But once a school has adopted school-based management, internal managing work becomes more complicated and heavy. Then new concepts and management skills are needed.

Use of Resources

In order to carry out universal education, most of the resources and expenses of public schools come directly from the government. The government needs to watch closely how the schools use the resources. As described by the Education and Manpower Branch and Education Department of the Hong Kong Government (1991), the use of resources of all Hong Kong public schools has to be under strict supervision, and the schools must consult or get approval from the central authority on nearly every aspect of school finance. In general, it is also not easy for public schools to procure new resources by themselves under the constraints of the central authority. Therefore, it is not surprising that schools cannot use their resources effectively in accordance with the needs of management and teaching activities. At the same time the central authority needs a lot of manpower and resources to supervise the use of resources in schools. Ever since the 1980s in England, Canada, Australia and the United States, different forms of School Self-Budgeting Programs have been started to let schools have greater autonomy to use and procure resources (Caldwell and Spinks, 1988). Hong Kong has also been working toward the increase of autonomy of schools in using resources (Education and Manpower Branch and Education Department, 1991). Self-budgeting may provide an important condition for schools to use resources effectively according to their own characteristics and needs to solve problems in time and pursue their own goals.

Role Differences

The role of the concerned school members is directly or indirectly determined by the school management policy of the government, the school mission, the nature of school activities, the school internal managing strategies and the style of using resources. Based on the discussion in above paragraphs, there should be obvious differences between school-based management and external control management in terms of the roles of the school, the central authority, administrators, teachers and parents.

Role of school.   The role of externally controlled schools is in passive and receptive style. Its major concern is to carry out assigned duties and to follow closely administration procedures to avoid making any mistakes. Even when some procedural rules may contradict the benefits of students and teachers, they will still be put in the first place. But school-based management aims at developing students, teachers and the school according to the school's own characteristics, therefore the role of the school is in initiative-developing style, solving problems and exploring all possibilities for facilitating teachers' effective teaching and students' effective learning.

Role of education department.   In external control management, the key actor is the central authority (or education department) whose role is a strict supervisor to control and supervise all school activities no matter how big or small, and the expansion of bureaucratic system is inevitable. In school-based management, the key actor is the school; the role of the central authority is only a supporter or advisor who helps schools to develop their resources and specialty to carry out effective teaching activities.

Role of administrators.   For externally controlled schools, school mission and goals are given from outside and the role of school administrators is a goal watcher whose job is to prevent the school from not abiding to the central orders or ordinances. They are also personnel supervisors and resource controllers who handle personnel affairs and resources by following the regulations. On the contrary, the role of administrators in school-based management is a goal developer and leader, a manpower starter and coordinator and also a resource developer. They develop new goals for the school according to its situation and needs and lead school members to proceed toward their goals with full collaboration and involvement in school functioning. They also broaden their resources to promote school development (Sergiovanni, 1984).

Role of teachers.   Under external control management, the role of teacher is employee, follower, and order receiver and implementer. They are passive and cannot participate in decision making. They only listen to orders and perform duties assigned by the school and the central authority. But in school-based management, the school ideal and managing strategies encourage participation and development, and the role of teacher is partner, decision maker, developer and, of course, implementer. They work together with shared commitment and participate in decision making to promote effective teaching and develop their schools with enthusiasm (Jones and Maloy, 1988).

Role of parent.   Although parents are subjects who receive the service of educating their children from schools, there are obvious differences of their roles in schools of different managing styles. In externally controlled schools, parents receive a kind of quantity services in terms of standard duration of a lesson, number of years, content of curricula, etc. Their role is as passive receiver. They cannot participate in the school process and express their expectations. There is no way for parents to inspect or supervise the school. On the contrary, in school-based management, parents receive a kind of quality service in which the students receive the education they need. The role of parents is partner and supporter. They can participate in the school process, educate students cooperatively, put efforts to assist the healthy development of the school by contributing resources and information, and support and protect the school in time of difficulties and crisis (Berger, 1987; Cheng, 1991g).

The change in management style may induce a change in the role of all school constituencies, particularly when school management is shifted from the external control management model to the school-based management model. The passive role of the school, administrators, teachers and parents should be changed to active roles. Only in this way, can resources be developed and used effectively to bring improvement to the school.

Human Relations

My previous study (Cheng, 1991c) on the organizational environment of Hong Kong secondary schools revealed that there are four types of school environmental climate: *commitment style, headless style, disengagement style* and *control style*. In terms of the nature of school-based management, human relations tend to be open and cooperative; team spirit and mutual commitment are emphasized, and the organizational climate seems to be the commitment type. In comparison, external control management emphasizes the hierarchical relationship and implementation of orders and there are different interests for higher and lower staff. Human relations tend to be closed and realistic. The organizational climate may not be good: if the principal is disengaged in the school, the climate will have a *headless style*; if most teachers tend to be disengaged or not interested in work, while the principal is not helping, the climate will have a *disengagement style*; if the principal shows suppressive management, and is indifferent to teachers' reaction, the climate will have a *control style*. All these three styles of organizational climate are harmful to the teaching and management of the school and thus affect school effectiveness (Cheng, 1991c).

Quality of Administrators

External control management and school-based management are two entirely different management models and the quality of administrators is much different. Since the external control model only emphasizes implementing assigned duties and avoiding mistakes, administrators with considerable relevant experiences, familiar with present ordinances and able to work according to regulations and prevent problems, are often regarded as very important. If there is not much change in system, they do not need to learn or to be retrained.

In the school-based management mode, schools have considerable autonomy. Participation and development are regarded as important in facing complicated education work and pursuing educational effectiveness. In this case, the requirement of administrator quality is very high. They not only should be equipped with modern management knowledge and techniques to develop resources and manpower, but also need to learn and grow continuously, to discover and solve problems for school improvement (Argyris and Schon, 1974). In short, in addition to being familiar with present school ordinance, they also need to broaden their views and open their minds to learning so that they can promote long-term development for their schools.

Indicators of Effectiveness

As discussed before, the development of school mission and goals may not be necessary for externally controlled schools. Hence academic achievements at the last stage of schooling are the only major indicator of school effectiveness rather than educational process and other important achievements. As discussed in Chapters 1 and 2, school effectiveness should be evaluated by multi-level and multi-facet indicators. In the school-based model, evaluation of school effectiveness should be a learning process and a method for helping school improvement. Therefore, evaluation of effectiveness should pay attention to multi-levels (i.e., the school, groups, individuals), multi-facet indicators including input, process and output of schooling in addition to academic development of students.

The Measurement of the Tendency towards School-based Management

Based on the conception of characteristics of school-based management and external control management, a measure can be developed to assess the tendency of a school's movement towards school-based management. As shown in Table 4.2 (pp. 50–51), eleven of the characteristics such as the school mission, the nature of school activities, the concept of school organization, the decision making style, the use of resources, the role of the school, the role of administrators, the role of teachers, the role of parents, human relations, and the indices of effectiveness can be selected and differentiated into two extreme ends of a spectrum with one end standing for school-based management and the other for external control management. A measure can be developed to assess the tendency of a school to move towards school-based management in terms of these key characteristics, including eleven items, each of which rated on a seven-point scale with one closest to school-based management and seven closest to external control management. The following is an example:

Role of teacher is partner, decision maker, developer and implementer	1 2 3 4 5 6 7	Role of teacher is employer, order receiver, and implementer

Before doing the statistical analysis, the scores of items are reversely recoded. Then the total score of the eleven items represents the tendency towards the mode of school-based management (see Table 4.2).

This measure was tested in one of my ongoing research projects (started from 1991) that aims to investigate a school management reform entitled 'School Management Initiative' in Hong Kong. The project involved 241 aided secondary schools (76 per cent of the school population), 127 supervisors, 204 principals and over 6300 teachers. About one-sixth (1092) of the sampled teachers were randomly chosen to complete this measure (and at the same time, the other teachers completed different sets of instruments). The scores of teachers within each sampled school were averaged, to yield a school score which reflected the school's tendency to use school-based management. Based on the individual teachers' responses, the estimated reliability (internal consistency) alpha was 0.932. It seems that the measure is quite reliable. Principal component analysis was further used to observe its factor structure. Only one principal component was extracted with eigen value 6.57 and explained variance 59 per cent. The finding supports the construct validity of the measure (Cheng, 1993l).

In order to further investigate its concurrent validity and predictive validity, the tendency towards school-based management was correlated with three categories of measures: *teacher performance*, *principal's leadership* and *organizational performance*. Teacher performance was assessed by the following measures:

- Sense of Efficacy — refers to a teacher's perceptions that his or her teaching is worth the effort, leading to the success of students and is personally satisfying. It is a four-item measure adapted from Newmann, Rutter and Smith (1989) and rated on a seven-point scale;
- Sense of Community — refers to the relationship of unity, belonging and cooperative interdependence among peers. The measure was adapted from Newmann, *et al.*, 1989, including five items and rated on a seven-point scale;
- Professional Interest — refers to the extent to which teachers discuss professional matters, show interest in their work and seek further professional development. This seven-item measure was adapted from Fraser and Fisher (1990) and rated on a seven-point scale.

Developed from Bolman and Deal (1991b) and Sergiovanni (1984), principal's leadership was assessed by the following dimensions (Cheng, 1993k):

- Human Leadership — refers to the extent to which the principal is supportive and fosters participation. It includes seven items and is rated on a seven-point scale;

- Structural Leadership — the extent to which the principal thinks clearly and logically, develops clear goals and policies, and holds people accountable for results; It includes seven items and is rated on a seven-point scale;
- Political Leadership — the extent to which the principal is persuasive and effective at building alliances and support and solving conflicts. It includes five items and is rated on a seven-point scale;
- Symbolic Leadership — the extent to which the principal is inspirational and charismatic. It includes six items and is rated on a seven-point scale;
- Educational Leadership — the extent to which the principal emphasizes and encourages professional development and teaching improvement. It includes five items and is rated on a seven-point scale.

Organizational Performance was assessed by the following variables:

- School's Organizational Structure — assessed by three measures adapted from Oldman and Hackman (1981) and Hage and Aiken (1967): formalization (four items), hierarchy of authority (two items), and participation in decision making (four items);
- Perceived Organizational Effectiveness of School — assessed by a measure adapted from Mott (1972) which describes the productivity, adaptability, and flexibility dimensions of effectiveness (eight items);
- Satisfaction to Principal — Teachers Relationship — assessed by a measure developed from a research project (Chan, Cheng and Hau, 1991) (ten items);
- Organizational Culture — assessed in terms of the strength of organizational ideology (Alvesson, 1987). Based on Price and Mueller (1986) an index of organizational ideology was developed in Cheng (1993h) and used to describe the strength of organizational culture in school;
- Clarity of School Management and Accountability — refers to the extent teachers know clearly the roles of management at higher levels, staff appraisal system, the school's financial situation, resources management, school plan and role expectations. It was developed for this project including thirteen items and rated on a seven-point scale;
- Need for Improvement — refers to the need for improvement in fifteen aspects of school functioning such as parental support, quality of student input, instructional resources, physical environment and facilities, staff professional development, morale, student performance, decision participation, teacher appraisal, and administrative procedures and management. It was developed for this project including fifteen items and rated on a seven-point scale.

The reliability and validity of the measures were documented. Most of them have been tested and used in previous studies. In order to reduce the response set and the time taken for completing questionnaires, the measures were grouped into four sets and completed by four groups of randomly assigned teachers within each

Table 4.3: Tendency towards school-based management as related to teacher performance, leadership and organizational performance

	Tendency towards School-based Management
Teacher Performance	
Sense of Efficacy	.3172**
Sense of Community	.3497**
Professional Interest	.3590**
Principal's Leadership	
Human Leadership	.3851**
Structural Leadership	.3348**
Political Leadership	.3411**
Cultural Leadership	.4057**
Educational Leadership	.3983**
Organizational Performance	
Principal-Teachers Relationship	.3674**
Hierarchy of Authority	−.2226**
Participation	.3892**
Formalization	.1521
Clarity of School Management and Accountability	.5012**
Organizational Effectiveness	.3685**
Strength of Organizational Culture	.3734**
Need for School Improvement	−.4825**

No. of Schools: 220   * $p < 0.01$,   ** $p < 0.001$

school. The responses of each measure were averaged within each sampled school to yield a score for the school. The unit of analysis is the school.

The results of Pearson correlation between the measure of school-based management tendency and the above measures are summarized in Table 4.3. The tendency towards school-based management is strongly correlated with nearly all the measures of teacher performance, principal leadership and organizational performance, except for formalization. The findings suggest that tendency of school-based management is positively related to teachers' sense of efficacy, sense of community and professional interest, the principal's human leadership, structural leadership, political leadership, cultural leadership and educational leadership, principal-teacher relationship, teachers' participation in decision making and clarity of school management and accountability, school organizational effectiveness and strength of organizational culture. But it is negatively related to the need for school improvement and hierarchy of authority. From its close relationship to positive teacher performance, strong principal's leadership in multi-dimensions, positive human relationship, teacher participation, clarity of accountability, effective organizational functioning and strong sharing of school values and beliefs, we can see that the concurrent validity and predictive validity of the measure of tendency of school-based management are strongly supported.

According to the upper 30 per cent and the lower 30 per cent of the scores of tendency towards school-based management, two groups of schools were classified as relatively *school-based type* and *external control type*. The profiles of these two groups in terms of measures of teacher performance, principal's leadership and

Table 4.4: Comparison between profiles of school-based type and external control type

	School-based Type Group Mean	External Control Type Group Mean	t-value
Teacher Performance			
Sense of Efficacy	.4383	−.3115	4.47***
Sense of Community	.4894	−.3649	5.05***
Professional Interest	.5352	−.3071	4.75***
Principal's Leadership			
Human Leadership	.5225	−.3842	5.55***
Structural Leadership	.4453	−.3406	4.78***
Political Leadership	.4658	−.3373	4.74***
Cultural Leadership	.5533	−.4507	6.57***
Educational Leadership	.5352	−.4058	6.27***
Organizational Performance			
Principal-Teacher Relations	.5079	−.4024	5.43***
Hierarchy of Authority	−.3298	.2790	−4.24***
Participation	.5264	−.2660	4.92***
Formalization	.2044	−.0082	1.26
Clarity of School Management Accountability	.5937	−.5646	7.72***
Organizational Effectiveness	.4802	−.4732	5.30***
Organizational Culture	.5291	−.2820	4.94***
Need for Improvement	−.6354	.5938	−8.06***

* $p < 0.05$, ** $p < 0.01$, *** $p < 0.001$

organizational performance were mapped and compared as shown in Table 4.4. All the measures were standardized with mean equal to 0 and standard deviation equal to 1.

As shown in Table 4.4, the profile of the schools in the school-based type is very different from that of the external control type in nearly all the measures of teacher performance, principal leadership and organizational performance, except formalization. In those school-based type schools, teachers tend to show higher sense of efficacy, sense of community, and professional interest and principals tend to have a stronger leadership in terms of structural, cultural, human, political and educational aspects. Principal–teachers relationship is positive and organizational effectiveness is high. There is strong sharing of school goals, values and beliefs among school members. Decision making is decentralized and teacher participation is encouraged. The need for improvement in these schools is perceived as not so strong.

Comparatively, in the schools of the external control type, teachers show less confidence in their work and less cooperative interdependence among colleagues and they are not so interested in professional development and professional matters. Principals lack leadership in managing schools in nearly all the important aspects and their teachers are not satisfied with the relationship with them. The schools are perceived as ineffective in terms of productivity, flexibility and adaptability. There seem no clear school mission, goals, values and beliefs shared among members. Decision making in these schools is quite centralized and teachers have few opportunities to participate. Teachers perceive that the schools need to be improved in most important aspects of school functioning such as parental support, quality of student input, instructional resources, physical environment and facilities, staff professional development, morale, student performance, decision participation, teacher appraisal, and administrative procedures and management. The above findings provide further evidence to support that the measure of tendency towards school-based management is valid in predicting some of the important characteristics of school management and organizational performance.

School-based Management as the Condition for Pursuing Effectiveness

School-based management and external control management are based on entirely different management theories. School-based management employs principles of equifinality and decentralization, assumes the school as a self-managing system and regards initiative of human factor and improvement of internal process as important. But external control management uses principles of standard structure and centralization, assumes the school as merely an implementing system, and pays major attention to structural control. Due to the differences in management theory, the characteristics of school functioning and internal management in the school are greatly different.

In school-based management, schools have clear school mission, strong organizational culture and school-based education activities. In these schools, managing strategies encourage participation and give full play to members' initiative. There is also considerable autonomy of using and procuring resources. The role of people concerned is active and developmental. Human relationship is open and cooperative with mutual commitment. The administrators should be of high quality and always willing to learn. Evaluation of school effectiveness should include multi-level and multi-facet indicators of input, process and output in order to help the school learn to improve.

In contrast, the school mission and organizational culture of schools under external control management tend to be vague. In these schools, internal activities which are determined by external factors might not match with school needs. Conservative managing strategies are often used for supervision, not for encouragement. The use of resources is formalized by the central authority and usually cannot be used effectively for development. The roles of the school and people concerned are passive and receptive. Human relationship is closed, alienated and difficult for cooperation. The requirement of administrator quality is not high so long as they are familiar with the existing regulations. One-sided indicators are used for evaluation of school effectiveness neglecting the process and development of the school and are thus rarely helpful to school improvement.

Obviously, school-based management with sufficient autonomy, flexibility and ownership in school functioning can provide the necessary condition for facilitating schools to achieve multiple goals and maximize effectiveness on multiple criteria in a dynamic way in the long run. External control management limits the initiative of schools and, of course, cannot encourage schools to learn, develop and pursue effectiveness on multiple goals. This is the reason why so many school reforms are making efforts to shift from external control management to school-based management in different parts of the world.

Chapter 5

Self-management at Multiple Levels

In Chapter 4, the basic theory of school-based management was introduced and discussed. The characteristics of school-based management can provide the necessary condition for facilitating schools to develop and pursue dynamic school effectiveness. In this chapter, the advantages of school-based management will be further developed with integration of the concepts of strategic management and self-management at multi-levels in school.

The Need for A Multi-level Perspective

Many contemporary school-based management studies address decentralization or self-management only at the school level and often assume that increased school autonomy and responsibilities will result in school effectiveness in producing quality educational outcomes (Cohen, 1988). Yet, this assumption is questionable. Regarding the effect of school-based management, investigators do not come to a convergent view. Some of them noted that school-based management is effective in enhancing the satisfaction level of teachers, parents and students as well as teachers' professionalism (see Brown, 1990; Collins and Hanson, 1991; David, 1989). On the other hand, some observed rather negative results. They found that the level of anxiety and overload is rather high and there is an absence of empirical evidence that school-based management is related to students' educational outcomes (see Arnott, Bullock and Thomas, 1992; Cheng, 1992a; Malen, Ogawa and Kranz, 1990; Mitchell, 1991). All these results reflect the need for further understanding school-based management.

Virtually, schools adopt school-based management and become self-managing under the blessing of centrally framed policies and endorsed structure. Thus, within these centrally set frames, schools are self-managing in their daily operations related to site level issues like the formulation of a school charter, program planning and implementation, budgeting, evaluation and monitoring (Caldwell and Spinks, 1992). If the main concern of school-based management in school is to pursue school effectiveness on multiple school functions at different levels in a dynamic way, we need to explore further how schools can fully use the strengths of school-based management to become effectively self-managing, particularly in dealing with issues related to staff performance and effectiveness not only at the school level but also at the group and individual levels. Despite this, there are exceptionally few studies addressing the conception of school-based management in terms of self-management at multi-levels in school.

Indeed, within the context of self-managing schools and the loosely supervised nature of teaching (Deal and Celotti, 1980; Owens, 1991; Sergiovanni, *et al.*, 1992; Weick, 1982), the initiative and commitment of individual teachers or groups of staff in discharging their daily duties is of prime importance in bringing about internal school effectiveness. This initiative of teachers can be considered as a kind of self-management of their professional task (Caldwell and Spinks, 1992; Stoll and Fink, 1992). It seems that school-based management should further be understood in terms of self-management at the school level, the group level and the individual staff level.

Self Management at the School Level: Strategic Management

As discussed in Chapter 4, the ongoing school-based management movement aims at creating conditions for the school to be responsive to the changing internal and external environments, to develop and achieve its goals and to have organizational development and learning. Thus, it is important to have an appropriate management process to ensure that effective self-management in school could be achieved. Regarding this, theorists (e.g., Caldwell and Spinks, 1992; Cheng, 1993c; 1994f; Holt, 1990) indicated that strategic management is effective in providing vitality for the school to meet external and internal challenges and maximize school effectiveness. It is a process that can keep a school as a whole appropriately matched to its environment, improve school performance, achieve school objectives and develop continuously. Therefore, school-based management, particularly self-management at the school level, should be based on a strategic management process, as shown in Figure 5.1.

Strategic management is a cyclic process which consists of five stages: environmental analysis, planning and structuring, staffing and directing, implementing, and monitoring and evaluating (Cheng, 1993c; 1994f). The major difference of strategic management from traditional management is the strong emphasis on development planning and strategies responding to the short- and long-term influences from the changing environments. Therefore, environmental analysis and the cyclic process are very important in strategic management. Other components such as planning, structuring, staffing, directing, monitoring and evaluating may be based on the traditional management process as described by Mackenzie (1969). In each stage of the management process, the contribution of participation and leadership is important and necessary.

Environmental Analysis

The initial stage of the strategic management process is environmental analysis in which the school (including the concerned school members) as a whole reflects on

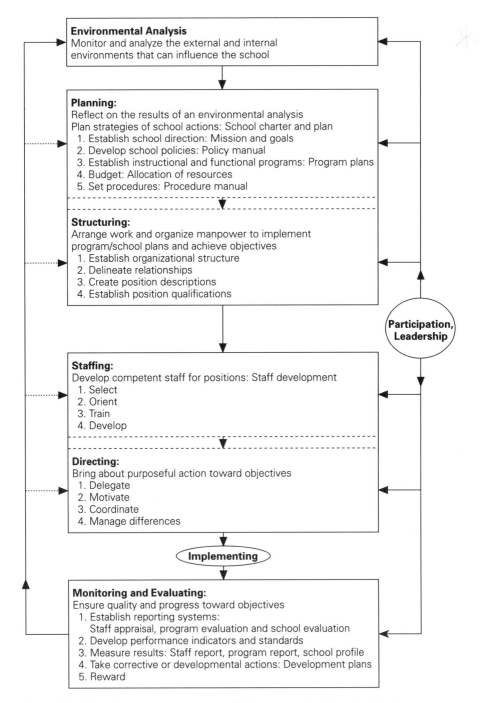

Figure 5.1: Strategic management process: Self-management at the school level

its internal and external environments relevant and crucial to its existence and also on its mission and goals in such environments.

At this stage, the external and internal environments are monitored and analyzed in terms of strength, weakness, opportunity and threats. The results of the analysis will serve as the bases for the planning stage. The external environment may include social, political, economic, cultural and technological development of the society, competitions from other schools, expectations of parents and members of the community, potential student population in the district, educational innovations, central education authority's direction in providing education services, etc. On the other hand, the school also analyses its internal environment in terms of human resources, financial resources, physical resources, student intake, school climate, its various education programs, etc.

In the process of environmental analysis, the school may have further under-standing of its effectiveness on the structural/technical functions, the human/social functions, the political functions, the cultural functions, and the educational func-tions at the different levels (see Chapter 1). Resulting from this analysis, the school further reflects on its mission and goals. In the analysis, development of meanings (such as why be it, what to value, why do it, etc.) for the school is very important for justifying the school's survival and effective implementation of all school activ-ities. Understanding positive meanings of school activities can help school members make sense of what they are doing and motivate them to be committed in school activities, to work hard, and develop themselves professionally. The developed meanings can guide the direction of all management activities such as planning, structuring, staffing, directing and evaluation, and also guide the direction of teach-ing and learning. The stronger the meanings are shared among staff, the stronger the school culture (i.e., the stronger the sharing of values, beliefs and assumptions). In other words, meaning developments start the building of school culture.

Planning and Structuring

The results of environmental analysis contribute valuable and powerful information for the school to plan strategies for school actions including establishing school mission, policies, programs, budget, organizational structure and work procedures in its existing external and internal environments. School mission and objectives can be established through participative decision making involving all important school members. School mission is a statement of school direction and purpose including such information as the scope of service, philosophy of the school, beliefs and values about education and management, school self-image, and guiding principles for school functions. To a great extent, school mission is a summary of meanings for all school activities, focusing all school members' attention and effort in a common direction.

Since every school has its own multiple environmental constraints, resource limitation, time boundary and different interest groups, it will experience pressure in setting up priorities for targets to be achieved in the dynamic process of pursuing multiple school effectiveness (see Chapter 3). This pressure may push various interest parties of the school to negotiate and agree to a shared priority of targets to be achieved within a certain time frame under the blessing of the school mission. During the process of decision making, all parties concerned participate and make use of the result of environmental analysis to draw up resolutions and establish school policies. The practice of participative decision making may develop a sense of ownership among those participating and the resulting resolutions will have a greater chance of successful implementation as compared to those imposed by external authority (Caldwell and Spinks, 1988; 1992; David, 1989; Fullan, 1992).

Based on the results of shared decision making, the school plans various functional and instructional programs and allocates resources to them. The establishment of an appropriate organizational structure and work procedures for achieving the set objectives is necessary. This includes also an appropriate communication flow, delineation of relationships, job specifications, position requirements, chain of command and other related issues. In sum, the planning and structuring process aims to make rational decisions on school direction and maximize the effectiveness of methods, resources and structure for achieving school goals and pursuing further development.

Staffing and Directing

With attainable school plans and appropriate structure, the self-managing process then proceeds to the staffing and directing stage. Staffing and directing are necessary for school development and effective implementation of school actions, aiming at developing competent staff and helping them bring about purposeful actions towards school objectives and effectiveness.

Staffing includes recruiting competent people for the positions, inducing new staff to the working situation, training staff to have the necessary knowledge and skills for performing their jobs, and providing opportunities for their professional development. Directing includes delegating responsibilities to staff, motivating staff towards outputting quality work, managing their differences by encouraging independent thought and resolving conflicts, coordinating efforts in effective combination, stimulating their creativity and innovation and providing directions to staff. Successful staffing and directing can maximize the effectiveness of all human initiative and power in implementing school plan and program plans, achieving school objectives, and pursuing long-term school development. The theory and practice of staff development will be introduced and discussed in Chapter 8.

Implementing

At this stage the school as a whole implements planned programs. Focus is put on ensuring the availability of necessary resources, guidance and support to successful launching of functional and instructional programs. The school coordinates the utilization of resources among different task/program groups and encourages effective use of all scarce resources. Additional resources, guidance and support may be provided whenever a need is identified. This stage ensures that the implementation of all programs are effective and consistent with the school policies and objectives.

Monitoring and Evaluating

At this stage, the performance of the school as a whole is evaluated and monitored to ensure the progress towards the goals and objectives according to programs and school plan. The school establishes its reporting and evaluation systems (for staff appraisal, program evaluation and school evaluation), the performance indicators and standards, and the reward system for individual staff and program teams. By means of these systems, the performance of the school is monitored, evaluated and regulated. The performance are summarized in staff reports, program reports and the school profile. The focus is to ensure the quality of school programs, take corrective actions and plan developments. The information obtained at this stage is useful for reflecting on the school's environments, reconsidering the school's direction, re-establishing policies, replanning action programs and reorganizing structures. In other words, the results of monitoring and evaluating will contribute to the start of the next strategic managing cycle. This stage can provide the necessary information for helping individuals, groups and the school to learn, improve and develop.

Leadership and Participation

Throughout the process, participation of school members and leadership of principal (/administrators) are necessary and crucial. Leadership is responsible for initiating and maintaining the strategic management process (Caldwell and Spinks, 1992; Cheng, 1993g) for developing school culture that facilitates the continuous pursuit of school effectiveness and development (Schein, 1992; Sergiovanni, 1984) and for ensuring quality and effectiveness in instructional activities and coordinating curriculum across the individual, program and school levels (Hallinger and Murphy, 1987). The contribution of leadership to strategic management will be further discussed in later chapters.

Participation involving multiple strategic constituencies such as teachers, students, parents and community leaders in the strategic management process (particularly the decision making component) is very important to the success of self-management at the school level. It is the involvement of school members or strategic constituencies in important activities related to decision making and planning such as searching for meanings, identifying problems, procuring and sharing information, developing ideas, making policy, planning actions or programs, and sharing responsibility and authority. In general, participation may serve the following functions for the management process and school effectiveness:

- Participation provides important human resources in terms of participants' time, experience, knowledge, and skills for better planning and implementation;
- Participation can produce high quality decisions and plans by involving different perspectives and expertise;
- Greater participation can promote greater responsibility, accountability, commitment support to implementation and results;
- Participation in planning and decision making is a form of meanings development or culture building that contributes to team spirit and organizational integration;
- Participation in management provides opportunities for individuals and groups to enrich their professional experience and pursue professional development;
- Participation in planning and decision making provides greater opportunities for schools to overcome resistance and change ineffective practices; and
- Participation is an important value or right for the concerned constituencies.

The Potential Advantages of Strategic Management in School

From the experience of using strategic management in the business sector or other organizations as described by Greenley (1986), the potential strengths of strategic management in school may be summarized as follows:

- increases school's ability to promote high quality learning and teaching;
- helps the school to allocate and use resources more effectively;
- boosts the commitment of school members to achieve long-term objectives through participative planning;
- helps the school to match the changing environment;
- signals that problems may arise before they happen;
- helps school administrators become more genuinely interested in the school;
- alerts the school to changes and allows for action in response to change;
- identifies any need to redefine the nature of education and management;
- improves the channeling of effort toward the attainment of predetermined objectives;
- enables school administrators to have a clearer understanding of school management;
- facilitates the identification and exploitation of future opportunities for school development and improvement;
- offers an objective view of management problems;
- provides a framework for reviewing the execution of the plan and for controlling activities;
- minimizes the ill effects of adverse conditions and changes;
- helps school members relate major decisions more effectively to established objectives;

- renders more effective allocation of time and resources to identified opportunities;
- coordinates the execution of the tactics that make up the plan;
- allows for the integration of all school functions into a combined effort;
- minimizes the resources and time that must be devoted to correcting erroneous *ad hoc* decisions;
- creates a framework for internal communication among personnel;
- allows for the ordering of priorities within the time frame of the plan;
- gives the school an advantage on long-term development;
- helps marshal the behavior of individuals in the school into a total effort;
- provides a basis for the clarification of individual responsibilities and thereby contributes to motivation;
- encourages 'forward thinking' on the part of personnel;
- stimulates a cooperative, integrated, and enthusiastic approach to tackling problems and opportunities.

The above five stages of strategic management process are sequential in order and each provides directions and a base on which the next stage is initiated. With this in mind, the strategic managing process or self-management at the school level is self-propelling and cyclic in nature. The above cyclic self-management process allows the school as a whole to be aware of changing challenges, to readjust its school mission, policies and action plans to these new challenges. In this way, self-renewal and learning occur as a result of the school's adaptability to the ever changing external and internal environments. The major characteristics of this cyclic self-management process at the school level are summarized in Table 5.1.

In addition to self management at the school level, effective school-based management can only be actualized through the performance of staff members in various work groups. The following section will therefore focus on developing the concept of self management at the group level and the individual staff level.

Self-management at the Group Level

In the past twenty years, there has been an increasing emphasis on employees' personal control and responsibilities, and numerous organizations have adopted strategies of greater self-management among managers and professional employees (Graen and Uhl-Bien, 1991b; Manz, 1983; Manz and Sims, 1987; Walton, 1985). This trend aims at developing a stronger concept of *self-management* as opposed to *management by others* in organizations. In the 1990s, the work world leans towards participative management through the introduction of self-managing work teams by empowering staff (Donovan, 1989; Odiorne, 1991) which elicits commitment and work initiative of employees (Hackman, 1986; Walton, 1985). Staff self-management is essentially required for top quality output of organizations (Manz, 1986; Sandy, 1990; Stewart, 1992).

The above development of staff self-management has its implications to the

Table 5.1: *Self-management process at different levels*

Stages of Self-Management	Process at the School Level	Process at the Group Level
Environmental Analysis	• reflect on the school's internal and external environment crucial to its existence • focus on its strengths, weaknesses, opportunities and threats as a school	• reflect on the group's internal and external environment crucial to its existence • focus on its strengths and weaknesses, opportunities and threats as a group
Planning and Structuring	• develop school mission, policies and action plans • negotiate and compromise in decision • focus on structural issues such as organizational structure, budgeting and allocation of resources	• develop group's direction and action plans consistent with the school's mission and policies • negotiate and compromise in decision • focus on issues like work designs, relationship delineation, and communication flows
Staffing and Directing	• recruit and deploy staff • focus on human resource aspects of management such as staff development and delegation	• deploy of members • focus on professional development of members and group learning

Stages of Self-Management	Process at Individual Level
Environmental Analysis	• reflect on personal attributes and external environment • focus on personal strengths, weaknesses, opportunities and threats as a member in the group and school
Planning and Affiliating	• develop personal goals and action plans within the frames delineated by the school and the group • focus on the technical aspects of planning and designing of educational programs • establish affiliation and relationship with colleagues, students, parents and community
Developing and Directing	• develop personal professional competence • allocate personal resources and attention • focus on personal learning

Table 5.1: (Cont.)

Stages of Self-Management	Process at the School Level	Process at the Group Level
Implementing	• ensure the availability of necessary resources, guidance and support • focus on issues related to actual launching of all programs	• ensure the proper allocation of resources • ensure mutual guidance and support among members to facilitate effective problem solving • focus on program implementation by the group
Monitoring and Evaluating	• set up work standards, monitor and control system for groups or programs • monitor and regulate pace of program implementation • evaluate the whole school performance • focus on ensuring quality of programs • use information to initiate next cycle of school self management	• set up work standards for members, self-monitor and regulate work pace of the group • evaluate performance of the group as a whole • focus on ensuring the group performance in delivering programs • use information to initiate the next cycle of group self management

Stages of Self-Management	Process at Individual Level
Implementing	• ensure effective use of allocated resources • have frequent rehearsal • focus on personal performance in the program or group
Monitoring and Evaluating	• set up personal performance standards • observe self, monitor and regulate personal work pace • evaluate personal performance • focus on ensuring personal performance • use information to initiate the next cycle of individual self management

Adapted from W.M. Cheung and Y.C. Cheng (in press).

education field. Teaching is a highly autonomous and loosely supervised profession. When performing their duties, teachers are relatively autonomous and normally receiving a low degree of supervision from their principals. The staff may be, to a certain extent, self-managing at both the group and individual staff levels.

A work group may be considered as a small organization in the school. Based on this, the conception of self-management at the school level might be extended to the group level. Thus, self-management of a work group may be conceptualized in a similar self-propelling and cyclic self-managing process as at the school level. Within the available autonomy and boundaries given in the school framework, self-management process at the group level (referred to as *group self-management* hereafter) is presented in Table 5.1 (see pp. 73–74).

In the first stage, the work group performs environmental analysis in the self-management cycle. It reflects on its strength, weakness, opportunity and threat as a group in its external and internal environment. External environment may include its relationship with other groups, the nature of students, parental expectations, school climate, etc. Internal environment may include the relationship among group members, group norm, commitment and professional competence of members, values and beliefs of members, etc.

Based on the reflection on the results of environmental analysis, the self-managing group plans its courses of actions to accomplish its assignment. It develops its own mission and goals that are expected to be consistent with the school mission. The shared mission and goals among members is crucial for effective functioning of the group (Hughes, 1991). With this mission in mind, the group plans activities, delineates relationships, designs work procedures and communication flows. Workload of members is self regulated within the group. Conflicts may be solved through negotiation and compromise in participative decision making by group members.

Following planning and structuring, staffing in the group is framed by the available manpower allocated by the school. Within this frame, the group deploys the appropriate staff to accomplish the group's assignment. To ensure the availability of competent staff, the group sets high priority in professional development of staff and group learning. To achieve this, on-the-job training of new members is frequently adopted.

In the implementation stage, the focus is to launch educational programs effectively. The group regulates its own implementation schedule and ensures the proper allocation and utilization of its available resources. Mutual support and guidance among members is also effected to establish a strong supporting network within the group.

In order to ensure high quality group performance, the work group sets up its own work standards and regulates its own work pace. Self-evaluation of the group's performance against the set work standards is frequently conducted. To achieve this, frequent exchanges between members in matters relating to the tasks are consistently conducted. In this way, the group accomplishes its assigned tasks through continuous refinement and adjustment of performance. Moreover, the information obtained at this stage propels the group to initiate the next cycle of group self-management.

One of the key characteristics of group self-management is that problems encountered are tackled within the group in the first place. Participative group decision making is the usual mode of problem solving. External assistance will be sought for if the group deems the problem impossible to be resolved within the group. Some of the key factors that enable group self-management process to be effective are that: throughout the whole process, school management does not intervene in the group as long as the group's direction and mission are in line with the school mission and policies; the school management respects members' interests and working style; the school management establishes an atmosphere of open communication; and the school management treats teachers as the owners of their tasks. Previous studies such as McConkey (1989) and Puckett (1989) also support this view.

With the above proposed self-managing cycle, groups can be aware of the ever changing internal and external challenges and develop group members to face and manage these challenges. In this cycle, groups are self-educating and self-renewing. This inevitably enhances and develops teachers' professionalism and in turn benefits the school as a whole.

Self-management at the Individual Level

The core components of a group are individual members. A self-managing group without self-managing individuals will not function effectively (Manz, 1991; Novak, 1991). In order to maximize the effectiveness of a group, self-management at the individual level should be necessary. A self-management process that facilitates the individual to be responsive to external challenges and enables individual continuous learning is important. The earlier presented group self-management process with appropriate modifications may serve this purpose. Self-management at the individual level (referred to as individual self-management hereafter) may be conceptualized as a cyclic process similar to that at the group level. Within the autonomy and boundaries given in the group and the school, individual staff work through their self-management process as follows:

At the initial stage, the individual staff members perform environmental analysis. Similar to group self-management, they reflect on their internal and external environment. Internally they reflect on their personal attributes in terms of strengths, weaknesses, opportunities and threats as a member in the group and the school. They focus on analyzing their own professional competence, their personal goals, values, and beliefs about education and management, etc. Externally, they reflect on their relationship with other members, students' abilities and parental expectations, competition and co-operation with colleagues, etc.

Bearing similar focus as the planning and structuring stage of group self-management process, individuals basing reflections on the first stage formulate their own directions and courses of action, such as the style of teaching, to accomplish the assigned tasks within the available autonomy and allocated resource. Of course, their action plans are also framed by the missions of the group and the school. They

focus on the technical aspects of planning and designing of functional and instructional programs through developing their own work schedule and procedures
and selecting their own teaching content, sequence and methodology. Apart from
these, they also establish good affiliation and relationship with colleagues, students,
parents and members of the community. This good affiliation is important to effective planning and later implementation of plans.

After planning and affiliating, the individuals move further to prepare themselves for accomplishment of their assignment. This stage is modified from the
staffing and directing stage of the group self-management process. Individuals invest
their effort in developing their professional competence through frequent attendance
in professional enrichment programs and exchange of experience with colleagues.
They also focus on directing themselves by proper allocation of personal resources,
such as time and attention. In this way, they are always and capable of meeting the
challenges of the external environment to achieve the assigned task.

In the implementing stage, individuals focus on personal performance in the
program or group. In order to have effective implementation, they ensure the effective use of allocated resources and personal resources. Through frequent rehearsals,
they refine their actual performance in implementing the program. It is also noted
that self-managing staff always use reward and punishment to reinforce and drive
themselves in the self-management process (Manz, 1986).

At the last stage of the individual self-management cycle, the individuals set
their own performance standards and regulate their personal work pace. They monitor
and evaluate their performance through self-observation in accordance with their
set performance standards. The focus is to ensure high personal performance. They
then use the results of self-evaluation to initiate their next self-management cycle.

The primary characteristics of the above individual self-management process
are summarized in Table 5.1. This self-management cycle is self-propelling. In the
cycle, individual staff may be aware of his or her limitations and strengths, and
become more flexible and adaptable in achieving his or her assignments. As a
result, he or she inevitably becomes self-educating and renewing.

The major source of vitality for achieving the school mission rests with the
work of the individual staff who make up the groups and the school as a whole.
Therefore, self-management at the individual level is the primary building block for
self-management at the group level, which in turn is the corner stone of self-
management at the school level.

Self-management at Multi-levels

The self-managed school conceptualized as above is a cyclic self-influence process
in which staff (including administrators), given a certain degree of autonomy, design
their own directions and manage their own performance at the whole school level,
the group level and the individual level. The overall view of this conception is
illustrated in Figure 5.2. It suggests that in order to have effective school-based
management, self-management at all these levels should be necessary, and they

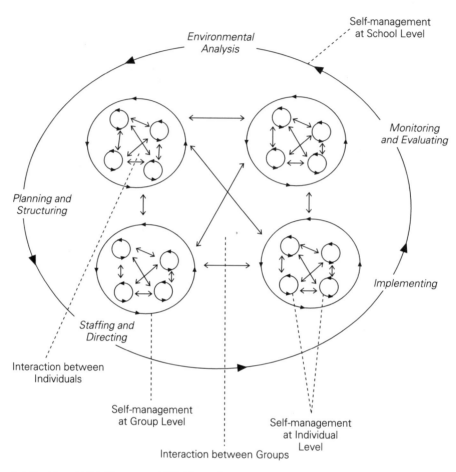

Adapted from W.M. Cheung and Y.C. Cheng (in press).

Figure 5.2: Self-management cycle at multi-levels

back up each other. The relationship between these self-management cycles is interlocking. In the first place, the extent of individual self-management is limited by the boundaries set by the group and school while that of group self-management is also framed by the boundaries set at the school level. These limitations are generally effected by the influence of the school on groups and the groups on individuals.

The results of school level environmental analysis will influence the groups' and individuals' directions, if not operationally, in performing their environmental analyses and action plans formulation. The next planning and structuring stage at the school level will also influence the functioning of the groups' and individuals' self-managing activities. In this way, we realize that the results of the various stages of the school self-management cycle will cast influence on the functioning of the group and individual self-management cycle. The similarity in nature of self-management cycles at the three levels allows us to assume corresponding influence from the groups on their members. Following the same line of reasoning, we may assume that each stage of the self-management cycle at an upper level has downward influences on a lower level cycle.

The school is a very complicated network in which staff interact with each other at various levels. The above proposed influence does not only happen downward. Similar but upward influence also occurs. For instance, individuals' environmental analysis results will shape their orientations when they participate in the school and group level activities. These orientations when consolidated as a whole will inevitably influence the direction and results of the decision making process at the school and group levels. In this way, individuals may influence upwardly the self-management process at group and school level. Similarly, we may assume that the same upward influence also exists between the group and school levels. Bearing this mutual influence in mind, it seems that in order to accomplish effective school-based management in school, a certain degree of consistency in the functioning of the self-management cycles across the three levels is essential. This may include the consistency in the school mission, group direction and individuals' goals; consistency in the work procedures formulated at school level and those at the group and individual levels; consistency in the directions of staff development across the three levels; and consistency in the pace of implementing educational programs.

Apart from upward and downward influence, a third type of influence: side-way influence can also be identified at both the group and individual levels. This influence is basically a result of inter- and intra-group interactions. According to Holt (1990), there are two types of interactions; namely the *required interaction* and the *optional interaction*. In either type of these interactions, individuals in groups interact with each other affectively, cognitively and behaviorally. In this way, the performance of individuals are influenced. At the group level, different groups may also bear influence in affective, cognitive and behavioral aspects on each other. These inter- and intra-group interaction effects, if observed and handled effectively, will have positive impacts on the successful implementation of self-management in school. On the contrary, if they are not observed and handled effectively, they may have detrimental effects on the effectiveness of self-management in school, especially when negative impacts that retard self-management are fused in the interactions.

Conditions for Facilitating Self-management

From the above discussion, we understand that effective self-management does not occur automatically in schools. It takes place when certain conditions are met. As a precondition, the central education authority should take the initiative to facilitate school-based management through decentralization of authority to the school level. With the appropriate autonomy, the school may initiate self-management at different levels. It has been stressed that the success of self-management rests largely on the performance of individual teachers in self-managing groups. Yet, without favorable and corresponding measures at the school level, successful self-management of teachers will be retarded (Jones and Meurs, 1991). Some of the critical measures and conditions at the school level that facilitate self-management of school at all levels are outlined below.

Conditions at the School Level

Participative decision making. A sense of ownership among staff is crucial in bringing about effectiveness (Fullan, 1992). Thus, the establishment of a mechanism of participative decision making which encourages school ownership is necessary. This may be achieved by establishing a school management council by inviting teachers and parents to serve as school managers. Parallel to this, routine school administration could be overseen by a school administration committee with the principal, panel chairmen and unit heads as members to contribute to the decisions related to school affairs. Other similar committees may be formed to serve different purposes, for example, a consultative council to resolve problems identified by teachers in their normal discharge of duties. Yet, the essence of participative decision making is the availability and openness of relevant information that will facilitate decision making.

Instructional autonomy. A mechanism which encourages autonomy in curriculum and instructional designs and delivery is of vital importance to activate professional self-management of the school. The school should delegate authority to curriculum developments and innovations and provide flexibility for the use of different types of resources within some given boundaries.

Open and autonomous school culture. The literature clearly indicates that the cultivation of an open and autonomous school culture is important in serving as a guidepost for the school and its staff to function effective self-management (Caldwell and Spinks, 1992; Deal and Peterson, 1990; Renihan and Renihan, 1984; Sergiovanni, 1984; 1990). Thus, the school should cultivate and sustain such a school culture in which staff members have shared mission and vision about education and self-management.

Strategic leadership. A new type of leadership, namely strategic leadership, is needed to initiate and direct the strategic management process or self-management at the school level. Strategic leadership may cover five different aspects such as technical leadership, human leadership, political leadership, cultural leadership, and educational leadership that can contribute directly to environmental analysis, planning and structuring, staffing and directing, implementing, monitoring and evaluating the strategic management process. The detail of strategic leadership will be discussed in Chapter 7.

Conditions at the Group and Individual Levels

School level measures will encourage self-management. The other conditions associated with the self-management at group and individual levels are also important and are outlined in terms of the affective, cognitive and behavioral areas as follows:

Affective conditions. Not everybody accepts the concept of self-management (Hughes, 1991). If self-management is to be successful, the affective readiness of individual staff and the group as a whole will be essential. This is a primary condition that facilitates the individuals and groups to accept and be ready to take up and commit to the responsibilities that come with self-management.

Cognitive conditions. Teachers' beliefs and values are important in determining their performance in school (Rosoff, Woolfolk and Hoy, 1991). In order to be effective self-managing individuals and groups, staff should have shared beliefs and values towards education services delivery (Caldwell and Spinks, 1992) and teamwork that are consistent with the school mission and objectives.

Behavioral conditions. Apart from cognitive and affective readiness, the group should also possess self-management competence and professional competence. Self-management competence at group level refers to the competent behavior of the group in 1) self-directing and planning (Graen and Uhl-Bien, 1991a; Latham and Locke, 1991; Manz and Sims, 1990); 2) self-regulating of work and pace (Salem, Lazarus and Cullen, 1992); 3) self-monitoring, control and problem solving (Graen and Uhl-Bien, 1991a; Sauers Hunt and Bass, 1990); 4) frequent exchange between members (Manz and Sims, 1990; Sauers, *et al.*, 1990); and training of group members (Salem, *et al.*, 1992). Based on the theory of Eraut (1993), professional competence refers to the competent mastery of professional knowledge (subject content) and process (teaching competency). In order that a group as a whole is behaviorally competent in self-management, its individual members should also be competent in the above mentioned self-management competence and professional competence.

Based on the conception of Manz (1983) and Manz and Sims (1990), self-management competence at individual level refers to the competent behavior of teachers in goal setting, management of cues, rehearsal, self-observation, self-reward, self-punishment, natural-rewards building and constructive-thought building. Profession competence refers to the mastery of professional knowledge (subject content) and process (teaching competency). It is believed that when individual teachers are competent in these two areas, they will be well equipped to be self-managing, perform their assignments competently and thus contribute to the group's performance as a whole.

From the above, we note that group self-management and individual self-management will not be attained unless the conditions at school level are first met and the above three conditions are also met. When any one of these conditions is not met, the effectiveness of self-management at the group and individual levels may be reduced.

Self-management and School Effectiveness

As discussed in Chapter 3, the dynamic perspective of school effectiveness emphasizes the sensitivity of a school to its changing environment and also the adaptation to internal and external constraints. Resolving inherent organizational conflicts and maximizing school effectiveness on multiple functions at multi-levels is possible in a long-term process. To a great extent, this line of thinking is consistent with the current emphasis on school-based management, strategic management or development planning in improving school performance.

As illustrated in Chapter 4 and this chapter, the ongoing school-based management movement aims at enhancing the autonomy of members at the site-level in creating advantageous conditions for participation, improvement, innovation, accountability and continuous professional growth. Through decentralization of authority from central offices and participation in decision making, school management tasks are set according to the characteristics and needs of the school itself and therefore school members (including the board of directors, supervisor, principal, teachers, parents, and students, etc.) have much greater autonomy and responsibility for using resources to solve problems and carry out effective teaching activities, and for the long-term development of the school.

To a great extent, the school-based management reform can release the tight external control on school functioning and encourage schools to become a multi-level self-managing system that has its own initiative to identify problems and needs, foster participation, make decisions, plan actions, improve performance, and pursue development and long-term effectiveness in a changing environment. In other words, self-management at multi-levels can facilitate the school, groups and individual members to learn, to adapt and to develop in the dynamic process for pursuing effectiveness on multiple criteria. Since school-based management or self-management in school emphasizes flexibility in the procuration, allocation, and use of resources, the participation of school strategic constituencies in decision making, internal process improvement, responsiveness to the changing internal and external environment, and the development and achievement of school goals, it provides a necessary condition for a school and its members to have autonomy and initiative to start the dynamic process of maximizing effectiveness on the criteria of the multiple models.

The contribution of self-management at different levels to different models of school effectiveness can be illustrated as follows:

- *The Goal Model*
  In strategic management or self management at different levels, school goals and objectives are necessary and should be planned to be achieved in a given time period. But the goals will be subject to review and redevelopment after implementation and cyclic environmental analysis. This practice includes the strength of the goal model.

- *The Resource-Input Model*
  Based on the conditions for school-based management, the school has the autonomy to procure more resources and the flexibility to use the resources

more effectively. Furthermore, the mechanism of environmental analysis and strategic planning can help the school to develop appropriate strategies for procuration of more resource input. Therefore, it contributes to the emphasis of the resource input model for school effectiveness.

- *The Process Model*
  In the self-management process at different levels, the school environment and its performance at the organizational level, the group level and the individual level are monitored, evaluated, analyzed and reported cyclically. The evaluation of strengths, weaknesses, opportunities and threats at different levels can provide very critical information to development planning. The practice can facilitate improvement and development of individuals, groups and the school. Obviously, it comprises the major concern of the internal process model of school effectiveness.

- *The Satisfaction Model*
  In school-based management, decentralization from the central authority encourages autonomy and initiative of the strategic constituencies at the site-level. Participation of the strategic constituencies such as parents, teachers, the community, and students in school decision making and development planning can increase their satisfaction and commitment. In other words, the major concern of the satisfaction model can be met.

- *The Legitimacy Model*
  The components of school self-management such as systematic environmental analysis, development planning, monitoring and evaluation help the school develop appropriate legitimate or marketing activities and also ensure accountability to the public. Through this mechanism, the school can establish good public relations, accountability, and school image, reputation, and status in the community and thus the emphasis of the legitimacy model in considering school effectiveness can be achieved.

- *The Ineffectiveness Model*
  The last component of the self management process — systematic school evaluation and monitoring — provides regular information for improving poor performances, solving problems, and eliminating difficulties at the school, group and individual levels in school. Through this self-management mechanism, ineffective practices and poor performances at the three levels can be eliminated. As such, the requirement of the ineffectiveness model of school effectiveness can be fulfilled.

- *The Organizational Learning Model*
  The self-management process at the three levels contributes directly to the concern of the organizational learning model because it is a continuous learning process that helps the whole school, groups and individuals to be aware of the changing environment and educational needs, overcome external constrains and internal barriers, improve performance and develop itself effectively.

- *The Total Quality Management Model*

  According to the total management model, a school is effective if it can involve and empower all its members in school functioning, conduct continuous improvement in different aspects of the school process, and satisfy the requirements, needs and expectations of the school's external and internal powerful constituencies even in a changing environment (see Chapter 2). It is an integration of the above models. Therefore, as illustrated above, the self-management process at multi-levels can contribute to the above models, and obviously, as a whole it can contribute to the total quality management model.

  From the above, we can see that the characteristics of school-based management or self-management at multi-levels can reflect the emphases and concerns of all the eight different models of school effectiveness. Since the categories of school effectiveness are closely associated with these models of school effectiveness, the self-management process can also help the school to maximize school effectiveness on different school functions in the long run. Through the strategic management mechanism, the school can identify the incongruence between effectiveness categories and its potential drawbacks, and then develop appropriate plans and actions to redress them. For example, a school may focus only on the internal effectiveness and efficiency and neglect the effectiveness at the societal level at the beginning. Later, this school may experience the pressure from the community or external environment because of the ignorance of the external effectiveness on criteria at the societal level. If this school can perform environmental analysis and development planning as described above, it can be aware of this pressure and develop appropriate measures to maximize effectiveness not only at the school level but also at the societal level.

  In sum, school-based management or self-management at multi-levels can provide the necessary condition and mechanism for a school to pursue development and long-term effectiveness along a spiral path as shown in Figure 3.2. The current emphasis of school-based management and strategic management or development planning is consistent with the dynamic perspective of school effectiveness, that a school can maximize effectiveness on multiple criteria derived from the multiple models and categories of school effectiveness through a dynamic process in the long run. Therefore, the integration of school-based management or self-management at multi-levels into the multiple conceptions of school effectiveness is very promising to the current educational reforms.

Chapter 6

A School-based Management Mechanism for Development

In addition to the theory of school-based management and the concept of self-management process at multi-levels, the inclusion of school process characteristics in establishing an effective school-based mechanism for pursuing school development and dynamic effectiveness is also critical. In this chapter, through generalizing the matrix conception of the school process, a new concept called *layer management* will be introduced and used to construct a comprehensive management unit of the school-based mechanism. Matrix conceptions of school technology and school culture will be developed to facilitate the understanding of internal school functioning and effectiveness. A principle of congruence will be proposed to explain the effectiveness of internal school process and direct the activities of management, teaching and learning. Finally, based on the school-based management theory, the multi-level self-management concept, the layer management concept, the matrices of school technology and school culture, and the principle of congruence, an effective school-based mechanism will be proposed for practice in school.

The Matrix of School Process

The school process may be divided into the following processes: management process — a process of principal and administrators influencing teachers in terms of leadership, management and staff development; teaching process — a process of teachers influencing students in terms of leadership, teacher–students relationship, and teaching strategies; and learning process — a process of student(s) learning in terms of cognitive, affective, and behavioral change and development. From this line of thinking, school process can be illustrated by a matrix including three dimensions: categories of actors, levels of processes, and domains of effects as shown in Figure 6.1.

Principal, school administrators, teachers, and students are the key actors in the school process. The principal and school administrators help school members to clarify the direction of education, provide the appropriate environment, technology and resources, and motivate them to teach, learn and develop. For example, the principal should be a structural, human, cultural, political and educational leader for excellent schooling (Bolman and Deal, 1991a; Cheng, 1994d; Sergiovanni, 1984). Teachers use appropriate teaching strategies, create suitable learning environments,

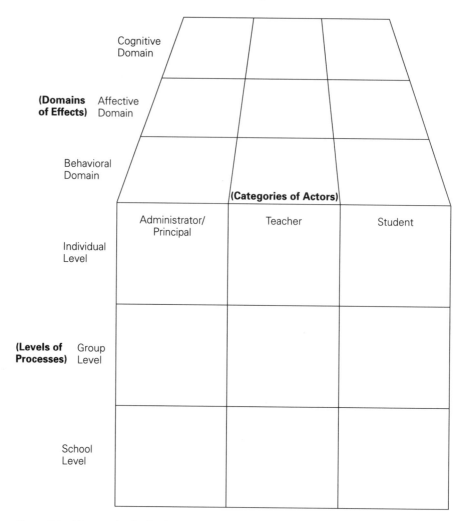

Figure 6.1: The matrix of school process

motivate students and help them to learn and develop. Students learn, experience, and develop according to the aims and content of education. Effectiveness of the internal education process can be affected by the performance of all these three categories of actors.

Traditionally the education process is often assumed to happen only at the individual level, such as that conducted by individual teachers and received by individual students. But this narrow conception is changing due to the induction of broader concepts of instructional management and education process. First, education can be planned and implemented at the program/group level or the whole school level. Currently the program planning or whole school approach emphasizing the planned collective efforts for effective education becomes more important. Second, education involves not only individual development but also group process and development. Classroom climate and school culture may have influence on education performance of individuals (Cheng, 1989; 1991c; 1993h; 1994a; Fraser, 1992; Fraser and Walberg, 1991). On the other hand, the climate and culture may be the collective outcomes of the school process. Therefore, school effects may happen not only at the individual level but at the group/classroom level and the school level.

The school process may have effects on different domains such as the behavioral domain, the affective domain and the cognitive domain of school actors. If the school process is a learning process for all those involved, then the effects may happen in the three domains of not only students but also teachers, administrators and principal. Furthermore, the effects may happen in the three domains of actors not only at the individual level but also at the group level or the school level.

Congruence in Process

According to the concept of congruence in system (Nadler and Tushman, 1983), effectiveness of education and the school process may be affected by congruence in process. Furthermore, based on Cheng (1987c; in press b), a principle of congruence can be proposed to predict the relationship of internal school effectiveness to the school process, as follows: *The greater the congruence in the school process, the higher the internal school effectiveness.*

The matrix of school process in Figure 6.1 suggests three types of congruence in process: the congruence across *domains*, the congruence across *actors* and the congruence across *levels*. The congruence across domains suggests that the effects of the school process produced or received are mutually consistent in the behavioral, affective and cognitive domains of each actor at each level. For example, what a student or teacher is doing should be consistent with what he or she is feeling and thinking if effectiveness of education or the school process is to be maximized. In Argyris and Schon's (1974) terminology, one's 'theory in practice' should be consistent with his or her 'espoused theory' for professional effectiveness.

The congruence across actors suggests that the performances of the principal, administrators, teachers and students are mutually consistent in each domain at each level. For example, principal's leadership style to teachers (democratic or autocratic) and teacher's leadership style to students (democratic or autocratic) should be consistent with expected student outcomes (democratic attitudes and values) in order to maximize effectiveness of civic education. It is ineffective for school administrators to use exploitative-authoritative management style to push teachers to adopt a democratic approach in teaching. Also it is ineffective for a teacher to use an autocratic approach to help students achieve democratic values in the learning (Cheng, 1987b; 1987c).

The congruence across levels suggests that the characteristics of activities at the individual level, the group level and the whole school level are mutually consistent for each actor in each effect domain. For example, a discipline policy should be implemented consistently by individual teachers, groups of teachers, or all teachers in the school if the effectiveness of this policy is to be maximized. For another example, if a set of education beliefs and values is held consistently by teachers at the individual, group and school levels, we can see that a type of school culture that can guide all the teaching efforts in a common direction and reduce internal operational and cognitive conflicts will exist among teachers.

The Layer Management Concept

Traditionally, education is often assumed to happen only in a few cells of the school process matrix (in Figure 6.1), relating to students and teachers only at the individual level and even only in one or two effect domains (for example, behavioral or cognitive achievements). The behavioral performance of individual teachers is used mainly to influence students' overt learning behavior and other possibilities are ignored. In this tradition, management is not an important concept in education and the unit of management in education is often limited to only some separate cells. As a result, the management methods or the pedagogic strategies suggested for education are often fragmentary, simplistic or trivial. The management concept based on separate cells sets a tight restriction to the enhancement of the effectiveness of education and school functioning through management because it ignores the organic relationship between levels, between actors and between domains. Without a full matrix conception of the school process, it is difficult, if not impossible, to conceptualize effective strategies to manage education.

Based on the matrix of process, a broader concept — *layer management* can be introduced to manage the school process. The matrix of process can be separated into actor layers such as the *administrator layer*, the *teacher layer*, and the *student layer* as shown in Figure 6.2. Or it can be separated into level layers such as the *individual layer*, the *group layer*, and the *school layer*, as shown in Figure 6.3. The management unit of school process is based on the layer instead of the cell of the matrix. This can provide a more comprehensive unit to think about the organic and dynamic nature of the school process, and contribute to the school-based management mechanism.

The Actor-Layer Management

As shown in Figure 6.2, the administrator layer influences the teacher layer through management and the latter affects the student layer through teaching. The student layer determines through learning the outcomes of education in the affective, behavioral and cognitive domains at all the individual, group and school levels. In general, the evaluation of educational effectiveness is based on the performance at the student layer. Even though we assume that the management process comes first, the teaching process second, and the learning process last, it is still possible that the performance of student layer affects back the teacher layer and the administrator layer, and also the teacher layer affects back the administrator layer.

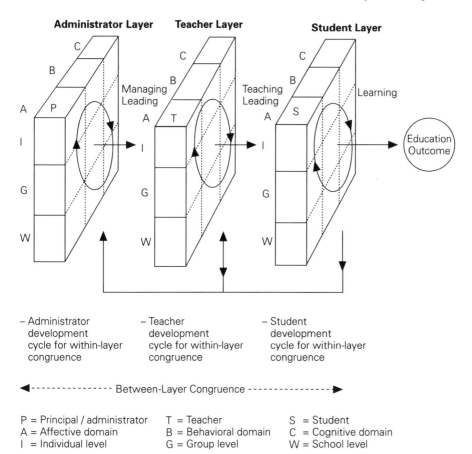

Figure 6.2: The actor-layer management

According to the principle of congruence, congruence in process is important to the effectiveness of education and the school process. Two types of process congruence can be identified in the school process:

Between actor-layer congruence. It refers to the congruence between the three actor layers in terms of consistency in the affective, behavioral and cognitive performance of the administrators, teachers and students at the different levels. For example, the understanding or beliefs (i.e., the cognitive domain) about education and management should be consistent between the administrator layer and the teacher layer if we want to enhance the effects of the management process and the teaching process. For another example, the teaching behavioral pattern (participative approach or student-centered approach) of the teacher layer should be consistent with the expected behavioral outcomes (active participation in learning) of the student layer, if the effectiveness of learning and teaching is to be maximized. The consistency in the affective and cognitive performance of actors is inevitably

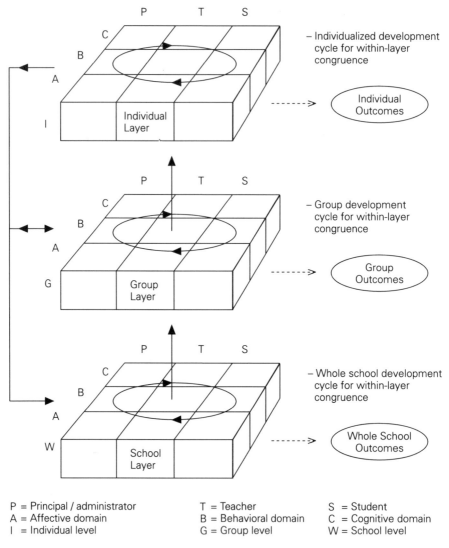

Figure 6.3: The level-layer management

reflected in the school culture, and the consistency in the behavioral performance is reflected in the school operation and technology of learning, teaching and managing. This will be further discussed in later parts of this chapter.

Within Actor-layer congruence. It refers to the consistency within one layer in terms of domain congruence (i.e., the consistency across the affective, behavioral and cognitive domains) and level congruence (i.e., the consistency across the individual, group and school levels). For example, in the student layer, the education activities or influences should be consistent at all the three levels and also in all the three domains if the effectiveness of education is to be maximized.

By the principle of congruence, we can predict that the greater the between actor-layer congruence and the within actor-layer congruence, the higher the internal school effectiveness.

The Level-Layer Management

As shown in Figure 6.3, the management mechanism can be based on the individual layer, the group layer, and the school layer. Each of the level layers includes the actors (such as administrators, teachers and students) and the domains (such as the affective, behavioral and cognitive domains). There are three different types of education outcomes at these layers: the individual outcomes, the group outcomes and the whole school outcomes in affective, behavioral and cognitive domains of students. Although we assume that the school level comes first, the group second, and the individual level last, it is still possible that the performance at the individual level may affect back the group level and the school level.

Similarly, there are two types of congruence in the school process important to internal school effectiveness:

Between level-layer congruence. It refers to the congruence between the individual layer, the group layer and the school layer in terms of consistency in the affective, behavioral and cognitive domains of school actors. For example, the behavioral performance or education beliefs of teachers at the individual level should be consistent with that at the group level or the school level. The congruence in the three domains can be reflected in the school culture and school technology. This will be further discussed in a later part of this chapter.

Within level-layer congruence. It refers to the congruence within one layer in terms of domain congruence (i.e., the consistency across the affective, behavioral and cognitive domains) and actor congruence (i.e., the consistency across principal, administrators, teachers and students).

According to the principle of congruence, the greater the between level-layer congruence and the within level-layer congruence, the higher the internal school effectiveness.

Ensuring Within-layer Congruence

In order to enhance school effectiveness, ensuring both between-layer congruence and within-layer congruence should be the key management strategy in the school process. In actor-layer management, ensuring congruence within each actor layer may be achieved through a dynamic development cycle that helps actors to perform consistently in all the three domains at all the three levels (see Chapter 8 for further detail).

For the administrator layer, a long-term program of administrator development may be established at the individual, group and school levels to facilitate their reflection on the existing practices, values and beliefs in morality, citizenship, education and management, identify inconsistencies in their own affective, behavioral and cognitive domains in the daily management arrangements and education processes, and make continuous improvement. Argyris and Schön's (1974) emphasis on reflection on theory in practice provides a strong support for such a development program for administrators.

Similarly, a long-term program of teacher development established at all the three levels is important for generating a continuous cycle for teachers to reflect on and to ensure congruence between values and congruence of performance in their affective, behavioral and cognitive domains. The current literature on various types of staff development support the importance of this line of thinking to effective schooling and curriculum change (Cheng, 1994c; Lieberman, 1988; Maeroff, 1993). The details about the management and practice of staff development will be further discussed in Chapter 8.

The design of education activities at the student layer, no matter in a formal program or not, should establish a continuous development cycle at the individual, group and school levels that helps students to learn, experience and develop.

Similarly in level-layer management, within-layer congruence can be ensured through establishing a continuous development cycle at each layer. At the individual layer, a program of individualized social interactions and developments may be set up to help individual administrators, teachers and students have social interactions, mutual understanding and opportunities for identifying and reflecting on inconsistencies (in the domains and values) and pursuing improvements and developments. At the group layer, a group-based program may be established to facilitate group interactions and developments among administrators, teachers, and students for group level effectiveness. For students, the group dynamics is often in forms of classroom climate (Cheng, 1994a; Moos and Trickett, 1974). For teachers, social norms play the key role in shaping teachers' group behaviors. Teachers' professionalism may be one of the critical elements at the group level (Cheng, in press c).

At the school layer, whole-school policies and programs may also be established to encourage social interactions and developments to pursue congruence at the school level. The recent emphasis on the whole-school approach to student counseling and guidance may reflect the increasing awareness of the importance of the school layer to education (Education Commission, 1990).

Ensuring Between Layer Congruence

Leadership as the driving force. The importance of leadership to effective schooling, staff development, school improvement and educational reforms have been supported in numerous studies (Caldwell and Spinks, 1992; Cheng, 1994d; Hallinger and Murphy, 1987; Sergiovanni, 1984). We may assume that the administrator layer is the driving force for ensuring between-layer congruence in the actor layer management. The administrators can establish the management mechanism based on the theory of school-based management (Chapter 4), the concept of multi-level self management (Chapter 5), school development planning, or strategic management (Hargreaves and Hopkins, 1991; Queensland Department of Education, 1992), from which the inconsistencies between layers and also within layers can be identified and reduced. Since the administrator layer is crucial in driving the teacher layer and then the student layer, it would be very important to ensure the congruence within this layer.

The school layer as the driving force. In level-layer management, the individual layer is driven by the group layer and the latter is driven by the school layer through development of school mission, policy, plan, organizational structure and management process. The importance of strategic management and development planning to school effectiveness is based on the assumption that a school can be improved and developed to be effective through appropriate management at the school level (Education and Manpower Branch and Education Department, 1991; Queensland Department of Education, 1992). This line of thinking suggests that in addition to the administrator layer, the school layer should be the driving force for ensuring between-layer congruence and indirectly contributing to within-layer congruence at the group layer as well as the individual layer. Whole-school policies and programs can be developed to encourage group layer congruence and individual level congruence and consequently to enhance effectiveness of school process at all the three levels. School culture that reflects the sharing of values, beliefs, assumptions, and norms among school members may be one of the salient indicators of congruence at the school layer. It is believed to have strong influence on the performance of school members at different levels (Cheng, 1993h). Therefore the development of school culture may be the key to enhancing effectiveness at the school level, driving the developments at the other levels (Beare, *et al.*, 1989; Cheng, 1989).

The Matrix of School Technology

In the above discussion, process congruence is strongly emphasized in pursuing internal school effectiveness. The behavioral congruence between the school actors and between the levels is the overt type of process congruence. The behavioral performance of administrators, teachers, and students for achieving school goals often depends on the technology they use.

As discussed above, the school process may be classified into the management process, the teaching process and the learning process. Therefore, the technology used in a school can be classified into managerial technology, pedagogic technology and learning technology.

If we take the strategic management process (Chapter 5) as the basis, then *managerial technology* should include the theories and techniques used in environmental analysis, planning and structuring, staffing and leading, and monitoring and evaluating. *Pedagogic technology* includes curriculum arrangement, teaching

(Learning Technology)

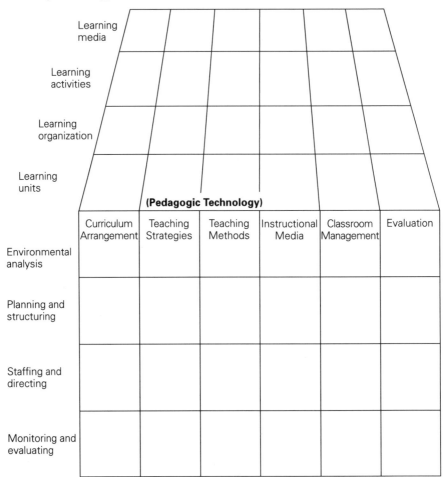

Figure 6.4:   The matrix of school technology

strategies, teaching methods, instructional media, classroom management and education evaluation (Farnham-Diggory, 1994). *Learning technology* refers to the use of learning units, organization of learning activities, such as individual learning or group learning, learning methods, learning media and facilities. These three types of technology can be used to form a matrix of school technology as shown in Figure 6.4.

In order to bring about good educational effects, the three types of technology should match with each other. Managerial technology should be used to support the nature and process of teaching and learning. Pedagogic technology should facilitate learning activities and provide the optimal opportunity for all students to learn according to the expected education content. Learning technology should fit the expected educational experiences and goals and facilitate learning of students with different personal characteristics and learning styles. There are two types of technology congruence that can affect the effectiveness of the internal school process:

Between-type congruence of technology. It refers to the congruence between managerial technology, pedagogic technology and learning technology in terms of mutual support and facilitation in operation; and

Within-type congruence of technology. It refers to the congruence between the components of one type of technology in terms of mutual support and facilitation in operation. For example, whether curriculum arrangement, teaching strategies, teaching methods, instructional media, classroom management and education evaluation are mutually supported and facilitated may affect the effectiveness of pedagogic technology.

According to the concept of congruence, the greater the between-type congruence and the within-type congruence, the higher the internal school effectiveness.

The Matrix of School Culture

According to the principle of congruence, process congruence is crucial to internal school effectiveness. The cognitive and affective congruence of school actors at the individual level, the group level and the school level is a hidden part of process congruence that is often related to school culture. To different people, the definition of school culture may be different. To a great extent, the sharing of beliefs, values and assumptions about education, management and the school process should be the core part of school culture because it can shape and determine the major characteristics of overt processes and artifacts in school (Alvesson, 1987; Cheng, 1989; 1993h; Schein, 1992).

The discussion of the internal process is also shaped by three basic questions: what to be conveyed, how to educate and how to manage in school. These questions are related to different sets of values and beliefs held in the school process. The first question is related to the specific content of the school process, particularly the moral and civic values and beliefs to be conveyed. The second question is related to the values and beliefs about the education process, and the third question to the values and beliefs about the management process held by the different actors in the school. We may assume that education is not only determined by its specific values and beliefs about education but also affected by the existing values and beliefs about morality, citizenship and management in the school. The dimensions of values and beliefs about morality, citizenship, education and management may form a 3-dimensional matrix of values and beliefs (as shown in Figure 6.5) that can contribute to the understanding of internal school effectiveness.

Values and Beliefs about Education

To different education philosophies, the sets of values and beliefs about education may be different in education aims, curriculum, pedagogic methods, roles of students and teachers, and ideal of education outcomes (Bottery, 1993; Tanner and Tanner, 1980). For example, according to Bottery (1993), there may be at least four different education philosophies, such as the cultural transmission code, the child-centered code, the social reconstruction code, and the gross national product code. For each code, the values and beliefs about education aims, roles of student, teacher, and the head and evaluation are different from other codes. To Tanner and Tanner (1980), education philosophies can be classified as Perennialism, Essentialism, Experimentalism, Reconstructionism, Romantic Naturalism and Existentialism, and their beliefs about education aims, curriculum, methods and ideals of the learner are different from each other. In general, the education values and beliefs may directly affect the pedagogic technology and learning technology to be used in the education process.

Values and Beliefs about Management

Similarly, for different management philosophies, the sets of management values and beliefs may also be different about human nature, human relationship, relationship to environment, universalism vs. particularism, priority of human needs, client-centered vs. career-centered, control vs. autonomy, formalization vs. flexibility, centralization vs. participation, teamwork vs. individual responsibility, resource adequacy, professional orientation and innovativeness (Cheng, 1989). The management values and beliefs may influence the management process which consequently affects teaching and learning, which in turn affect the outcomes. Currently, the strong emphasis on the contribution of organizational culture or climate to effective schooling supports the importance of management values and beliefs to the effectiveness of the internal school process (Cheng, 1993; Sergiovanni, 1984).

Values and Beliefs about Morality and Citizenship

In the education process or management process, there should be a specific set of values and beliefs about morality and citizenship to be conveyed. Particularly, in moral education, a set of values and beliefs about caring, judging and acting is emphasized and conveyed to students (Hersh, Miller and Fielding, 1980). In civic education, democracy, social responsibility, equity and freedom are often important values. There may be different conceptions and classifications of values and beliefs about morality and citizenship (e.g., Allport, Vernon and Lindzey, 1960; Braithwaite and Law, 1985; Harding and Phillips, 1986; Kluckholn and Strodtbeck, 1961; Lorr, Suziedelis and Tonesk, 1973; Rokeach, 1973). To Allport *et al.* (1960), the values can be classified as theoretical, economic, aesthetic, social, political and religious values. But to Braithwaite and Law (1985), the values can be categorized as goal values (including international harmony and equality, national strength and order, traditional religiosity, personal growth inner harmony, physical well-being, secure and satisfying interpersonal relationships, social standing and social stimulation) and mode values (including a positive orientation to others, competence and effectiveness, propriety in dress and manners, religious commitment, assertiveness and getting ahead).

As shown in the matrix in Figure 6.5, there are three sets of values and beliefs dominating the internal school process. They may or may not be consistent in nature. It would be interesting to know what combination of these three sets of values and beliefs can maximize the effectiveness of the internal process including management, teaching and learning. Specifically, what kinds of values and beliefs in education and management can most benefit the transmission of a given set of moral and civic values is still an unknown area for investigation.

Congruence in Values and Beliefs

The values and beliefs about morality, citizenship, education and management in school may or may not be mutually consistent (Bottery, 1993; Cheng, 1987c). According to the matrix of values and beliefs in Figure 6.5, there may be two kinds of congruence in values and beliefs:

Between-type congruence of values and beliefs. It refers to the congruence between different types of values and beliefs of education, management, and morality/citizenship. For example, the congruence of management values and beliefs with education values and beliefs belongs to the between-type congruence. The congruence of education values and beliefs with moral and civic values and beliefs is another example. Whether the existing values and beliefs in education and management are consistent with the given set of values and beliefs of morality and citizenship to be conveyed is crucial to the effectiveness of moral and civic education. If they are inconsistent, the moral and civic education may be ineffective. For example, it is ineffective to use autocratic management to push teachers to be democratic when leading students. Also, using an authoritative style to help students achieve democratic values is not effective. In Cheng (1987b; 1987c), there are examples to illustrate how the consistency of philosophy of management, leadership, school climate, classroom climate, teacher-student relationship, teaching strategies, and roles of teacher and student is important to the effectiveness of civic education. These examples support the validity of the theory of congruence.

Within-type congruence of values and beliefs. This refers to the congruence of values and beliefs within the same type. The congruence across the educational values and beliefs (about aims, curriculum, methods, roles of teacher and student, and ideal of education outcomes) belongs to the within-type congruence, and this may shape the educational process in a consistent pattern and affect its effectiveness.

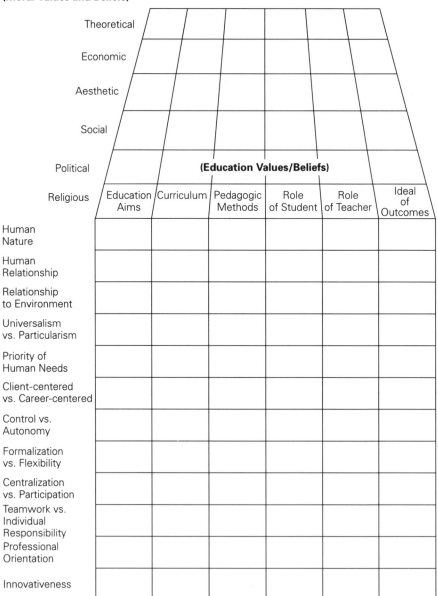

Figure 6.5: The matrix of school culture

The greater the congruence, the more effective the educational process. The congruence across management values and beliefs may shape the overt characteristics of the management process that may influence the educational process and then the education outcomes. The greater this congruence is, the more facilitating the management process is for teaching and learning. The congruence across the given set of values and beliefs of morality and citizenship indicates the potential acceptability of these values and beliefs to be conveyed in the education process. We can assume that congruent values and beliefs are more easily conveyed than incongruent ones.

According to the principle of congruence, ensuring cognitive and affective congruence of school actors, or ensuring the between-type and within-type of congruence of values and beliefs in education, management, morality, and citizenship is very important to enhancing internal school effectiveness. To a great extent, the congruence of values and beliefs in these three areas can contribute directly to the strength of school culture. The greater the congruence, the stronger the school culture. According to the literature of organizational culture, strong school culture is associated with high school performance (e.g., Cheng, 1993h; Sergiovanni, 1984).

A School-based Management Mechanism

Based on the integration of the key concepts and theories proposed in Chapters 3, 4, 5 and 6, a school-based management mechanism for continuous pursuit of school development and effectiveness can be developed, and it should have the following characteristics:

- *School-based management principles*. This mechanism is supported by the theories of school-based management including the principle of equifinality, the principle of decentralization, the principle of self-managing system, and the principle of human initiative, as illustrated in Chapter 4;
- *School profile*. The school profile of the mechanism is characterized by school mission, nature of activities, management strategies, use of resources, roles of different constituencies, human relationship, quality of administrators and evaluation indicators, as shown in Table 4.4 (p. 62);
- *Strategic management*. The mechanism is based on a strategic management system at the school level including components such as environmental analysis, systematic planning and structuring, appropriate staffing and directing, constructive monitoring and evaluating, leadership and participation, as conceptualized in Figure 5.1;
- *Self-management at multi-levels*. The mechanism can facilitate self-management at multi-levels in school, and the characteristics of self-management at these levels are mutually consistent and supports the continuous learning, improvement, and development of individuals, groups and the whole school, as described in Chapter 5;
- *Pursuing dynamic effectiveness*. The mechanism can help the school to adapt to the internal and external environment and maximize the different

categories of school effectiveness, as conceptualized by the eight different models in a dynamic process illustrated in Chapter 3;

- *Layer management.* The management unit of this mechanism should be the layer of the school process matrix instead of the separate cells. The integration of the concepts of actor-layer management (Figure 6.2, p. 89) and level-layer management (Figure 6.3, p. 90) into the school-based management mechanism can provide a more comprehensive unit to manage the organic and dynamic nature of the school process;
- *Principle of congruence.* The mechanism functioning is based on the principle of congruence. Ensuring congruence in categories of school effectiveness, congruence in models of school effectiveness (Chapter 3), and congruence in school process (Chapter 6) (including congruence in technology, values and beliefs) is critical for internal school effectiveness; and
- *Driving forces.* The administrator layer and the school-level layer should be developed as the driving forces to ensure between-layer congruence in the school process, and the development cycles should be established at each layer to ensure within-layer congruence, as explained in Chapter 6.

This school-based management mechanism has integrated the important elements of the recent development and research on school effectiveness and school-based management. It can provide a new and comprehensive perspective to understand school effectiveness and manage the internal school process for the continuous pursuit of school development, school effectiveness and education quality. In the coming chapters, we will discuss in detail the practice related to the application of these ideas. Specifically, leadership for the school-based management mechanism, management of staff development, management of school-based curriculum change, management of organizational change and monitoring of school effectiveness and educational quality will be discussed.

Part III

Practice

Chapter 7

Leadership for the School-based Management Mechanism

In Chapters 1 to 6, the ideas of school effectiveness, school-based management, multi-level self management, layer management, and principle of congruence have been introduced and the school-based management mechanism for development and effectiveness have been developed. Since the proposed management ideas and mechanism are very different from the traditional concepts, there should be an urgent need to reconceptualize school leadership for this new mechanism. In the light of the above ideas and the new development in leadership theory, this chapter will provide a new conception of school leadership in terms of layer leadership and strategic leadership. The reconceptualization can contribute to the practice and research on leadership for implementing the new school-based management mechanism.

Traditional Concepts of Leadership

The role of leadership is crucial for school effectiveness and school improvement (Bass and Avolio, 1994; Cheng, 1994d; Louis and Miles, 1990; Schein, 1992). But the concept of leadership is often very different to different researchers or scholars (Yukl, 1994). The following are some typical examples: leadership is the process of influencing the activities of an organized group toward goal setting and goal achievement (Stogdill, 1950); leadership is the initiative of a new structure or procedure for accomplishing an organization's goals and objectives or for changing an organization's goals and objectives (Lipham, 1964); leadership is the process to act for certain goals that represent the values and the motivations — the wants and needs, the aspirations and expectations — of both leaders and followers (Burns, 1978); and leadership is a force that can initiate action among people, guide activities in a given direction, maintain such activities and unify efforts towards common goals (Kenzevich, 1975). Searching for the one and only proper and true definition of leadership seems to be fruitless (Bass, 1990).

Even though there are differences between definitions, two characteristics of leadership can be observed: Leadership is related to the process of influencing others' behavior; it is also related to goal development and achievement. There are many methods to influence followers or other people to work. Based on different perspectives, different approaches may be developed to lead, to manage or to control. For example, from the classical theory of management, a leader may initiate formal structures such as policies, rules, regulations, rewards, punishments or roles to manage followers' behavior. From the tradition of the human relations movement, a leader has to satisfy followers' social needs in order to motivate them to work. What methods and processes are used to influence followers becomes one of the two critical elements of leadership. The other element is goal development and achievement. How to set goals, create meanings, direct actions, eliminate uncertainty or ambiguity, and achieve goals are also the core part of leadership.

Leadership as studied through traditional theories such as the Ohio State University studies (see Halpin, 1966), the managerial grid model (Blake and Mouton, 1985), and the contingency theories (see Fiedler, 1967; 1971; Hersey and Blanchard, 1972; House, 1971) is often assumed to occur between a leader and a face-to-face group in a steady situation where a task is given to complete in a relatively short time period (Hampton, Summer and Webber, 1987). Inevitably, some limitations exist in these traditional theories:

Limitations of transactional leadership. Explicitly or implicitly, the theory often focuses on the transactional process in which a leader gives something to followers in exchange for their satisfactory effort and performance in the task. For example, the path–goal model of leadership effectiveness (House, 1971) is based on the expectancy theory of motivation and cost-benefit formulations. Transactional leadership style is encouraged and assumed to be effective. As a transactional leader, he or she tends to survey followers' needs and clarify how their needs can be fulfilled in exchange for their performing task, and set goals for them on the basis of the effort he or she can expect from them (Bass, 1985). In terms of Zaleznik's (1977) category, a transactional leader is a manager but not a leader. As Bass pointed out,

> The past half-century has seen the refinement of the use of more carrot and less stick. Contingent reinforcement has been the fundamental concept of consequence. Followers are rewarded for fulfilling roles based on agreements reached with their leaders. Reaching such agreements through democratic processes have been encouraged. But even in the best of circumstances there seem to be limits on what contingent reinforcement of followers can achieve with this transactional arrangement between followers and leader (1985: p. xiii).

The traditional leadership theory concentrates on leaders' management techniques and interpersonal skills. This conception assumes that leaders should adapt their behavior to the situation, do not question the goals of their organizations, do not expect their followers' performance beyond the ordinary limits, and do not transform the situation nor their followers' beliefs, values, attitudes, motives and confidence. It seems that an organization has no hope to be excellent under transactional leadership (Bass, 1985).

Limitations of the contingency theories. The contingency theories assume that the relationship between leadership style and organizational outcomes is moderated by situational factors, and therefore the outcomes cannot be predicted by leadership style unless the situational variables are known. They suggest that leaders have to adapt their behavior to the situation and should not change the situation. For example, leaders' styles have to fit the followers' characteristics such as needs, arousal levels and current competency, etc. Therefore, these theories may not be true for those leaders who can transform the situations (Bass, 1985; Bennis, 1984). From a research perspective, Hackman (1985) made a sophisticated critique of the limitations of the contingency theories. He pointed out that the contingency models sometimes are generated out of a researcher's desperation because variation in findings across studies and samples may be explained successfully only by individual differences and situation attributes. He contended that two questions may be used to assess the usefulness of a contingency model: 1) Does the model predict the outcomes of interest more powerfully than simpler 'main effect' models that address the same phenomena? 2) Is the model framed in a way that makes it usable by practitioners in their work? He found that the general direction in this kind of research 'has been to make more and more distinctions and to add ever more conditions and qualifications to general propositions' and as a result, 'increments in explanatory power come more slowly than increase in model complexity' (p. 141). Moreover, it also seems very difficult to use complex contingency theories as behavioral guides. Based on the multiple possibility theory and notion of equifinality, he questioned the traditional stimulus–response models in which situational causes are tightly linked to behavioral effects directly or contingently (p. 142).

Alternative Perspective of Leadership

The drawback of the traditional theories is that they fail to pay attention to the transformational function of a leader. An alternative perspective of leadership is emerging (Bass, 1985; Bennis, 1984; Tichy and Ulrich, 1984; Zaleznik, 1977). This perspective argues that a leader is one who not only adapts his behavior to the situation but also transforms it. A leader is more than a manager (Zaleznik, 1977). A leader is proactive about future organizational goals, shaping the people's beliefs, values and attitudes and developing options for future, while a manager is reactive about organizational goals, using transactional approach to motivate his followers. In the fifties, Selznick (1957) contended that the major function of leadership is to infuse the organization with value beyond the technical requirements at hand, that is, to build upon people's need for meaning and create institutional purpose. He noted,

> The inbuilding of purpose is a challenge to creativity because it involves transforming men and groups from neutral, technical units into participants who have a peculiar stamp, sensitivity, and commitment. This is ultimately an educational process. It has been said that the effective leader must know the meaning and master the techniques of the educator . . . The leader as educator requires an ability to interpret the role and character of

the enterprise, to perceive and develop models for thought and behavior, and to find modes of communication that will inculcate general rather than merely partial perspectives (pp. 149–50).

This passage highlights the importance of a leader in shaping organizational culture and defining the mission of his organization (Schein, 1992; Sergiovanni, 1984). Therefore, a leader is in nature a transformational leader or a cultural leader. As we have pointed out, no matter which perspective is used, there are two elements of leadership: the process of influencing followers and others, and goal development and achievement. We can use these elements to compare and evaluate the traditional theories of leadership and the new idea of transformational leadership.

Traditional theories assume that organizational goals and tasks are static, well defined and recognized, and given to be achieved, therefore the main function of a leader (and also the theory of leadership) is to focus on the process of influencing his or her followers to complete these given tasks. In this tradition, the approach a leader can use to motivate followers or other people is inevitably based on the cost-benefit exchange theories — a transactional model. Bargaining and negotiation are inevitable in the leadership process.

As a contrast, the new perspective treats these two elements of leadership in a dynamic way. The organizational goals and tasks are often ambiguous, situation-varied and not well defined. Even though there may be some formal goals and tasks specified by some of the organizational authorities, not all followers or constituencies understand them and accept their meanings. Therefore a leader has to clarify the ambiguity and uncertainty to help constituencies to develop an organizational mission and goals. The process of goal development and clarification can contribute to motivating and influencing the constituencies, whereas the process of influencing followers is to shape organizational culture, transform their needs, beliefs and values, encourage commitment and provide opportunities for them to experience the meaningfulness of the tasks. Proposing, educating and transforming are important elements in the leadership process. According to Bass (1985), a transformational leader is one who motivates people to do more than they are originally expected to do by any one of the following ways:

- raising their level of awareness and consciousness about the importance and value of designated outcomes, and ways of reaching them;
- getting them to transcend their own self-interest for the sake of the team, organization, or large polity;
- altering their need level on Maslow's (1943) hierarchy or expanding their portfolio of needs and wants from low level, such as physiological or safety needs, to high level, for example, esteem or self-actualization needs.

From this perspective, leadership is not only a process to influence the behavior of followers or constituencies but also their attitudes, values and beliefs; not only individual members but also the whole organization; not only the goal achievement but also goal development and organizational culture building.

Multi-dimensions of Leadership

In traditional theories, duality of leadership is often emphasized in terms of the concern for people and the concern for task (Blake and Mouton, 1985; Halpin, 1966; Stogdill, 1974). This may be too simplistic for understanding the complexity of leadership process as described above. It ignores the cultural and political aspects of the organizational process in general and school life in particular, therefore, it is insufficient to form strong comprehensive leadership for the school-based management mechanism to pursue dynamic school effectiveness and long-term school development.

A Five-dimension Model

According to the alternative perspective of leadership, the cultural and transformational aspect of leadership should be important. Based on the four frames of understanding organizations, Bolman and Deal (1991a; 1991b) suggested that there may be four leadership orientations in organizations: the structural leadership, the human resource leadership, the political leadership, and the symbolic leadership. For educational organizations, Sergiovanni (1984) proposed a five leadership forces model to explain how the principal's leadership is related to excellent school performance. In this model, there may be five aspects of principal leadership: technical leadership, human leadership, educational leadership, symbolic leadership and cultural leadership. It seems that school leadership should be multi-dimensional. Integrating the above two models, we may assume that school leadership should be composed of five dimensions: structural leadership, human leadership, political leadership, symbolic leadership and educational leadership. The first four dimensions can be defined by the Bolman and Deal (1991b) framework and the last by the idea of Sergiovanni (1984). With this integrated model, we may describe and understand school leadership from five critical dimensions that have roots in different organizational theories and specific nature of educational organizations. Specifically, the five dimensions of school leadership can be described as follows:

Human leadership. The school leader is supportive, fosters participation, enhances staff commitment and satisfaction, and encourages positive interpersonal relationship;

Structural leadership. The school leader thinks clearly and logically, develops clear goals and policies, holds people accountable for results, and provides suitable technical support to plan, organize, coordinate and implement policies in school;

Political leadership. The school leader is persuasive and effective at building alliances and supports and resolves conflicts among school constituencies;

Cultural leadership. The school leader is inspirational and charismatic, and builds a school culture which transforms the mission, values, and norms of individuals or groups; and

Educational leadership. The school leader encourages professional development and teaching improvement, diagnoses educational problems and gives professional opinions and guidance to school instructional matters.

Multi-dimensional Leadership and School Performance

Based on this conception of multi-dimensionality, I have studied the relationship between principal leadership and school performance at the student level, the teacher level and the organizational level in a sample of 190 primary schools, involving 190 heads, 678 classes of mainly grade six students, 21,622 students, and 3872 teachers (Cheng, 1994d). The results of the Pearson correlation analysis are summarized in Table 7.1.

Organizational performance. As shown in Table 7.1, the structural, human, political, cultural and educational dimensions of principal leadership are strongly related to the school's perceived organizational effectiveness, principal-teacher relationship, strength of organizational culture, the authority hierarchy (negatively) and teacher participation in decision making, mainly at the 0.001 significance level. It seems that the stronger the dimensions of leadership, the more effective the school organization perceived, the more satisfactory the principal–teachers relationship, the more sharing of the school's mission and values, the less hierarchical the school authority and the more the teachers participate in decision making.

The above findings support the importance of strong leadership in terms of the structural, human, political, symbolic and educational aspects to organizational functioning and performance (Bolman and Deal, 1991a; 1991b). To the school's organizational effectiveness, the findings are consistent with Cheng's (1991b) result that principal leadership behavior in initiating structure is positively related to school organizational functioning, and principal's cultural leadership has substantial contribution to school development and improvement. To school organizational culture, the findings reinforce the current belief in the principal's leadership role in developing, shaping and transforming members' shared assumptions, values and beliefs about the school's mission, organization, technology of teaching and learning, interpersonal relationship and daily functioning (Bass, 1985; Bennis, 1984; Conger, Kanungo and associates, 1988; Schein, 1992; Sergiovanni, 1984). As found in Chan, Cheng and Hau (1991), whether teachers are satisfied with the social and working relationship with their principal is very sensitive to the principal's managerial style. In terms of organizational structure, strong leadership seems to be more preferable for decentralization and encouragement of teacher participation in decision making. In this sense, it supports the theory that strong leadership tends to encourage and involve teachers but not to establish a high hierarchy of authority or a highly centralized system. The findings further suggest that strong leadership does not mean great formalization of procedures, instructions and communication in school.

Table 7.1: Multi-dimensional leadership and school performance

	Human Leadership	Structural Leadership	Political Leadership	Cultural Leadership	Educational Leadership
Organizational Performance					
Organizational effectiveness	.2175*	.3297**	.2398**	.3172**	.3044**
Organizational culture	.4166**	.4513**	.4173**	.4656**	.4517**
Principal–teacher relationship	.6725**	.6410**	.6405**	.6019**	.6198**
Formalization	-.0024	.0434**	.0603	.0745	.1246
Hierarchy of authority	-.3682**	-.2766**	-.3156**	-.2691**	-.2556**
Participation	.3548**	.2992**	.3366**	.3051**	.3287**
Teachers' Group-level Performance					
Intimacy	.0808	.0407	.0997	.1129	.1375
Esprit	.4460**	.4712**	.4487**	.4913**	.5101**
Disengagement	-.2632**	-.3337**	-.2859**	-.3207**	-.2754**
Hindrance	-.3149**	-.3000**	-.3036**	-.2528**	-.1670
Professionalism	.3557**	.3853**	.3720**	.3824**	.3192**
Teachers' Individual-level Performance					
Extrinsic satisfaction	.3075**	.2502**	.3454**	.3148**	.2724**
Intrinsic satisfaction	.2435**	.2406**	.2508**	.2417**	.2587**
Influence satisfaction	.4229**	.3744**	.4013**	.3782**	.3846**
Social satisfaction	.1377	.1046	.1554	.1652	.1808
Job commitment	.3407**	.3167**	.3639**	.3555**	.3587**
Feeling of fair role loading	.3483**	.2981**	.2945**	.2670**	.2307**
Feeling of job meaning	.2036*	.1610	.2025*	.2343*	.2022*
Students' Performance					
Self concept	.0676	.0493	.0414	.0570	.0461
Attitude to peers	.0692	.0840	.0965	.1232	.0791
Attitude to school	.2495**	.2863**	.2130*	.2500**	.2243*
Attitude to teacher	.1824*	.2207*	.1837*	.1696	.1309
Attitude to learning	.1522	.1641	.1818*	.1866*	.1323
Feeling of homework overload	-.0869	-.0871	-.0597	-.0303	-.0504
Intention to dropout	-.1103	-.1332	-.1307	-.1714	-.1475

No. of Schools = 164   * $p < .01$,   ** $p < .001$
Adapted from Y.C. Cheng (1994d).

Teacher performance. As shown in Table 7.1, the five dimensions of leadership are strongly related to four measures of teachers' group level performance such as teachers' spirit, disengagement (negatively), hindrance (negatively) and professionalism at the 0.001 significance level. The stronger the human, structural, political, symbolic and educational dimensions of leadership, the higher the teachers' working morale, the greater the professionalism among teachers, and the less the disengagement and feeling of unnecessary overload shown by teachers. The social relationship (or intimacy) between staff seems to be unrelated to all dimensions of the principal's leadership.

The five dimensions of principal leadership are positively related to most measures of teacher performance at the individual level, such as intrinsic satisfaction, extrinsic satisfaction, influence satisfaction, job commitment, feeling of fair role loading and job meaning. It seems that when the human, structural, political, symbolic and education aspects of principal leadership are stronger, the teachers tend to be more satisfied with extrinsic and intrinsic rewards of their job and opportunities of autonomy and participation in decision making. They are more committed to their jobs and have a better feeling of job meaning and fair role loading. But teachers' personal satisfaction with social relationship in their job is not related to any dimensions of principal leadership. This finding is consistent with the negligible correlation between leadership and teachers' intimacy found at the group level. It is possible that principal leadership may affect the principal–teacher social relationship more easily than the teacher–teacher social relationship.

Student performance. As shown in Table 7.1, there is a moderate correlation between principal leadership and some of the measures of student performance. All the dimensions of principal leadership are related to student attitudes towards their school at the 0.01 significance level. The stronger the human, structural, political, symbolic and education aspects of the principal's leadership, the more the students are committed to the school, satisfied with the school arrangements and activities and enjoying school life. The human, structural, and political dimensions of leadership are related to students' positive attitude to teachers, and the political and symbolic dimensions of leadership are related to students' positive attitude to learning.

As shown in this study, the multi-dimensional model should be appropriate to the practice and study of leadership for school-based management.

The Layer Leadership

In light of the alternative perspective of leadership and the characteristics of layer management, we can reconceptualize leadership to contribute to the school-based management mechanism and long-term school development and effectiveness. From the concept of layer management (Chapter 6), school leadership may be based on the administrator layer including three levels (the individual, group and school level) and three domains (the affective, behavioral and cognitive domain), as shown in Figure 7.1. This may be called *layer leadership* with leadership influence from the *leader layer* to the *matrix of school constituencies*. The explanation is given as below.

The Leader Layer

In this layer conception, the leader may not be limited to an individual. The leader may be the principal/individual administrator (teacher), a group of administrators (teachers), or all the administrators (teachers) in school. If participative management or collaborative management is implemented in the school, most of the teachers may be administrators or leaders in some management activities and at the same time they are also members in other management activities. This practice becomes popular particularly when professionalism and participation are strongly emphasized in schools. As suggested by Barth (1988), there should be a community of leaders in schools. But in the traditional concept, the category of leaders may be limited to the principal or individual administrators.

In the layer conception, the leaders exercise their leadership through their affective, behavioral and cognitive performance. The affective performance often refers to the personal commitment, attraction or charisma at the individual level and to the team spirit, social attitudinal norms and social intimacy at the group and school level. The behavioral performance refers to the general leadership behavior, (such as consideration, initiating structure, etc.) or management skill practice, (for example, planning, supervision, etc.) at the three levels. The cognitive performance refers to the understanding, proposing, meaning development, clarification of uncertainty and ambiguity, and building values and beliefs about education and management. Affective and cognitive performance is often expressed in popular terms such as human, cultural, symbolic or charismatic leadership (see Bolman and Deal, 1991b; Conger, *et al.*, 1988; Sergiovanni, 1984; 1990; 1992). Behavioral performance is often named as technical or structural leadership (see Bolman and Deal, 1991b; Sergiovanni, 1984) or leadership style in some overt behaviors, (such as the Leader Behavior Description Questionnaire, LBDQ of the Ohio State University Studies, Halpin, 1966). To a great extent, behavioral performance is parallel to the traditional concepts of leadership, and affective and cognitive performance is in line with the emphasis of transformational and cultural leadership.

The Matrix of Constituencies

As shown in Figure 7.1, the school's constituencies to be led or influenced by the layer leadership include those often in school such as staff and students and those often outside school such as parents, members of the school management board, officers of the Education Authority, people of social service organizations, people of business and industrial organizations and the public, etc. Traditionally, the discussion of school leadership is often limited within the school and ignores the importance of the impact and support of some external 'hidden' strategic constituencies

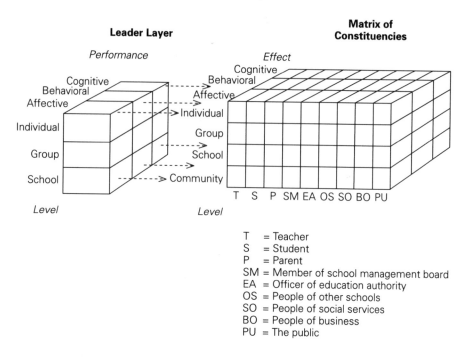

Figure 7.1: The layer leadership

to the effectiveness and survival of a school. As pointed out in the resource-input model, the satisfaction of the strategic constituencies model, the legitimacy model, the total quality management model of school effectiveness in Chapter 2, these external strategic constituencies are very important to school effectiveness in terms of resource support, expectations of school functions or goals, legitimacy for survival and accountability. Therefore, the school leaders work not only for the internal constituencies but also for the external constituencies, if they want to influence the environment and get support from the external constituencies for school's long-term development and effectiveness. This direction of leadership has been reflected in terms of environmental leadership or strategic leadership in some recent literature (Caldwell and Spinks, 1992; Goldring and Rallis, 1993).

The level of internal and external constituencies includes the individual level, the group level, the institutional level and the community level. The leadership for the community is not a new concept. As we know, there are many famous schools playing a leading image and role for their community. But in the traditional concept, the community level is often ignored.

In the layer conception, the domains of school constituencies to be led or influenced include not only the behavioral aspects but also the affective and cognitive aspects. In other words, the layer leadership may influence not only how school constituencies behave, but also how they feel and think and what they value and pursue. In terms of Sergiovanni's (1984) typology or Bolman and Deal's (1991b) typology, the effect of leadership on constituencies include the technical/structural aspect, the human aspect, the political aspect, the cultural aspect and the educational aspect. In the traditional conception, leadership focuses mainly on the technical/structural aspect or the behavioral aspect.

In the layer conception, the leadership process is an influencing process from the whole leader layer (including the affective, behavioral and cognitive performance of different leaders at the individual, group and school level) to the whole matrix of school constituencies including the affective, behavioral and cognitive effect domains at multi-levels, as shown in Figure 7.1. But in the traditional concept, the leadership process is an influencing process from only one or two cells of the leadership layer to some cells of the matrix of constituencies. One typical example of the traditional concept of leadership is the principal who uses his or her leadership behavior, for example, initiating structure, to influence teachers' teaching behavior.

From the above discussion, the major differences between the traditional leadership concept and the layer-leadership concept can be summarized as shown in Table 7.2. The layer concept can provide a more comprehensive approach to understanding the complex nature of leadership process and leadership effect. It can contribute to the effective practice of leadership particularly in school-based management or self-management at multi-levels.

The Strategic Leadership

In Chapter 5, strategic management is strongly emphasized as the critical component of the school-based management mechanism. This part will explain how multi-dimensional leadership can contribute to the strategic management process.

Conception of Strategic Leadership

Currently, the discussion of strategic leadership is still meager and the domain of studying strategic leadership is relatively diffuse and uncharted (Hambrick, 1989). In general, we may say that as strategic management emerges, leadership at the level of top management may be considered as strategic leadership. Following the conception of self-management at the school level as described in Chapter 5, strategic management process in school includes the stages such as environmental analysis, planning and structuring, staffing and directing, implementing, monitoring and evaluating. This process can keep the school as a whole appropriately matched to its environment, improve school performance, achieve school objectives and develop itself continuously. Then, *strategic leadership* in the school can be considered as the leadership for initiating, developing and maintaining of the strategic management process.

As discussed above, the five dimensions of school leadership are important to effective management process. Therefore, applying structural leadership, human

Table 7.2: The traditional leadership concept and the layer-leadership concept

	The Traditional Leadership Concept	The Layer-Leadership Concept
Level of leader	• Individual leaders	• Individual leaders • Groups of leaders • A school of leaders
Category of leader	• Mainly the principal or a few administrators	• The principal • Administrators • Teachers
Leader performance	• Mainly behavioral performance	• Affective performance • Behavioral performance • Cognitive performance
Level of constituencies	• Often at the individual level or the group level	• Individual level • Group level • School level • Community level
Category of Constituencies	• Internal constituencies (teachers, students, etc.)	• Internal constituencies • External constituencies (parents, officers of Education Authority, members of school management board, people of social service, business and industrial organizations, and the public, etc.)
Domain of leadership effect	• Mainly behavioral aspect	• Affective aspect • Behavioral aspect • Cognitive aspect
Nature of leadership	• Based on the separate cells • Composed of individual level, behavioral performance and behavioral effect domain • Related mainly to the technical/structural aspects of management	• Based on the whole layer • Composed of multi-levels, multi-performance and multi-effect domains • Related to the technical/structural, human, cultural, political and educational aspects of management
Process of Leadership	• Leadership is an influencing process from a cell of the leadership layer to some cells of the matrix of constituencies	• Leadership is an influencing process from the whole leadership layer to the whole matrix of constituencies

leadership, political leadership, cultural leadership and educational leadership to the strategic management process, we can have a matrix conception of strategic leadership as shown in Figure 7.2.

Each column of the matrix represents the contribution of one dimension of leadership to each major stage of the strategic management process. The whole matrix represents the contributions of the five dimensions of leadership to the entire strategic management process. This conception reflects that each dimension of leadership has its unique and important contribution to the strategic management process in school. Compared with this comprehensive matrix, the traditional duality of leadership (concern for people and concern for task) seems to be far too simple.

	Educational leadership	Technical leadership	Human leadership	Political leadership	Cultural leadership
Environmental analysis					
Planning and structuring					
Staffing and directing					
Monitoring and evaluating					

Figure 7.2:   The conception of strategic leadership in schools

From the alternative perspective of leadership and the concept of layer leadership, the five-dimension leadership model should be more comprehensive and powerful to facilitate strategic management or school-based management. The following parts will explain the contributions of the five dimensions to strategic management in detail.

The Contribution of Cultural Leadership

As cultural leaders, school leaders are inspirational and charismatic to build school culture which transforms the mission, values, and norms of individuals or groups. As Sergiovanni (1984) suggested, leaders' cultural role and symbolic role are important for excellent school performance. They assume the role of *chief* by emphasizing selective attention and signaling to others what is of importance and value. They also assume the role of *high priest*, seeking to define, strengthen and articulate those enduring values, beliefs and cultural strands that give the school its unique identity (Sergiovanni, 1984). The contribution of cultural leadership to the strategic management process can be summarized as follows:

To environmental analysis.   In the process of environmental analysis, the school leaders can:

- draw the attention of members to the internal and external changes that affect the school;
- help members to understand the importance of environmental analysis to the development of the school;

- help members to be aware of the environmental changes upon which the school is highly dependent;
- highlight the meanings of the school's strengths, weaknesses, opportunities, and threats for all members;
- guide the environmental analysis towards a meaningful direction for school development;
- ensure that environmental analysis is making sense of what the school is achieving and pursuing.

To planning and structuring.   In the process of planning and structuring, the school leaders can:

- focus members' attention to what is most important to the school's future from the findings of the environmental analysis;
- envision the school's future and uniqueness and encourage members to pursue school excellence;
- help members to establish the school mission and goals and be committed into actualizing them in planning and structuring;
- raise members' level of awareness and consciousness about the school goals and transcend their own self-interests for the sake of school development in the process of planning and structuring.

To staffing and directing.   In the process of staffing and directing, the school leaders can:

- articulate the meanings of professional growth and school development in the light of the school's future;
- act as role models for members by demonstrating high standards of ethical and moral conduct;
- ensure staffing and directing as important process for school development of school culture;
- ensure the staffing and directing processes are consistent with the school mission and goals.

To monitoring and evaluating.   In the process of monitoring and evaluating, the school leaders can:

- articulate the meaning and importance of monitoring and evaluation to the school's development and future;
- emphasize the value of learning and continuous development inherent in the process of monitoring and evaluating;
- focus members' attention on what is most important to the school's development in the different activities of quality assurance in school;
- guide the activities of monitoring and assessment towards meaningful direction for the development of individuals, groups and the school.

Moreover, Yukl (1994) recognize the importance of getting accurate information from members who may be reluctant to provide it. It is essential to react to information about problems in a constructive, non-punitive manner. Cultural leaders should therefore create a culture in the school to encourage members to report problems and mistakes in the process of monitoring and evaluation.

The Contribution of Political Leadership

In the political perspective, school leaders react to strategic management process in different ways. The concerned issues focus on conflict or tension among different constituencies, interest groups or organizations; competing interests and agendas; disputes over allocation of scarce resources; games of power and self-interest (Bolman and Deal, 1992). Political leadership contributes to resolving conflicts among teachers or groups. The underlying assumption about politics taken is that school members can be empowered through an understanding of the positive side of politics, where positive politics evolve when individuals choose actions that appeal to higher motives and higher stages of moral judgment (Block, 1987; Burns, 1978). Also, a shared vision can help members recognize that they must work together to create the best solution (Tjosvold, 1992). Since conflict is not going to go away from a school, the question is how individuals and groups can make the best of it (Bolman and Deal, 1991a). Leaders should strive for 'win-win' and cooperative solutions and discouraged those efforts to pursue individual objectives at others' expense (Covey, 1989; Tjosvold, 1992). Under the above assumptions, the contribution of political leadership can be summarized as follows:

To environmental analysis. In the process of environmental analysis, the school leaders can:

- encourage positive attitudes of members to face up to the conflicts in environmental analysis;
- help members be aware of the environmental impacts on the common interests of all of them;
- help members to understand the importance of their consolidation in facing up to the external challenges and internal difficulties;
- consolidate the interest of different parties and help them to contribute to the environmental analysis;
- balance and integrate the diverse interests in identifying the strengths, weaknesses, opportunities and threats of the school;
- facilitate the resolution of conflicts aroused in the process of environmental analysis in a 'both win' manner.

To planning and structuring. In the process of planning and structuring, the school leaders can:

- encourage constructive views and attitudes towards the conflict in planning and structuring for school development;
- build strong alliance among different parties to support the development of school mission and goals;
- help members to understand that diversity can be an important asset if we can manage it;
- emphasize the common interests in the process of developing school goals, establishing programs and organizing resources;
- minimize the adverse conflicts between programs in planning and between roles in structuring by encouraging the 'win-win' thinking.

To staffing and directing.   In the process of staff and directing, the school leaders can:

- manage the conflicts of interests among different parties in a positive way in the staffing process;
- build consolidation and encourage collaboration among staff in program implementation;
- emphasize the common interests of all concerned in solving conflicts and ordaining different actions;
- facilitate members to manage differences occurred among groups and individuals using the 'both win' approach.

To monitoring and evaluating.   In the process of monitoring and evaluating, the school leaders can:

- minimize the internal and external resistance to the activities of quality assurance in the school through appropriate legitimacy;
- build strong support from different constituencies to the implementation of monitoring and evaluation programs;
- emphasize the common interests and long-term advantages brought from the monitoring and assessing activities to all school members;
- help members to solve conflicts and prioritize the areas for evaluation in a 'both-win' approach;
- balance and integrate the diverse interests of members in the process of selecting performance indicators.

The Contribution of Human Leadership

From the human resource perspective (Bolman and Deal, 1991a), an effective school is one characterized by highly motivated individuals who are committed to school objectives from which they derive satisfaction. These individuals are linked together into highly effective work groups. The work groups are characterized by commitment to common objectives, group loyalty and mutual support (Sergiovanni,

1984). People are primarily motivated by social needs and obtain their basic satisfactions from relationships with others, therefore meaning must be provided in the social relationships of the job (Mayo, 1945). Human leadership thus emphasizes enhancing teachers' commitment, personal growth and interpersonal relationship. They support the activities of coaching, training, mentoring and career counseling that can be used to increase a person's skills and facilitate his or her job adjustment and career advancement (Yukl, 1994). Therefore, its contribution to the strategic management process is listed as follows:

To environmental analysis. In the process of environmental analysis, the school leaders can:

- create or foster an open climate for members to reflect on the problems and needs of the school;
- ensure that environmental analysis and problem identification to be conducted in good interpersonal relationships among staff;
- encourage participation of all members in the reflection on and analysis of the environmental impacts on the school's future;
- ensure that environmental analysis is a positive learning experience for members.

To planning and structuring. In the process of planning and structuring, the school leaders can:

- foster an open climate among staff in discussing and establishing the school mission and goals;
- encourage participation of members in planning and structuring school's development;
- encourage team spirit not only in program planning but also in school planning;
- ensure that the planning and structuring activities are opportunities for learning and growth for members.

To staffing and directing. In the process of staffing and directing, the school leaders can:

- recognize the importance of members' participation in the staffing and directing activities;
- emphasize the importance of development of interpersonal relationship and team spirit in the process of staffing and directing.
- provide challenges to member's work in accordance with their abilities;
- stimulate creativity and innovation in achieving school goals and activities.

To monitoring and evaluation. In the process of monitoring and evaluating, the school leaders can:

- encourage cooperation, teamwork, and commitment in the process of monitoring and evaluation;
- emphasize the contribution of monitoring and assessment to the development of human resources in the school;
- cultivate an open climate of learning and development in assessing the performance of individuals, groups, and the whole school;
- provide praise, recognition and tangible reward for encouraging outstanding performance at different levels.

The Contribution of Technical Leadership

Technical leadership emphasizes providing suitable technical support to plan, organize, coordinate and implement teaching and learning activities in the school. Technical leaders are competent in manipulating strategies and situations to ensure optimum effectiveness (Sergiovanni, 1984). Relevant leaders' actions include division of labor, role clarification, proper communication channels, allocating resources (Sergiovanni, 1984), clarifying policies and procedures, budgeting (Bolman and Deal, 1992), informing, monitoring, consulting and delegating (Yukl, 1994), etc. As a result, through planning, time management technologies, organizing and scheduling, the contribution of technical leadership to the strategic management process is listed below:

To environmental analysis. In the process of environmental analysis, the school leaders can:

- facilitate members to handle the techniques for the analysis of school situation;
- arrange opportunities for members to identify and discuss the problems or needs in the school;
- facilitate the gathering of information about the external and internal factors that influence the school.

To planning and structuring. In the process of planning and structuring, the school leaders can:

- arrange resources and opportunities for members to reflect on the finding of environmental analysis, develop school mission and goals, and establish programs, policies and procedures;
- maximize the effectiveness and efficiency in structuring the necessary human resources for school management and program implementation;
- provide technical support for members to formulate school policies, programs and procedures; and
- ensure role clarity and accountability for every member in the organizational structure.

To staffing and directing. In the process of staffing and directing, the school leaders can:

- provide technical support for members to organize staff induction, job orientation, training or development programs for colleagues to effectively implement programs and school actions;
- allow members to have substantial responsibility and discretion in carrying out work activities, handling problems and making important decisions to attain school goals;
- clarify all the role responsibilities and help them to have relevant competence for personal performance and program implementation;
- provide appropriate coordination and communication network for school members to implement the plans.

To monitoring and evaluating. In the process of monitoring and evaluating, the school leaders can:

- provide technical support to members in collecting information about school performance with different indicators according to the school plans, program plans, and individual developments;
- delegate appropriate members responsible for conducting school self-evaluation, facilitating external inspection and preparing the school's accountability report and development report;
- coordinate all the efforts of monitoring and evaluating, minimize technical difficulties and ensure the effectiveness and efficiency of the monitoring and evaluating process;
- ensure the application of the findings of school evaluation to the continuous improvement of the school, programs and individuals as indicated in the strategic management cycle.

The Contribution of Educational Leadership

As educational leaders, the school leaders encourage professional development and teaching improvement, diagnose educational problems, and give professional opinions and guidance to school instructional matters. They stimulate, support and supervise teachers and help them to perform effectively (Grift, 1990).

In order to exercise this professional supervisory responsibilities, educational leaders need to have a strong sense of the purpose of schooling given in its neighborhood context, the socio-economic realities of the community, the cultural make-up of its families, and the human potential and social capital such a community represents (Sergiovanni and Starratt, 1993). They are responsible for establishing educational goals, framing and communicating these goals to all school members (Achilles, 1987; Hallinger and Murphy, 1987). The contribution of educational leadership to the strategic management process is listed as follows:

To environmental analysis. In the process of environmental analysis, the school leaders can:

- help members to be aware of the social, economical, technological, and political changes that affect education;
- help members to be aware of internal problems in instructional matters and critical educational issues in school evaluation reports;
- help members in identifying the strengths, weaknesses, opportunities and threats of the school's educational process;
- identify the educational needs of students and the developmental needs of teachers.

To planning and structuring. In the process of planning and structuring, the school leaders can:

- facilitate members to establish appropriate educational mission and development goals for students and teachers from the reflection on the external and internal environmental impacts;
- ensure the development of school plans and instructional program plans closely related to the established educational goals;
- maximize opportunities for student learning and staff development through appropriate structuring.

To staffing and directing. In the process of staffing and directing, the school leaders can:

- maximize opportunities for learning and development for students and teachers in staffing and directing;
- ensure the fitness of staffing and directing to the educational needs of instructional program plans and structure;
- ensure that staffing and directing activities can contribute to the professional development of staff and learning effectiveness of students;
- encourage teacher professionalism through appropriate staffing and directing activities.

To monitoring and evaluating. In the process of monitoring and evaluating, the school leaders can:

- help members to understand the contribution of monitoring and evaluation to the improvement of the instructional process and development of staff;
- help members to become familiar with recent developments of educational evaluation and monitoring and their applications to enhance educational effectiveness and professional development;
- facilitate members to link up the monitoring and evaluating process to the educational process and the established instructional goals;

Table 7.3: Models of school effectiveness and leadership roles

	Conception of School Effectiveness	Leadership Role
Goal Model	• Achievement of stated goals	• School goal developer • School goal leader • School planning facilitator
Resource–Input Model	• Achievement of needed resources and inputs	• Resource developer • Resource allocator
Process Model	• Smooth and healthy internal process	• Process engineer • Process facilitator
Satisfaction Model	• Satisfaction of all powerful constituencies	• Social leader • Social satisfier
Legitimacy Model	• Successful legitimate or marketing activities for school survival	• Public relations manager • Environmental leader • Accountability builder
Ineffectiveness Model	• Absence of characteristics of ineffectiveness in school	• Supervisor • Dysfunction detector • Problem shooter
Organizational Learning Model	• Adaptation to environmental changes and internal barriers	• Environmental analyzer • Learning promoter • Organizational developer
Total Quality Management Model	• Total management of internal staff and process to meet strategic constituencies' needs	• Total quality leader

- facilitate members to use the educational indicators to monitor and improve the teaching process and educational outcomes.

Leadership and Different Models of School Effectiveness

The idea of layer leadership provides a comprehensive view to conceptualize and practise leadership for the school-based management mechanism. Based on the five-dimensional leadership model, school leaders can make the necessary contribution to the implementation of strategic management or school-based management in the school, as discussed above.

In Chapter 2, eight models of school effectiveness were introduced to describe the different conceptions of and approaches to pursuing school effectiveness. Obviously, based on the different models of school effectiveness, the required role of leadership is different. In order to facilitate the application of leadership, it would be interesting to discuss the leadership roles in the eight models of school effectiveness.

The relationship between leadership roles and models of school effectiveness is summarized in Table 7.3.

School Goal Developer

According to the goal model, a school is effective if it can accomplish its stated goals. Since the educational environment is changing, school goals are not static and often need to be clarified, developed and established. Therefore, school leaders should play the role as goal developer, goal leader, and school planner and facilitator. They help school constituencies to develop appropriate school mission and goals that can fit the needs of the external and internal constituencies and the characteristics of the school. They direct all school members' attention and effort to the achievement of school goals. Inevitably, they need to facilitate school planning and ensure that the priorities of school goals are set appropriately, the school outcomes are clear and the effectiveness criteria are available and accepted by all strategic constituencies, at least in the given time period.

Resource Developer

The resource input model assumes that more scarce and valued resource input are needed for schools to be more effective. A school is effective if it can acquire its needed resources and inputs. Therefore, school leaders should play the role as resource developer and resource allocator. They clarify the connections between school inputs and outputs, and determine what resources are critical to the school's survival and development. They make all efforts to develop and utilize the scarce resources from outside and allocate these resources to support effective internal functioning and produce high quality school outcomes.

Process Engineer

To the process model of school effectiveness, the nature and quality of school process often determine the quality of output and the degree to which school goals can be achieved. A school is effective if its internal functioning is smooth and healthy. Therefore school leaders should play the role as process engineer and facilitator. They engineer the school process including all activities of managing, teaching and learning, and facilitate effective communication, participation, coordination and social interactions in the school.

Social Leader and Satisfier

According to the satisfaction model of school effectiveness, a school is effective if all its strategic constituencies are at least minimally satisfied. School leaders should play the role of social leader and social satisfier. They help the internal and external constituencies to communicate their expectations, understand the strengths and weaknesses of the school and set appropriate targets for the school to satisfy their needs and expectations. If there is serious conflict between the demands of different strategic constituencies, school leaders help them to resolve the problem and sustain good social relationships. They try their best to satisfy the needs of different strategic constituencies.

Environmental Leader

The legitimacy model assumes that successful legitmate or marketing activities are very important to the school's survival and development. Therefore, school leaders play the role of public relations manager, environmental leader and school accountability builder. They have to manage the school's external environment, build up good relations with all strategic external constituencies, market the school's strengths and contributions to the community, establish the school's public image and ensure the school's accountability to the public.

Supervisor

From the concept of the ineffectiveness model, a school is effective if there is an absence of characteristics of ineffectiveness in the school. The role of school leaders should be supervisor, dysfunction detector and problem solver. They have to supervise school activities, identify weaknesses, conflicts, dysfunctions, difficulties and defects and help members to eliminate and solve the problems.

Organizational Developer

The organizational learning model assumes that the impact of environmental changes and the existence of internal barriers to school functioning are inevitable. A school is effective if it can learn how to make improvement and adaptation to its internal and external environments. School leaders play their role as environmental analyzer, learning promoter and organizational developer. They help school constituencies to be sensitive to environmental changes and internal barriers, analyze them, reflect on findings, draw implications, establish strategies, plan actions and develop the school organization.

Total Quality Leader

As discussed in Chapter 2, the total quality management model of school effectiveness is an integration of the other models, particularly the organizational learning model, the satisfaction model, and the process model. This model emphasizes the total management of the internal environment and process to meet the strategic constituencies' needs. A school is effective if it can involve and empower all its members in school functioning, conduct continuous improvement, and satisfy the needs of external and internal strategic constituencies. School leaders need to play the role as a total quality leader that includes nearly all the roles of the other seven models, such as school goal developer, resource developer, process engineer, social leader and satisfier, environmental leader, supervisor, learning promoter and organizational developer.

Chapter 8

Management of School-based Staff Development

In the theory of school-based management mechanism, human initiative is strongly emphasized in the development of self management at the individual level, the group level and the school level. In this chapter, I will discuss the concepts, management and practice of staff development that are consistent with the theory of the school-based management mechanism for long-term school development and effectiveness.

The Needs for Staff Development

During the 1980s and 1990s, society and education environment have changed very quickly, not only in the Western countries, but also in the Asia–Pacific regions. Accordingly, educational goals become more complicated, educational tasks are harder, expectations from the public are higher, and school accountability to the public is heavier than any time before. Facing these challenges, both policymakers and educators are aware of the need of in-service staff development activities to cope with the increasingly demanding school work, and also to give full play to their potential. In many countries, staff development is only at its starting point. Not many people realize its importance to school effectiveness and development, and therefore it is not yet successfully carried out to improve the quality of education.

The study of organizational behavior has a profound influence on organizational management and staff development. From different viewpoints, the human needs theory of Maslow (1943) and Alderfer (1972), Herzberg's (1966) two-factors theory of motivation, McGregor's (1960) Theory X and Theory Y of human nature assumptions, Hackman and Oldman's (1976) job design theory, the participative management theory of Likert (1961; 1967) and Tannenbaum (1968), and the quality work life studies of Cammann, Fichman, Jenkins, and Klesh (1983) have all illustrated the importance of developing staff potential and human resources. According to the perspective of human resources (Bolman and Deal, 1991a), staff are the important resources of a school. If these human resources are properly developed, the school will perform more effectively and achieve better results. Therefore, in the management process, a school must pay more attention to staff motivation, their feelings and their needs for development and growth, and create opportunities for them to develop their potential and make more contribution.

Currently, there are several important factors reinforcing the demands for staff development in schools, including the changes in educational environment, changes in school values and personal values, and changes in school management models.

Changes in Educational Environment

The changes in educational environment often happen in terms of rapid development of technology, demand for accountability to the public, developments in curriculum, diversity in student quality and diversity in teacher quality.

In a continuously expanding modern world, the role of the school is changing and teachers need to expand their knowledge domain and develop a variety of new competence to keep pace in their teaching. Since taxpayers are responsible for school expenditure, school performance and effectiveness have become the main concern of the public. Higher accountability to the public is required of the school. Teachers need to develop various competence to satisfy the diverse expectations from students, partners, education authorities, the community and the public.

Due to the demands of society's development, the increase in knowledge, and the advances in educational theory and teaching strategies, the change of curriculum and educational processes are inevitable. Teachers have to pay attention to these changes and meet new demands so as to maintain their teaching effectiveness. Diverse and poor input of student quality is also a big challenge to our teachers. Teachers often come across student problems like 'behavioral problems', 'low achievement', or 'low motivation'. Both administrators and teachers need to develop new ideas and skills to solve the problems. In developing countries, the number of teachers grows rapidly when education expands, and variation in teacher quality become greater and more obvious, and so are their viewpoints of education, even in the same school. It is necessary to enhance the quality of teachers by carrying out school-based staff development activities in order that school effectiveness can be enhanced.

Changes in School Values and Personal Values

In recent years, the school values emphasized in school management have been changed. For example, achieving long-term school development and effectiveness, pursuing educational professionalism, having quality staff conditions, meeting constituencies' needs, participating in decision making, and providing services to the community have become some of the major school values for teachers and administrators. Staff development is often assumed as the necessary condition for the realization of these school values. Also, there are changes in teachers' personal values. Apart from the basic needs of life, teachers are now concerned about the need of higher-level growth such as full use of ability, professional growth and sense of achievement. Learning and development become the core of personal values and needs. Whether these needs are satisfied will influence teacher effectiveness.

Therefore, development and growth opportunities are critical to teachers' motivation, satisfaction, commitment and performance. All these changes in school values and personal values have aroused the school's concern about the need for staff development.

Changes in School Management

The recent school management reforms and teacher professionalization movements have brought about a fundamental change of the role of teachers. In the 1980s, school-based management, collaborative management or shared decision making were commonly advocated all over the world (Caldwell and Spink, 1988). Since then, teachers have more opportunities to participate in decision making and school management. More than that, the role of teachers as school leaders has been gradually treated as more important. Barth (1988) proposed the concept that school is a community of leaders, under this circumstance all teachers should have the ability to be a leader.

As discussed in Chapter 5, the success of implementing school-based management or self-management at the individual, group and school levels depend on a number of conditions. Among these conditions, staff participation and readiness are very important. In order to prepare staff to implement school management changes or educational reforms, staff development is necessary. The details will be discussed in Chapter 10.

The role of a teacher is changing. The new role includes being an education professional, learner of new knowledge and technology, education partner, reform initiator, decision maker and realizer of school ideals. Staff development can assist teachers in changing their roles. Responding to the changes in education environment, school values and personal values, school management and staff development become necessary for long-term development and effectiveness of the school.

Concepts of Staff Development

General Ideas

In the literature, the theories of staff development held by different scholars are in fact compatible. For example, Warren-Piper and Glatter (1977) regarded staff development as carrying out a set of systematic activities to satisfy the personal interests, wants and needs of staff and at the same time satisfy the future needs of the organization. Arends, Hesh and Turner (1980) also suggested that there should be two major aims for staff development: maintaining staff working efficiency (i.e., the organizational aim) and supporting personal growth (i.e., the personal aim). Sparks and Loucks-Horsley (1990) defined staff development as those processes that improve the job-related skills, knowledge and attitudes of staff.

The area of staff development activity can be very broad. Sparks and Loucks-Horsley (1990) summed up the current staff development activities into five major models: the individually guided staff development model, the observation/assessment model, the development/improvement process model, the training model and the inquiry model. All these activities are formal, systematic with overt goals. If we believe that the whole school process has educational functions and developmental meanings to the staff, then the staff development aspect should be taken into account while arranging any school activities. In the daily school functioning and teaching, teachers should have the opportunities to reflect, learn and grow in the informal, natural and unconscious contexts of the school. This informal process of staff development activities should be at least as important as the formal staff development programs. The influence of school culture or participative management on school members is currently emphasized. This has reflected indirectly the importance of the staff development function of the informal or hidden school process (Cheng, 1992b).

Alternative Concepts of Staff Development

Traditionally, staff development is often regarded as externally controlled and planned by the central education authorities. Top-down management is emphasized in staff development management. The targets are mainly teachers, without considering the development need of school administrators. The content of the development activities is confined to knowledge and skills. As Combs (1988) pointed out, educational reforms may have great difficulties because they concentrate too much on the training of knowledge and skills; they are based on one-sided or even wrong assumptions, and they are carried out by top-down methods. He suggested that successful educational reforms should consider the need of each basic level in a school (including administrators, teachers and students), and should also give consideration to the change in cognition and behavior of participants.

Starting from the 1980s, staff development has been gradually moving away from the external-control tradition to enter into a school-based development mode run mainly by the staff themselves. The new concept of staff development emphasizes a school-based format, in which the conception, management and evaluation of staff development all take place in the school and are conducted directly by the staff. Based on Oldroyd and Hall (1991) and Cheng (1993e); the comparison between the traditional concepts and the new concepts can be summarized, as shown in Table 8.1.

As in Table 8.1, the differences between traditional and new concepts of staff development are the changes from an externally controlled and top-down imposition to school-based management, from remedial purposes to developmental purposes, from temporary and unsystematic arrangements to continuous and systematic organization, from fragmentary content to continuous and comprehensive content, from passive attendance to active participation, from focusing only on individuals to individuals, groups and the whole school, from the training of knowledge and technology to the affective, cognitive and behavioral development of staff, from teachers only to teachers, administrators and supporting staff inclusive, from learning

Table 8.1: Traditional concepts and new concepts of staff development

Traditional concepts of staff development	New concepts of staff development
1. *Externally controlled* • The central education authorities plan and manage the activities with emphasis mainly on policy concern • Staff are not willing to participate and give opinions • Activities cannot meet the needs of the staff • Activities are held outside the school, participants must be absent from their duty and normal school work is affected	1. *School based* • The staff plan and manage the activities and the content is designed according to the needs of the staff of each school • Staff are willing to participate and contribute their ideas • Activities meet the needs of the staff • Activities are mostly carried out in the school, teachers need not be absent from their duty and can have immediate practice
2. *Remedial* • Activities are arranged for remedial purposes when the education process goes wrong • Only take care of problems in general, not particular needs of each school	2. *Developmental* • Activities are planned for development purposes on the needs of the school, groups and individuals • Serve the needs of the school
3. *Temporary, not systematic* • Activities are mainly temporary, planned and carried out by outside experts • Has no long-term strategy for development and no systematic management	3. *Continuous, systematic* • Activities are included in the annual school plan, fully supported by school administration • Has long term strategies and systematic management
4. *Content* • Fragmentary • Stress too much on achievement of technical knowledge and behavioral changes	4. *Content* • Continuous and comprehensive • Development of techniques, affects, values and beliefs are all taken into account
5. *Focus on individuals* • Emphasize improvement of individual members but ignore the development of groups and the whole school	5. *Focus on individuals, groups and the school* • Emphasize development at all the individual, group and whole school levels
6. *For teachers only*	6. *Not only for teachers, but also administrators and supporting staff*
7. *External speakers mainly* • They are not familiar with the school situation, and irrelevant examples are used	7. *Both internal and external speakers* • The content fits the needs of participants and the real cases they share are helpful in practice
8. *The role of staff is passive*	8. *The role of staff is active*
9. *Simplistic types of activities* • Lectures mainly	9. *Various types of activities* • Seminars, talks, workshops, coaching, quality circle, classroom research, evaluation, etc.
10. *Motivation* • Encourage staff participation by extrinsic rewards such as promotion and reduction of work load	10. *Motivation* • Staff participation is self-motivated by intrinsic rewards such as professional growth and ownership

Adapted from Y.C. Cheng & W.M. Tam (1994).

through lectures only to various types of development activities, and from encouragement by extrinsic incentives to self-motivation by intrinsic rewards in the participation of staff development activities. These changes show that the new concept of staff development gives consideration to the needs of various subjects at different levels, and new staff development activities are set to enhance effectiveness in various aspects of staff and their school.

Integrating the above discussion about the concepts of staff development, we may define staff development as follows:

Staff development is the process including various activities that help the staff (teachers and administrators) to learn and develop to be more effective individual staff and more effective groups in teaching students, managing the process of schooling, and helping the school as a whole to be effective in facing the changing educational environment.

The Functions of Staff Development

Referring to the new concepts in Table 8.1 and the Scottish experience on staff development (Scottish Education Department, 1991), some important functions of staff development at different levels can be summarized as follows:

For Individual Development and Effectiveness

- to encourage individual staff to be more motivated and committed to their job;
- to contribute to the growth of the knowledge, skills and expertise of staff;
- to assist individual staff in their career development;
- to help individual members reflect on the aims and objectives of current school policies and practices;
- to develop the potential of each staff member;
- to maintain and improve personal satisfaction in job;
- to enhance personal confidence.

For Group Development and Effectiveness

- to encourage cooperation in the group;
- to build up team spirit;
- to foster friendship and intimacy;
- to learn from other team members;
- to understand and accept alternative ideas in the group;
- to improve coordination in the group;
- to solve group conflicts;
- to have better communication among group members;
- to generate better ideas, solutions or decisions in the group.

- to ensure/enhance the quality of learning and teaching in the school;
- to improve the management of staff;
- to build up a strong school culture;
- to develop positive and open human relationship in the school;
- to provide the opportunity for communicating and developing school mission and goals;
- to help school members to implement school changes or educational innovations;
- to meet long-term development needs of the school;
- to achieve wider participation and involvement in the school.

Of course, the development and effectiveness at the individual, group and whole school levels are mutually reinforced. The better the individual development, the better the group or school development. The reverse is also true.

The Matrix Conception of School-based Staff Development

Borrowing the matrix conception of school process in Chapter 6, we can propose a school-based staff development matrix to further illustrate the new trend of staff development on one hand, and serve as a theoretical framework for practice and management of school-based staff development on the other.

The Staff Development Matrix

The school process matrix, as shown in Figure 6.1 (see p. 86), is now applied to the staff development matrix which may include three dimensions: domain of development, category of actors and level of development, as shown in Figure 8.1.

The matrix assumes that the main actors involved in staff development activities may include students, teachers and administrators, with the latter two as the centre and each of the three having different development needs. The performance and development in a school may be considered in terms of the individual, group and school levels. The objectives, practices and management of staff development for each of these three levels might not be similar. The outcomes of staff development are shown in three major domains: the technical or behavioral domain, the affective domain and the cognitive domain. In the behavioral domain, changes of staff behavior are regarded as important, and therefore overt performance, passing on of knowledge, mastering of techniques, and behavioral efficiency are usually important. In the affective domain, the feeling of involvement, sense of achievement, confidence, organizational climate and human relationship are regarded as important. In the cognitive domain, staff's beliefs and values, reflection on their job, and cognitive growth are often important.

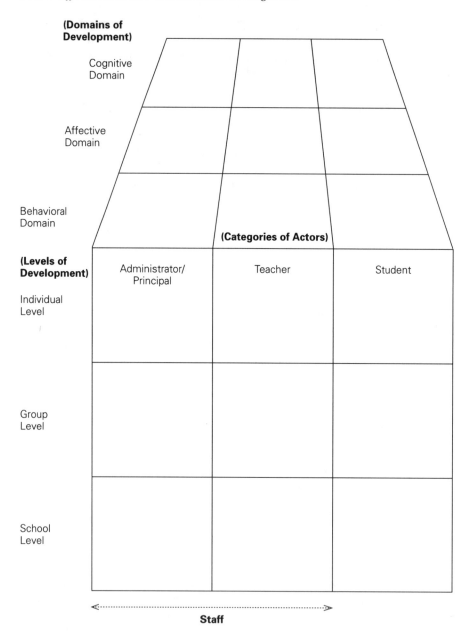

Figure 8.1:   *The matrix conception of school-based staff development*

Category of actors in staff development. The major school mission often aims at facilitating student development. Staff development which involves administrators, teachers and supporting staff inevitably has a final aim to support student development. The development needs between teaching staff to administrative staff are different. The development needs of teaching staff may be related mainly to classroom teaching activities, such as teaching techniques, classroom management, subject matter knowledge, curriculum design, dealing with teacher–student relationship, fostering learning climate, and helping emotionally disturbed students and slow learners, etc. The development needs of administrative staff may be related to school management including team collaboration, leadership, planning, staff evaluation, etc.

Levels of development. There are three levels of staff development: the individual, the group and the whole school level. Traditional staff development focuses mainly on the technical training of individual teachers. The development need in team collaboration between teachers and other members is neglected, as are the roles that members play in achieving the overall goals of a school. Staff development is now beginning to address the development needs at the group level as well as the school level.

As suggested in Carnegie Task Force on Teaching as a Profession (1986), team collaboration within the school is critical for the improvement of teaching quality so that on one hand, novice teachers may learn from experienced and expert teachers, and on the other hand, principals can give full play to their role as teaching supervisors. In fact, the significance of teacher professionalization is not confined to individual teachers having specific knowledge and teaching techniques, but also to being a professional individuals who can influence the performance of colleagues through team collaboration. All three levels, the individual, the group and the whole school, must be considered at the same time in the management of staff development. Individual development and effectiveness must be supported by the collaboration of a team and the whole school. Without collaboration, individual development will be limited, and the functioning of a school will not be efficiently organized. The situation will become one of putting in more effort but having little or no effect, and of course the learning of students will be negatively affected.

If only group development is emphasized, neglecting individuals and the entire school, different self-interest groups or parties will be formed in the school hindering cooperation among teachers. The worst situation will be that disagreement among different interest groups will turn into malicious attacks on each other and damage the development of the school as a whole. If only school development is addressed, neglecting the development needs of groups and individuals, it is impossible to achieve any development without the support from groups and individuals. Therefore, when we plan and manage staff development, all three levels should be considered.

Domains of development. The effects of staff development may take place in different domains. There are the technical/behavioral domain, the affective domain and the cognitive domain in staff development. In general, the behavioral development of staff is shown overtly, either in the classroom or in the school organization. Classroom-related behavior may include teaching techniques, classroom management, teacher–student interactions and teaching behavior, etc. The organization-related behavior may include punctuality, cooperation, participation, communication, presiding, planning, etc. All these are often the criteria schools use for teacher appraisal.

The affective development of staff may be related to personal interest, sense of satisfaction, organizational commitment, teacher–student affection, sense of involvement, relationship with colleagues, team spirit, organizational climate, etc. All these may affect the behavioral development and performance of the staff. Cognitive development is often implicit and hidden. It may include developments in staff reflection on school practice, judgment of professional issues, values and beliefs in teaching and management, and understanding of the school process and school mission, etc. The cognitive development of staff is often very important because it will support the internalization of behavioral development and affective development and also contribute to the formation of school culture.

The Content of Staff Development

Based on the matrix conception of staff development, various forms of development activities can be designed to achieve different development objectives for teachers and administrators at different levels, as shown in Table 8.2. Some objectives of the development activities for teachers and administrators should be similar. Therefore, Table 8.2 lists only those which might be different examples.

Principles of Congruence for Staff Development

As shown in Table 8.2, various types of activities can be conducted in the area of staff development. But how would it be most effective to promote these activities? This issue can be judged by the Principle of Congruence proposed in Chapter 6 (see p. 87). The principle of congruence applied in staff development includes three types of congruence in the matrix of staff development: *category congruence, level congruence* and *domain congruence*.

Category congruence means that the purposes of the development activities for administrators and teachers in the three domains at different levels should be congruent with that of students. For example, in the development activities for administrators, the management principles, for example, internal control/external control, to be encouraged should be congruent with the principles of classroom management (self discipline/punishment) and the learning of students (active/passive). *Level congruence* means that the development activities at different levels should be congruent with each other. For example, when a whole-school approach to guidance is to be carried out in the school, it would be successful only when it gains unanimous support from each functioning group, and teachers carry it through to the end in contact with individual students. Therefore, the staff development activities arranged for implementing the whole-school approach to guidance should take into consideration the congruence across the individual, group and school levels at the same time. *Domain congruence* means that the influence of staff development activities on the behavioral, affective and cognitive developments of participants should be congruent with each other and at the same time. For example, in staff development, a principal uses clinical supervision as a means to improve teachers' teaching. Clinical supervision should not be limited to improving their teaching behavior only, but also to changing their attitudes and beliefs about teaching if an optimal effect on teachers is expected.

Category congruence, level congruence and domain congruence are the factors that judge whether the staff development activities in the school work or not. The degree of congruence in development activities also reflects whether the school culture is strong or weak, because it represents the unanimous orientation of school members in behavioral, affective and cognitive development at different levels.

Staff Development Cycles

According to the matrix conception, staff development should be an interactive developmental process in multi-domains at multi-levels. As shown in Figure 6.2 (p. 89), the staff development matrix can be cut into three layers: the administrator layer, the teacher layer and the student layer.

Staff Development Cycle at the Actor Layer

As discussed in Chapter 6, within actor-layer congruence, i.e., the consistency within one layer in terms of domain congruence and level congruence is very important to the effectiveness of the school process. Also, within actor-layer congruence can be achieved by a development cycle which can help staff to perform consistently in all the three domains at all the three levels to enhance effectiveness. Staff development activities can be designed according to this concept of the development cycle.

Take the administrator layer as an example. The school can establish an administrator development program on the individual, group and school levels to provide administrators with opportunities to learn new management ideas and competence, establish better human relationship, examine regularly their management style, review school policies, reflect on school culture and make self improvement. In order to achieve long-term effect, the development activities may focus on improving individual behavior of administrators at the beginning, and extend to the aspects of their affects and beliefs later on. Of course, it is also important that the development activities should be extended to the group level and then the school level so that all administrators learn to have unanimous education beliefs, management philosophy and ways of running the school. When the administrators have

Table 8.2: Activities and objectives for staff development

	For teachers	For administrators
Behavior (Technique)	• Increase knowledge, techniques and specialty of teaching and learning • Find out the factors hindering the full play of teacher's competence • Improve teaching performance • Encourage participation and development • Assist the work of colleagues	• Enhance administrative efficiency • Improve leadership • Master techniques of planning and management • Improve supervision style • Encourage open mind and learning • Assist the development of colleagues
Affective	• Reinforce confidence as a teaching professional • Enhance satisfaction in teaching • Increase personal commitment to education	• Reinforce confidence as administrative leader • Enhance satisfaction in administration • Increase the concern and support for colleagues • Increase personal commitment to education and administrative work
Cognition	• Understand current educational trends • Understand current school policies and objectives of school functions • Recognize the values of teaching and establish personal beliefs about education • Provide teachers with opportunities for role clarification • Identify with the school mission • Self-evaluate and reflect on educational work • Responsible for outcomes of teaching	• Understand current educational trends • Reflect on current school policies and objectives of school functions • Recognize ethical and moral issues on administration • Recognize the values of administration • Establish personal beliefs about leadership • Clarify the role of administration • Self-evaluate and reflect on administration • Be responsible for colleagues' performance and administrative results

INDIVIDUAL

		Column 1	Column 2
G R O U P	*Behavior (Technique)*	• Provide opportunities for members to learn from each other • Work together to teach and develop curriculum • Provide inter-class visits • Learn to share and participate	• Solve internal conflicts and improve communication • Lead group/team work • Learn to delegate and distribute work
	Affective	• Establish team spirit • Encourage mutual trust of members • Foster friendship	• Establish team spirit • Encourage mutual trust of members • Foster friendship
	Cognition	• Discuss and understand the relationship between group work and school policies • Evaluate the effectiveness of group work • Analyze strengths, weaknesses and development of the group • Ensure the role and value of group work • Commitment to group effectiveness	• Discuss and ensure the relationship between groups and school policies • Recognize the values of collaborative management and participative decision making • Evaluate strengths and weaknesses of each policy • Ensure the role and value of the administrative group • Commitment to policy effectiveness
S C H O O L	*Behavior (Technique)*	• Provide opportunities for whole-school teaching collaboration • Improve the use of whole school resources • Find out whole-school factors unfavorable for teaching	• Provide opportunities for whole-school collaboration for teaching and management • Improve the management of whole-school resources • Find out and prevent factors unfavorable for the full development of staff • Develop the whole-school image
	Affective	• Foster a sense of belonging to the school • Establish whole-school collaborative climate among teachers • Develop a homely atmosphere in the school	• Establish whole-school climate and a sense of belonging • Establish close relationship between administrators and teachers • Develop a homely atmosphere in the school
	Cognition	• Evaluate school effectiveness • Participate in developing school mission and goals • Ensure the values of school education • Identify with the unique mission and vision of the school	• Lead the discussion and reflection on school policies • Lead the staff to develop school mission and goals • Lead and ensure the values of school education • Lead and ensure the unique mission and vision of the school

Adapted from Cheng and Tam (1994).

reached a mutual understanding, they will be more involved in their work and the school, and their collaboration will be more effective. When the functioning of the whole administrative system is smooth, the performance of individuals and groups will be further developed. Groups will be more congruent among themselves and more willing to propose new ideas and give room for innovation. Individuals will be more self-confident, more willing to accept new things, and more willing to further develop their professional competence. In such a way, a development cycle is formed which starts from the individual administrator to groups and to the whole school, then back to the individual again. There may also be mutual reinforcement among individuals, groups and the entire school. The domain of development may start from behavior to affect, then cognition and back to behavior again, and there may be mutual influence among the three domains. In short, it is a dynamic development cycle which pushes forth the development of administrators and reinforces the congruence in the school management process.

Similarly, the school can carry out development cycle for teachers by establishing a teacher development program to provide development activities according to their behavioral, affective or cognitive needs at the three levels.

Staff Development Cycle at the Level Layer

In addition to the concepts of the actor layers, we can divide the staff development matrix into the *school layer*, the *group layer* and the *individual layer*. As discussed in Chapter 6, within level-layer congruence is also important to the effectiveness of the school process. Staff development cycles can be established on each of these layers (see Figure 6.3, p. 90) to ensure the within level-layer congruence and contribute to school effectiveness and development.

The development activities designed for administrators, teachers and students on the individual layer should meet their different behavioral, affective and cognitive needs. The development cycle can start from improving administrators' performance, and then extend to the activities designed for improving teachers' teaching performance. When teachers possess effective teaching skills, ideas and attitudes, they will influence the learning behavior of students more effectively, so that students will become more interested and confident in learning and think more positively. The progress of students will inspire teachers to be more confident in teaching and develop more positively and quickly. It is not a surprise that the successful development of teachers will affect the belief, commitment and development of administrators. Thus a development cycle for staff is formed on the individual layer.

Similarly, a development cycle can be designed on the group layer according to the needs of groups. To administrators and teachers, the areas of group development may include peer group climate, team building, interpersonal relationship, social norms and team spirit, etc. Group activities such as team cooperation, working committee and social activities can be conducted to develop human relations, ease uptight emotions, solve problems and work effectively. Many studies on staff development pointed out that participating in team cooperation activities can stimulate thinking and provide new perspectives that are important to staff professional development (see Little, 1982; Shulman and Carey, 1984).

Also, it is possible to establish a staff development cycle at the school layer. Whole school policies and programs on staff development can be set up to encourage social interactions and developments and pursue congruence at the school level. Similarly, the congruent behavioral, affective and cognitive developments of students, teachers and administrators at the school level can make contribution to the development and effectiveness of the school as a whole.

A Summary of the Matrix Conceptions

The matrix conception of staff development, the principle of congruence, and the idea of development cycle can provide a comprehensive framework for understanding, planning, managing and implementing staff development activities.

From the matrix conception, we understand that staff development is not confined to the technical behavioral domain or to the individual level, but should have multi-actors, multi-development domains and multi-development levels. Although the administrator layer, teacher layer, and student layer have their own development models, they are mutually supporting and reinforcing. Similarly, the school layer, group layer and individual layer do not have the same development functions, but they are also mutually influencing and reinforcing. Therefore, when there is a lack of development in any layer, the effectiveness of the staff development program will be decreased.

The principle of congruence for staff development guides planners to set effective staff development strategies. In addition to considering the needs of the school, the staff and the students, they should also pay attention to level congruence and domain congruence.

The concept of staff development cycle helps us to look at staff development and the school process from a dynamic viewpoint. According to the dynamic perspective of school effectiveness discussed in Chapter 3, an effective school, even when faced with pressures from inside and outside in the changing education environment, can maintain dynamic development and maximize effectiveness on multi-criteria. The staff development cycle should be the critical element for helping the school to pursue dynamic effectiveness and development. Therefore, quite a number of studies have discovered that many important school efforts such as the development of school culture, organizational change, and curriculum change, all need the support from staff development to achieve the expected results (e.g., Cheng, 1994c; Fullan, 1991; Joyce, 1989; Slater and Teddlie, 1992).

Establishing a Staff Development Program

To put these concepts of staff development into practice, a staff development program is needed. Staff development programs aim to provide some systematic activities and opportunities to develop individual staff and groups, consequently the school as a whole becomes more effective in achieving the expected school goals and developing new goals for the future. Concerning the effectiveness of a staff development program, we have to consider the following issues:

- Does it meet the development needs of individuals, groups and the school as a whole?
- If the resources are limited and the development needs are many, how does one identify and prioritize the different needs?
- Is there a positive climate among the staff supporting the meaning and implementation of the program?
- If not, how does one establish a positive climate?
- Is the staff development program well designed and implemented with clear policies, appropriate resources and arrangements?
- How does one establish and manage an appropriate staff development program?
- Since participative management encourages participation, involvement, team building and group process, is it available in the school for creating development opportunities for staff?
- How does one encourage participation in management?
- Can the role of staff be conceptualized as partner, learner, initiator, leader, professional and implementer in organizing the staff development program?
- Is it necessary to redefine the role of staff in school functioning?
- Can the school leaders inspire the staff, create a climate to bring out the meaning and prospect of staff development, set up a staff development program and encourage the staff to take part and make decisions?

The above questions provide some important guidelines to design a staff development program. Specifically with reference to the Scottish experience (Scottish Office Education Department, 1991), the development of a staff development program may include the following steps, as shown in Figure 8.2. In each step, staff participation in management is necessary; staff should be the partner, learner, initiator, leader, professional and implementer of all staff development activities.

Review of the Existing Practice

The planners should review the existing policy, procedures and arrangements of staff development activities. According to the school mission and goals, the school development plan, the matrix conception of staff development, and the above questions, planners can analyze the strengths, weaknesses, opportunities and threats of the existing practice.

Identifying and Prioritizing the Development Needs

Due to the limitation of school resources, it is impossible to satisfy all the development needs in school at the same time. For planning staff development activities

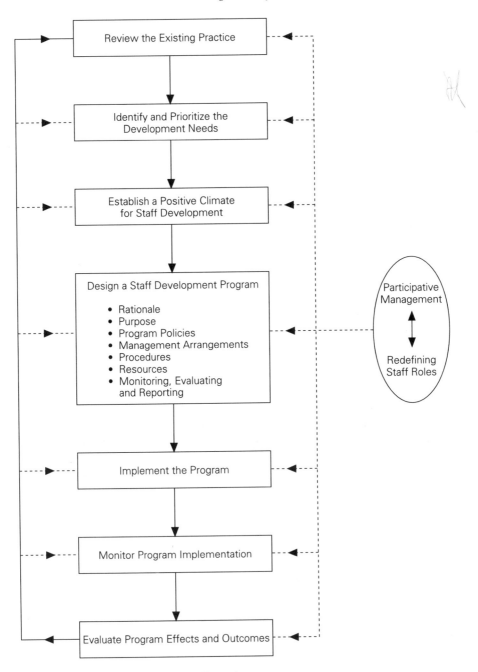

Figure 8.2:   Steps of establishing a staff development program

in a fixed period of time, for example, one year, identifying the important development needs and prioritizing them is necessary. The identifying and prioritizing process can be based on the following considerations:

- draw implications from the review results of the existing staff development practice;
- take the priorities of school objectives or program objectives as the critical reference for prioritizing the staff development needs;
- use the knowledge of teacher effectiveness and educational effectiveness (e.g., Cheng, 1991a; Creemers, 1994; Wang and Walberg, 1991) as guidelines to understand and identify the staff development needs;
- use all the relevant sources of information to identify and prioritize the staff development needs. The following are some examples of the important sources: education department reports and policy papers; Education Inspectorate audit report; annual school report; reports from working groups or program teams; curriculum audit or analysis; examination or test results (external and internal); program evaluation or review; pupil progress data; individual appraisal processes; feedback from parents; staff self-evaluation, etc. A balance between the needs of the school as a whole and those of groups and individuals should be important.

Establishing Positive Climate for Staff Development

Positive social climate in the school is an important factor for the successful introduction of a staff development program. When establishing a staff development program, it is necessary to encourage mutual trust, ownership, participation, consultation and involvement among staff. At the beginning, staff should be encouraged to participate in decision making on the direction and policy of staff development. They are facilitated to exchange ideas and information and understand the aims and importance of staff development to their professional development and school effectiveness. In discussion of staff development activities, staff should be fully involved and consulted.

Designing the Staff Development Program

The design of staff development may use the program planning technology including the following components:

- *rationale*: To explain the logic, background, and significance of staff development;
- *purposes*: To list the specific objectives of staff development activities;
- *program policies*: To formulate the basic principles and policies to guide the management and implementation of staff development;

- *management arrangements*: To describe the necessary arrangements to manage, support, and implement the staff development activities;
- *procedures*: To list the necessary steps and procedures to carry out staff development activities;
- *resources*: To budget and plan the necessary resources for the activities;
- *monitoring, evaluating and reporting*: To describe the methods for monitoring, evaluating and reporting the effectiveness of staff development activities.

Implementing, Monitoring, and Evaluating the Program

According to the plan of the program, staff development activities can be implemented, monitored and evaluated. In the implementation process, the principal, senior teachers or the staff development task group should play the leading role in facilitating staff participation in the activities. There may be various types of school-based development including formal and informal types, external and internal types, such as workshops or short courses conducted by staff members, mutual lesson observation, teaching experience exchange, classroom action research, cooperative teaching, whole-staff conference, departmental meetings, program team meetings, policy groups, new teacher induction or new position holder induction, rotation of responsibility, curriculum development meetings, visits to other schools, outside short courses, educational seminars or conferences, secondments of exchanges with other schools, participation in local or international working committees and service to education organizations or professional associations.

A teacher education network may be established to support all school-based or external staff development activities by providing in-service teachers with various forms and opportunities for professional development. (Cheng, 1992b). Individual schools, colleges or schools of education, teacher center, education department, professional associations and other organizations can join together to form a teacher education network. The connection and mutual support among schools can provide teacher development activities, such as exchange of teachers, joint seminars, exchange visitings, etc. The mutual support between schools and colleges of education can provide services such as guidance for student teachers, school consulting services, research, seminars, workshops and lectures by experienced teachers and principals, etc. Other linkages between education organizations and schools can have various types of joint seminars and conferences, forums or research projects. In this way, the linkages can be mutual support to each other. Therefore, the staff development network can have the following advantages:

- providing more alternatives for meeting the diverse needs of staff development;
- enriching the content of staff development activities;
- disseminating the successful experiences, ideas and skills more rapidly to schools;
- decreasing the cost of staff development activities.

The changes in education environment, school and individual values, school management model and the professional growth of teachers all urge the need of staff development. Without staff development, it is impossible to enhance school effectiveness or promote school development.

Recently, the concept and practice of staff development have been changing. The traditional concept of staff development pays attention to external-control, remedy, technical knowledge training and change of behaviors of individuals. The role of staff is passive. The new concept emphasizes school-based development and growth in multi-domains at multi-levels where the role of staff is active.

The matrix conception of school-based staff development provides a new and comprehensive framework to understanding, managing and practising staff development. The principle of congruence can be a guide for carrying out staff development activities. Effective staff development should include level congruence and domain congruence. Based on the staff development matrix, a development cycle can be established to develop administrators, teachers and students from individuals to groups and to the whole school. Based on these new concepts, staff development programs can be established and implemented to help all the staff and the school as a whole to pursue development and effectiveness.

Chapter 9

Management of School-based Curriculum Change

Curriculum change and development is an important activity for the improvement of educational processes and pursuit of school effectiveness. In this chapter, the management and effectiveness of school-based curriculum change will be discussed in light of the concepts introduced in the previous chapters.

The changing educational environment, the diverse educational needs of students, the high expectations from the public and policy reports strongly demand educational change, not only at the education system level, but also at the school-based level in many countries. For example, some efforts on curriculum change have been done at the system level. School-based curriculum development has also been strongly encouraged in both primary and secondary schools in Hong Kong and some Asia–Pacific countries. Curriculum change as a form of planned change in the school may meet resistance, and its implementation may be affected by different organizational factors (Cheng and Ng, 1991a). Though there are some curriculum evaluation studies, very few provide guidelines or models for practitioners or researchers to effectively implement and manage curriculum changes in the complex context of school organization in which there are multi-level influencing factors. Without a theoretical model linking organizational factors and curriculum change, it is very difficult, if not impossible, to understand the dynamic and effectiveness of curriculum change.

This chapter will apply the concepts of the school-based management mechanism to the understanding and management of curriculum change. First, it will clarify the concepts of curriculum, curriculum effectiveness and curriculum change at different levels, and then illustrate how the school-based management mechanism can contribute to the management and effectiveness of curriculum change and development.

Concept of Curriculum Effectiveness

To different researchers and practitioners, the definition of curriculum may be different. It may be defined narrowly as a specific set of knowledge, skills and activities to be delivered to students, or it may be defined broadly as a set of planned activities to foster teachers' teaching and students' learning. It may be further defined as national curriculum at the nation level, or as school curriculum at the school level, or as subject curriculum at the subject level. Since our focus will be limited to the school level, *curriculum* is defined as a set of activities and content planned at the individual level, the program level, or the whole-school level to foster teachers' teaching and students' learning. Therefore, the discussion of curriculum change in this chapter will not go beyond the school level even though curriculum change at the national level is also important for study. In other words, school-based curriculum change will be the only focus.

To a great extent, curriculum development or change aims to maximize the effectiveness of teaching and learning through change in planned content, activities and arrangements for educational processes. If we accept this line of thinking, the discussion of curriculum change should be related to another concept — curriculum effectiveness. It is crucial to know what and how curriculum is effective for teaching and learning and what main factors contribute to curriculum effectiveness. My previous conception of curriculum effectiveness may be helpful to our discussion (Cheng, 1986a). The structure of curriculum effectiveness can be illustrated as shown in Figure 9.1. Based on this structure, a curriculum is effective if it can appropriately interact with teachers' competence to facilitate teacher performance, help students gain learning experiences that fit their needs and produce expected educational outcomes, under the constraints of preexisting characteristics such as national goals, school goals, school management, subject content, educational technology and resources. The structure suggests that the evaluation of curriculum effectiveness may include process and outcome criteria such as teacher performance, student learning experience and outcomes. The variables that can be manipulated, changed or developed to improve teacher performance and student learning experience and outcomes are curriculum and teacher competence.

Approaches to Curriculum Change

From this conception of curriculum effectiveness, we may categorize the approaches to maximizing teaching effectiveness and learning effectiveness through curriculum change into the following three kinds:

The Simplistic Curriculum Change Approach

Curriculum should be developed or changed at the individual, program, or school level to fit in with teacher competence and student characteristics in addition to its consistency with school goals. This approach assumes that teachers are passive, teacher competence is static, and curriculum change can be planned and implemented effectively by administrators or external experts.

The Teacher Competence Development Approach

Teacher competence should be developed to meet the demand of the curriculum. This approach assumes that curriculum change is imposed by administrators or external experts and teacher competence can be developed easily to satisfy all the needs of the changed curriculum.

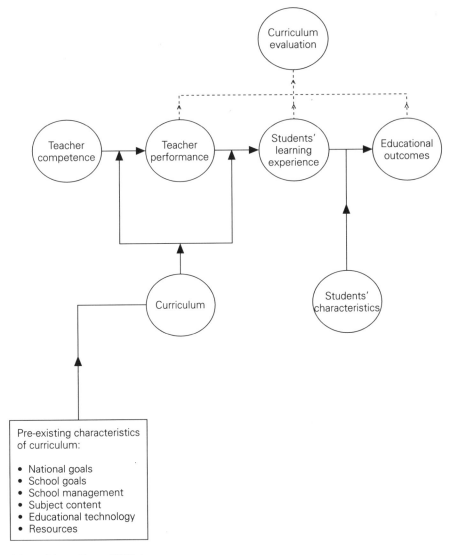

Adapted from Cheng (1986a).

Figure 9.1: The structure of curriculum effectiveness

The Dynamic Curriculum Change Approach

Both curriculum and teacher competence should be developed and changed in order to maximize curriculum effectiveness in terms of facilitating teaching and learning. This approach assumes that:

- curriculum effectiveness is a dynamic concept involving a continuous and cyclic process for developing both curriculum and teacher competence;

Table 9.1: Comparison between the approaches to curriculum change

	Simplistic curriculum change approach	Teacher competence development approach	Dynamic curriculum change approach
Nature of change	• One-way change	• One-way change	• Two-way change, dynamic
Focus of change	• Curriculum	• Teacher competence	• Curriculum and teacher competence
Ways of maximizing effectiveness	• Curriculum adapts to teachers and students	• Teachers adapt to the changed curriculum	• Both curriculum and teachers should be developed
Initiator of change	• Change planned by administrators or external experts	• Change imposed by administrators or external experts	• Teacher participation in planning change
Teacher role	• Passive implementer	• Passive implementer	• Active implementer and planner
Time framework	• Short-term	• Short-term	• Long-term, continuous, cyclic

Adapted from Y.C. Cheng (1994c).

- curriculum can be developed and changed effectively only when teachers (i.e. implementers) are sufficiently involved in the process;
- teacher competence should be developed not only to satisfy the demands of the existing curriculum or the changed curriculum but also to develop the curriculum more appropriately to fit students' characteristics, school goals, and preexisting school conditions in the long run;
- effective curriculum change should involve not only administrators or external experts but also teachers in curriculum planning and decision making.

The comparison between the approaches is summarized in Table 9.1. The first and second approaches employ a short-term, mechanical perspective to conduct curriculum change and implementation. They ignore the dynamic nature of curriculum change and teacher development and the importance of teachers' active role, involvement and commitment to curriculum planning and their own professional development. Because of this ignorance, curriculum change through these two approaches may not bring long-term effectiveness to teaching and learning, even if it is not frustrated by resistance including teacher sabotage, slowdown, protest and apathy (Cheng and Ng, 1991a).

The dynamic curriculum change approach uses a long-term perspective and is consistent with the concepts of school self-management at multi-levels in Chapter 5 and the emphasis on staff development in Chapter 8. The active role and participation of teachers are assumed to be really important in curriculum planning and change. Comparatively, this approach seems to be more promising to effective teaching and learning through development and change in both curriculum and teacher competence.

Contribution of School-based Mechanism to Curriculum Change

Even though the dynamic approach may be more powerful in conceptualizing curriculum change, some important questions remain unanswered. As mentioned above, curriculum change and teacher competence development are important for effective teaching and learning, but how can they be effectively initiated and maintained towards achievement of planned school goals? How does the school-based management mechanism contribute to the dynamic approach to curriculum change?

Inevitably, all forms of school curriculum change happen in a complex organizational context including teachers' personal factors, group norms, organizational structure, school culture, leadership, etc. How are curriculum change and teacher development related to organizational factors? Specifically, how can they be facilitated but not hindered by organizational factors? As described in the previous chapters, the school-based management mechanism can initiate and sustain a continuous process for school development including curriculum change and teacher development. Based on the concepts of self-management at the individual, group and school level, the contribution of the school-based management mechanism to curriculum change can be illustrated as shown in Figure 9.2 and explained as follows.

A Three-Level Organizational Context

Curriculum change and teacher competence development happen in a three-level context of school organization including the individual level, the group level/program level, and the whole school-level as shown in Figure 9.2.

Mutual Development

Curriculum change and teacher competence development are mutually developed and reinforced at each of the three levels of school organizational context in the long term.

Hierarchy of Influence

Curriculum change and teacher competence development at the individual level are influenced by those at the group or program level and all at these two levels are affected by those at the whole-school level. There is a hierarchy of influence across these levels.

Effectiveness and Interaction

The effectiveness of curriculum change at the classroom or individual level (i.e., effects on teaching and learning) is directly determined by the interaction between

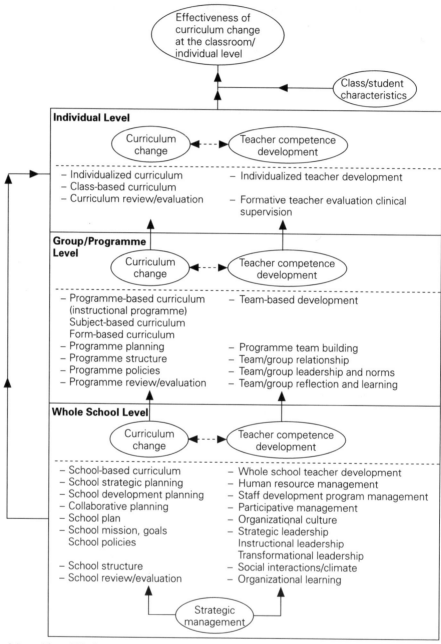

Adapted from Y.C. Cheng (1994c).

Figure 9.2: The organizational model of curriculum change

Table 9.2: *The congruence matrix*

		CONGRUENCE	
		<- ->	
		Curriculum Change	Teacher Competence Development
^ ¦ ¦ CONGRUENCE ¦ ¦ v	Individual Level		
	Programme/Group Level		
	School Level		

changes in curriculum and teacher competence and characteristics of students and the class; and is also indirectly affected by curriculum change and teacher development at the group/program level and the whole school level.

Congruence

According to the principle of congruence in the school-based management mechanism, the effectiveness of curriculum change may be affected by two types of congruence: congruence between curriculum change and teacher competence development and congruence between levels. They form a matrix of congruence as shown in Table 9.2. Congruence is defined in terms of conceptual (cognitive) consistency in goals, objectives, values and assumptions (about change, development, management, teaching and learning) and operational consistency (for example, coordination, to a great extent, congruence reflects the strength of school culture, (i.e., the strength of sharing of values, beliefs, and assumptions among members, Schein, 1992) and is believed to be a determinant of school effectiveness (Beare, *et al.*, 1989; Cheng, 1993h). The greater the congruence between and across levels of change and development, the greater the effectiveness of curriculum change for teaching and learning.

Characteristics At Different Levels

The characteristics of curriculum change and teacher development are different at different levels, shaped by a variety of organizational factors.

At the *individual* level, curriculum change is often understood in terms of individualized curriculum, class-based/ability-based curriculum and related curriculum review or evaluation. Teacher competence development is often individualized in terms of formative teacher evaluation or clinical supervision (see Bollington, Hopkins and West, 1990; Cheng, 1993e; Valentine, 1992).

At the *program* level, the focus of curriculum change is on instructional program that includes a set of curriculum units such as subject-based curriculum or form-based curriculum for some specific program goals. For example, the science education program may include curriculum units such as biology, physics and chemistry. Another example is the grade 11 program in high schools including a combination of different curriculum units or subjects. In general, there may be many instructional programs and non-instructional programs in a school. The mechanism of curriculum change at this level is composed of program planning, structure, policies and review/evaluation (Cheng, 1993d). Specifically, instructional planning as the critical component is a process of establishing program direction and curriculum objectives, developing teaching and learning activities and content, organizing instructional facilities and resources and setting implementation procedures. Teacher competence development at the group level is group, team-based or program team building (Dyer, 1987; Maeroff, 1993). The mechanism of development consists of group relationship, leadership, norms and reflection and learning. As discussed in Chapter 8, it is also possible to establish a program specifically for team/group development.

As discussed in Chapter 5, at the whole-school level, curriculum change and development can be conducted in terms of school strategic management or school development planning with emphasis on analysis of the school's internal and external environment and long-term perspective (Hargreaves and Hopkins, 1991). The important components that can contribute to curriculum change include collaborative planning, school plan (including school mission, goals, policies, strategies), school structure and school review/evaluation (see Chapter 5). Teacher development at this level is the whole-school teacher development. The components contributing to teacher development may include human resource management, staff development program management, participative management, organizational culture, social interactions, leadership and organizational learning (see Chapter 8).

Curriculum change and teacher competence development focus on two different aspects of effective schooling: One on the structural and planning aspect and the other on the human aspect. Both of them may be based on the school-based management mechanism.

As discussed in Chapters 5 and 6, the school-based management mechanism includes strategic management at the school level and self-management at the group and individual levels. Strategic management is a process that can keep a school as a whole appropriately matched to its environment, improve school performance, achieve school objectives and fulfill school mission. It includes the sequential components such as environmental analysis, systematic planning and structuring, appropriate staffing and directing, and constructive monitoring and evaluation. It is a cyclic learning process that contributes to continuous curriculum development and staff development at the individual, program/group and whole school levels. As discussed in Chapter 5, self-management at the group level and the individual level is also a cyclic learning process that contributes to a cycle of curriculum change and staff development at these two levels. Figure 9.3 shows a typical example of a cyclic process at the program level that includes components such as program analysis, planning, implementation, monitoring and evaluating. The process can provide a cyclic mechanism to change and develop curriculum at the program level.

In general, the length of each cycle for curriculum development may vary

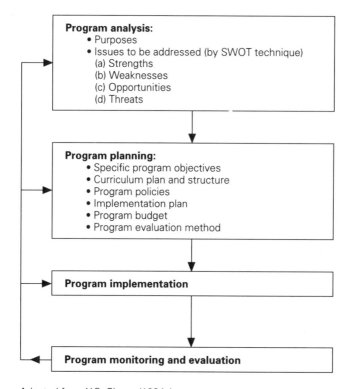

Adapted from Y.C. Cheng (1994c).

Figure 9.3: An example of cyclic process at the program level

from one to three years and may also vary across levels, programs, and individuals. But strategically, the cycle at the school level should drive those at the program and individual levels, and the program level should drive the individual level. These cycles provide opportunities for continuous improvement and development in curriculum and teacher competence.

As noted above, the congruence between curriculum change and teacher development and the congruence across levels in terms of conceptual consistency and operational consistency are important for ensuring the effectiveness of curriculum change. Congruence is often ensured through development of school mission, goals, and policies and sharing of school values, beliefs and assumptions among school members. This is the reason why recently, development of school culture has been strongly emphasized for effective schooling (Beare, *et al.*, 1989; Cheng, 1989, 1993h; Schein, 1992).

Leadership and Participation

In order to initiate and use school-based management for the effective management of curriculum change, layer leadership and strategic leadership should be necessary and important (for detail, please see Chapter 7). Particularly, leadership is responsible for facilitating instructional activities and coordinating curriculum across the individual, program and school levels for ensuring congruence through defining the school mission and goals, managing the instructional programs and promoting a positive school learning climate. It is what we often call instructional leadership (Hallinger and Murphy, 1987). Successful curriculum change inevitably involves transformation of teachers' behavior, skills, motivation, conceptions and beliefs about management, teaching and learning. Therefore, transformational leadership is also an important component of leadership for the process of curriculum change and teacher development (Bass, 1985; Bennis, 1984). As explained in Chapter 7, instructional leadership and transformational leadership have been included in the concepts of layer leadership and strategic leadership.

Teacher participation or teacher leadership is strongly emphasized in effective schooling and educational change (e.g., Conley and Bacharach, 1990; Lieberman, 1988; Mortimore, 1993). In planning and managing curriculum change whether at the individual, program or whole school level, teacher participation (and also participation of parents, students or alumni, where appropriate) may make the following contributions to curriculum change:

- provide important human resources in terms of participants' time, experience, knowledge and skills for better planning and implementation of curriculum change;
- produce high quality decisions and plans of curriculum change by involving different perspectives and expertise;
- promote greater responsibility, accountability, commitment and support to implementation and results of curriculum change;
- participate in planning of curriculum change and provide a form of meaning development or culture building;
- participate in management of curriculum change and provide opportunities for individuals and groups to enrich their professional experience and pursue professional development;
- participate in planning and decision making on curriculum change and provide more information and greater opportunities to overcome technical and psychological resistance and change ineffective practices at different levels;
- participate in planning to help ensure congruence between curriculum change and teacher development and congruence across levels, which is critical to effective change.

This chapter has shown how the school-based management mechanism provides a comprehensive framework to manage curriculum change. In Chapter 10, the management of organizational change in the school will be discussed, suggesting ideas and techniques of changes helpful to the practice of curriculum change.

Management of School-based Change

In Chapter 9, we have discussed the management of school-based curriculum change. Obviously, curriculum change is only one part of school change that helps the school to adapt to the changing environment and meet the changing educational needs. There may be two types of school change: externally imposed school change and school-based change. The former refers to the change that is initiated and imposed by an external agent on the school and the latter refers to the change that is initiated and implemented mainly by school members. Since the concept of school-based management is emphasized in this book, internal school-based change will be the focus of discussion. In this chapter, we will discuss the nature, management and effectiveness of school-based change, particularly on the organizational aspects in the light of the dynamic perspective of school effectiveness and the concepts of school-based management mechanism.

The Needs for School-based Change

Following the tremendous economic and technological developments in society, the expectations on education have become more demanding and more diverse. The school has to change and develop continuously to satisfy the rapidly growing needs of education. Therefore, school change is an inevitable trend all over the world.

Whether a school should implement changes or not depends on one hand on the external factors (political, economical and social changes) which directly or indirectly push the school to respond and on the other hand, on the internal factors (appointment of new principal or supervisor, decline in school performance, etc.) which cause the school to change its organizational structure and process.

The needs for school-based change may be explained by Parsons' (1966) social system theory. According to this theory, a school should possess the following four functions for its survival:

1 Adaptation: it can adapt to the changes in internal and external environments for continuous development and effective survival;
2 Goal achievement: it can continuously enhance the ability of teachers and students to achieve school goals;
3 Integration: it can maintain an open and co-operative school climate in which school members feel satisfied and happy, and absenteeism or drop-out can be reduced to the least;

4 Pattern maintenance: it can maintain the loyalty and pride that school members take in their school, such that the good traditions encourage everybody to do their best.

The adaptation function suggests that a school needs to respond to the changes in its environments and therefore school change is inevitable. If a school is weak in the other three functions — goal achievement, integration and pattern maintenance, its survival will be threatened. Therefore school-based changes are needed particularly in these three aspects.

In Chapter 3, a dynamic perspective of school effectiveness has been introduced to explain that continuous school development and change is needed to pursue long-term school effectiveness on multiple school functions at multiple levels. Specifically, this perspective can explain the need for school-based change: due to multiple environmental constraints and constituencies, a school often has to pursue multiple and contradictory goals. Dilemmas and problems are unavoidable in school functioning and they cause the school to make changes in order to solve them. In the process of pursuing multiple school goals, the school experiences different pressures from the multiple and conflicting environmental constraints and constituencies. Since school resources are often very limited and not sufficient to support achievement of all school goals at the same time, the school has to develop different priorities for goals to be pursued according to the strengths of the pressures in a given time frame. When some specific goals are strongly emphasized and more resources and efforts are given to them, the school will experience greater pressure from ineffectiveness of achieving other goals. This inevitable unbalanced pressure brings about the need for school-based change. According to the dynamic perspective of school effectiveness, school-based change is inevitable for effective schools to pursue long-term and dynamic school development and effectiveness.

The Meanings of School-Based Change

According to Crandall, Eiseman, and Louis (1986), there are two categories of school-based change: the *pedagogic focus change* and *the organizational focus change*. The former focuses on changes in classroom arrangements, instructional process and teaching methods, etc., and the latter on changes in school organizational structure and process such as management style, hierarchy of authority, communication channels, decision making style and school climate, etc. From the above discussion, we may define *school-based change* as a process which includes a set of planned systematic activities conducted by school members to change the school's pedagogic and organizational processes in order to solve the school's dilemmas and problems and maximize effectiveness of functioning at the individual level, the group level and the school level (Cheng and Ng, 1991a; Levy, 1986).

There are three different perspectives that can be used to understand the complex nature of school-based change: the technological perspective, the cultural perspective, and the political perspective (House, 1981).

The Technological Perspective

This perspective regards school-based change as a technical task based on rational analysis. Its focus is on the technological aspect of the school change process and it emphasizes the matching between new technologies and school members. The key to success of a school-based change depends on its systematic planning, clear goals, sufficient resources, reasonable expectations for achievement, appropriate task allocation, good time management and support by policies and regulations. This perspective assumes that both people and organization are rational and they can handle the uncertainties of change through information, look at the school change from a rational model, care about the outcomes of change, regard change as the means of pursuing efficiency and effectiveness, and can control change by means of systematic methods and feedback. As a whole, this perspective lays stress on the contribution of technological factors (such as models of change, information systems, measures and analyses, and decision making techniques) to school-based change (Attewell, 1992; Gattiker, 1990; Noori, 1990; Sankar, 1991).

The Political Perspective

According to the political perspective, schools are coalitions composed of various individuals and interest groups and there are enduring differences among individuals and groups in their values, preferences, beliefs, information and perceptions of reality (Bolman and Deal, 1991a). Since the school resources are often scarce but the differences are enduring, conflicts are inevitable in school functioning. The happening of school-based change, particularly on the organizational aspects, is the reaction to pressures from the external environment, and is the reflection of change in the power structure and the use of different means to pursue interests of different groups and individuals in the school. School-based change involves the redistribution of school resources and therefore influences the relationship between individuals, groups and the school and creates conflicts. In the process of school change, powers and political activities, such as coalition building, bargaining, negotiation and jockeying for position, etc. are often essential tools to influence the success of change. Coalitions, conflicts and competition become the major components of school-based change. According to this perspective, leaders should choose appropriate political strategies, and in making the choice for school change, they should put politics in the first place and technology the second (Child, 1972). Since the power relationship between individuals and groups involved in the change may be very subtle and uncertain, it is usually difficult to wholly understand and control the process of school change. The goals of school-based change are often the interactive outcome of negotiation among internal members and coalitions, not rationally planned, and they may change according to the shift of power relationship among coalitions (Blase, 1989; 1991; Greiner and Schein, 1989).

The Cultural Perspective

The cultural perspective assumes that the overt behavior or performance of school members at the individual, group or whole-school level is often shaped by school culture, i.e., the sharing of values, beliefs, norms and assumptions about education, school management and life among school members (Cheng, 1989; Schein, 1992). According to this perspective, school-based change cannot be understood only from the overt performance, objectives, procedures and behaviors in the change process. It should be studied from the hidden school culture. A successful school-based change is a process involving changes not only in superficial behavior but also in the values and beliefs of school members. In other words, a school-based change is in itself a cultural change. Therefore, whether a school-based change can be successfully implemented depends not only on the change in technology but also the corresponding changes in school culture. Some scholars even suggest that the existing cultural factors should be mastered first if success is to be brought to school-based change (Firestone and Corbett, 1988; House, 1981; Hoy, 1994).

The above three perspectives have their strengths and weaknesses, reflecting the different aspects of the complex school-based change. In order to have a more comprehensive view, all of them should be used to understand and manage the practice of school-based change. In other worlds, we pay attention to the technological aspect of school-based change, but we are also concerned with the political dynamics and cultural factors in managing the change process.

From Laughlin's (1991) classification of organizational change, we may divide school-based change into two basic types: *change in school technology* and *change in school culture*.

The Technological Changes

As discussed in Chapter 6, school technology is the basic means to maintain daily school functioning and achieve school goals. Technology used in the school can be classified into school management technology, pedagogic technology and learning technology as shown in the matrix of technology in Figure 6.4 (see p. 94).

Management technology includes the theories and techniques used in the strategic management process including environmental analysis, planning and structuring, staffing and leading, and monitoring and evaluating. Pedagogic technology includes curriculum arrangement, teaching strategies, teaching methods, instructional media, classroom management and education evaluation. Learning technology refers to the use of learning unit, organization of learning, learning methods, and learning media and facilities. In order to bring about good education outcomes, these three types of technologies, aiming at facilitating teaching and the learning process, should match each other. Educational changes are often planned to change some components of management, pedagogic or learning technologies for maximizing the educational outcomes of the school process. Some changes may emphasize the improvement in learning style or tools at the individual level; some changes may pay attention to the change in teaching methods or learning curriculum at the classroom level; and others may focus on the reform of management pattern or planning decision at the school level. Obviously, curriculum change (Chapter 9) is one type of technological changes.

As discussed in Chapter 6, there are two types of technology congruence that can affect the effectiveness of the internal school process: the between-type congruence of technology (refers to the congruence between the managerial, pedagogic and learning technology in terms of mutual support and facilitation in operation); and the within-type congruence of technology (refers to the congruence between the components of any one type of technology in terms of mutual support and facilitating in operation).

According to the concept of congruence, the greater the between-type congruence and the within-type congruence, the higher the internal school effectiveness. If there is any incongruence in technology, technological changes in management, teaching or learning are needed and should aim at ensuring these two types of congruence and maximizing effectiveness of the use of managerial, pedagogic and learning technology.

The Cultural Changes

According to Laughlin (1991), the overt technological changes, named as *first-order changes*, are in general easily achieved and analyzed. Those hidden changes involving school culture are often difficult to be achieved and analyzed and can be called *second-order changes*. Technological changes if not involved with the corresponding changes in school members' values and beliefs, often become superficial and the effects of change are usually short-term and limited, if not ineffective. Therefore, a successful school-based change should bring about not only technological changes but also cultural changes at the same time in order to achieve their planned goals and produce persistent and effective improvement (Laughlin, 1991).

As described in Chapter 6, school culture refers to the system of shared norms, values, beliefs and assumptions among school members that can shape school members' performance and behavior explicitly or implicitly (Cheng, 1993h; Schein, 1992). As shown in the matrix of school culture in Figure 6.5 (see p. 98), school culture can be characterized by three sets of values and beliefs: moral, education and management values/beliefs. Moral values/beliefs include theoretical, economic, aesthetic, social, political and religious aspects. Management values/beliefs may include those assumptions about human nature in management, human relationship, relationship to environment, universalism vs. particularism, priority of human needs, career-centered vs. client-centered, control vs. autonomy, formalization vs. flexibility, centralization vs. participation, teamwork vs. individual responsibility, professional orientation, and innovation. Education values/beliefs may include values/beliefs in education aims, curriculum, pedagogic methods, role of student, role of teacher, and ideal of educational outcomes.

According to the principle of congruence in the school process, congruence among the beliefs and values about management, education, morality and citizenship is critical to school performance and effectiveness. As discussed in Chapter 6, there are two kinds of congruence in values and beliefs: the between-type congruence of values and beliefs (referring to the congruence between different types of values and beliefs of education, management and morality/citizenship); and the within-type congruence of values and beliefs (referring to the congruence of values and beliefs within the same type).

If there is any incongruence, cultural changes in the school are needed and should aim at ensuring these two types of cultural congruence in management, education, morality and citizenship.

The Matrix of School-based Change

School-based change can be a change in the school process involving different levels (i.e., individual, group and the school), different school members (i.e., principal, administrators, teachers and students), and different domains (i.e., affective, behavioral and cognitive). Borrowing the idea of the school process matrix in Chapter 6, we can propose a matrix of school-based change to further our understanding of the technological and cultural changes in the school. The matrix of school change includes three dimensions: category of change actor, level of change and domain of change, as shown in Figure 10.1. (The meanings of the arrows in the figure will be discussed in a later part of this chapter.)

Category of Change Actor

There are three categories of actors in school-based change: *change initiator/implementer, change supporter* and *change receiver/target*. Generally these three actors refer to the principal, administrators, teachers and students of a school organization who are playing different roles in school-based change. Traditionally administrators play the role as initiator or implementer whose responsibility is to set strategies and programs of school change. They are leaders of change management and implementation. Teachers are usually supporters or receivers who take part in the change process and make changes in their teaching, such as using new teaching skills, improving their classroom management and curriculum design, increasing their subject knowledge and developing better learning environment for students. Students play the role as change receiver or change beneficiary whose learning behavior and experience could be improved according to the goals and content of school changes. Obviously, this appears to be a top-down school change, however, it is also possible that teachers are the initiator of school-based changes while the school administrators who understand the nature and meaning of the changes become supporters to help the change implementation. Besides, in some high schools, students even play the role as change initiator supported by their teachers to make changes in their school life. No matter what role each category of change actor

Domain of Change

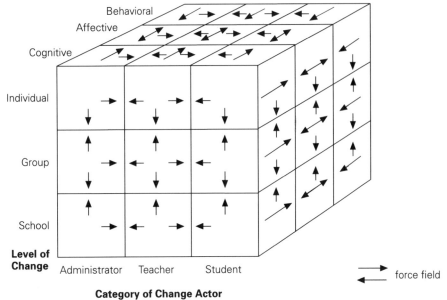

Adapted from K.H. Ng & Y.C. Cheng (in press).

Figure 10.1: The matrix of school-based change

plays, the success of change depends on the performance of all these three categories of actors.

Level of Change

School-based changes may happen at three different levels: individual, group and school level. It means that the change initiator or change receiver may be individual school members, a group of school members, or the entire school. It is often that some school-based changes are initiated by the school principal or only one senior staff (i.e., individual level) and the change target or receiver is a group of teachers or students. Of course, it is not rare that the school-based change is initiated by a group of staff, supported by the principal, then extended to the entire school. There are different possible groupings of who will be the initiator, who will be the supporter and who will be the receiver at different levels in a school-based change. Table 10.1 summarizes the possible groupings and can be used to clarify categories of change actor and levels of change, and develop appropriate strategies to manage the process of school-based change.

In general, changes at all three levels are important. It is nearly impossible to make changes at one level without changes at the other levels. Therefore, in planning school-based change, we should pay attention to the mutual influence between

Table 10.1: *Category of change actor and level of change*

Role	Administrators			Teachers			Students		
	I	G	S	I	G	S	I	G	S
Initiator									
Supporter									
Receiver									

I = Individual level; G = Group level; S = School level

the changes at all these three levels and should not focus on one and ignore the others.

Domain of Change

School-based changes can happen in three different domains of school members: the cognitive domain, the affective domain, and the behavioral domain. Cognitive changes of school members are often hidden. Typical examples are obtaining new values and beliefs on education and management, further understanding of education development, and rediscovering the new meanings of school life or teaching activities. Cognitive change is very important because it may be the basis for initiation and internalization of behavioral and affective changes. Affective change refers to the change in school members' satisfaction, commitment, motivation and human relationship. Behavioral change is often overt, related to the change in members' behavior in managing, teaching, learning and social interactions. In general, school technological changes are related to the behavioral changes of school members at the individual, group and school levels. School cultural changes are often reflected in the cognitive and affective changes of school members at the three levels. Therefore, the discussion of technological changes or cultural changes can be based on this matrix of school changes in terms of different actors, domains and levels.

The Matrix of Force Field

As discussed previously, there are different internal and external factors driving schools to make changes. At the same time, some restraining forces may exist to resist any changes in school for different reasons (Cheng and Ng, 1991a). In general, we have to analyze the potential driving forces and restraining forces before we implement any school-based change. As shown in Figure 10.2, the potential driving forces and restraining forces act in opposite directions and form a force field.

If the strength of driving forces is *equal* to that of the restraining forces, the situation will be in equilibrium and the school change initiator has to increase the driving forces in order to start the school-based change. If the strength of driving forces is *larger* than that of the restraining forces, then the school-based change

Driving Forces   Restraining Forces

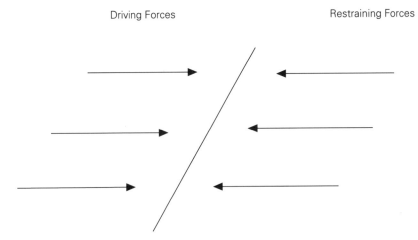

Figure 10.2:   The force field of school change

will start. But if the strength of the driving forces is *less* than that of the restraining forces, then the change initiator has to decide whether to:

- give up the change;
- increase the strength of the driving forces;
- minimize the strength of restraining forces; or
- convert the restraining forces into driving forces (i.e., change the direction of the restraining forces).

Of course, these alternatives may be associated with different costs depending on the context in which school-based change is implemented. Therefore, a careful analysis of the force field, available alternatives, and their related costs is necessary in planning a school-based change.

Based on the matrix of school-based change, a matrix of force field can be proposed to facilitate the analysis of potential driving forces and restraining forces particularly in the school-based change context, as shown in Figure 10.1. The arrows in this figure represent the potential driving forces and restraining forces existing between different actors, different levels and domains.

In the matrix of force field, there are driving forces and restraining forces between cells. In addition to the force field between cells, there may be three basic types of force field that should be analyzed in managing school-based change: the force field between actor layers, the force field between level layers, and the force field between domain layers (see Figure 10.1, p. 163).

The Force Field between Actor Layers

There may be differences in interests, roles, values, beliefs and perceptions among different actors within a school which will become apparent and cause force wrestling among actors in school change. As discussed in Chapter 6 (Figure 6.2, p. 89), the matrix can be divided into the administrator layer, teacher layer and student layer. Between these layers, there may be force fields composing of driving forces and restraining forces. For example, if administrators promote a school change but the change is not accepted by the affected teachers and students, a rival situation will exist between the driving forces from the administrator layer and the retraining forces from the teacher layer and the student layer. In another example, if teachers initiate a school change that is resisted by administrators and students, then the driving forces will come from the teacher layer and the restraining forces come from the administrator layer and the student layer. Of course, it will be in the optimum situation that no matter where the school change is initiated, all forces on the three layers are driving forces.

The Force Field between Level Layers

According to the political perspective, a school-based change may arouse conflicts between individuals and between groups due to the potential influence of change on resource allocation and constituencies' interests. It is also possible that the aroused conflicts exist between individual and group, individual and the school as a whole, and group and the school. As shown in Figure 6.3 (see p. 90), the matrix of change can be divided as the individual layer, the group layer, and the school layer. Then in a school change, there may be force fields existing between these three layers.

The Force Field between Domain Layers

Even though many people may assume that a person's cognition, affection, and behavior should be consistent, it may not be true. A person's behavior may not reflect exactly what he or she thinks and feels. In the late fifties, Festinger proposed the cognitive dissonance theory to illustrate this inconsistency that causes psychological problems to a person (Robbins, 1993). When facing a school-based change, a school member's cognition, attitude and behavior towards the change may not be consistent, consequently the changes in these three aspects may also be inconsistent.

Similarly, we can divide the matrix of school change into three layers: the affective layer, the behavioral layer, and the cognitive layer. Due to the potential inconsistency in the affect, behavior, and cognition of school members towards a school-based change, there may be force fields existing between these three layers (see Figure 10.1 (p. 163)), in which some are driving forces and some are restraining forces of the change. For example, teachers may rationally know the meaning of a school-based change, but are emotionally uneasy about it and resist the change. In such a case, they may take part in overt action, but at the same time try to postpone the change. This conflict in cognition, behavior and affect of school members towards a school change is indeed not rare.

We can analyze the above force fields, whether between the actor layers, between the level layers or between the domain layers, and plan the change strategies. If the strength of the restraining forces is larger than that of the driving forces, the school-based change will fail. As discussed above, in order to achieve the change (if not to give up), three possible ways could be attempted: 1) to increase driving forces; 2) to decrease or even remove restraining forces; 3) to change the direction of restraining forces into driving forces. Although the reason for promoting change by increasing driving forces is obvious, most literature focuses on how to decrease the restraining forces and control their direction (Corbett, Firestone and Rossman, 1987) for two reasons: first, the cost of increasing driving forces by developing new techniques or changing organizational structure is considerably high; second, the increase in driving forces may stimulate the increase in the restraining forces correspondingly and the input effect may be balanced out. Therefore, in order to achieve success in the change, it is necessary to identify the potential driving and restraining forces, analyze and understand the characteristics of the force field before planning any change strategies. The matrix of force field provides a comprehensive framework for the analysis.

Staff Development for Effective School-based Change

As discussed above, the success of school technological and cultural changes are closely related to the affective, behavioral and cognitive changes of school members. Also, according to the matrix of force field, it is necessary to increase the driving forces and decrease (or change the direction of) the restraining forces between different layers in order to start a school change and achieve its goals. The optimum situation is that all the forces in the matrix are driving forces to support the change. How to increase driving forces, decrease restraining forces, and convert resistance into driving forces is a critical question in the management of school-based change. The ideas of school-based staff development in Chapter 8 should be helpful in answering this question.

Many scholars have suggested that staff development is an important means to prepare and implement the technological and cultural changes in a school (see Fullan and Hargreaves, 1992; Hargreaves, 1994). In Chapter 8, a matrix theory has been proposed to understand and implement staff development. The principle of congruence and the idea of development cycles on the layers can be used to conduct staff development activities for effective school-based changes.

Based on the principle of congruence, the effectiveness or the success of a school-based change with the help of staff development will be affected by two types of congruence in change and development: *within-matrix congruence* and *between-matrix congruence* (see Figure 10.3).

The within-matrix congruence refers to the mutual consistency and support among the components on each dimension (i.e., within-type congruence) and/or among the dimensions (i.e., between-type congruence) of a matrix. In the matrix of

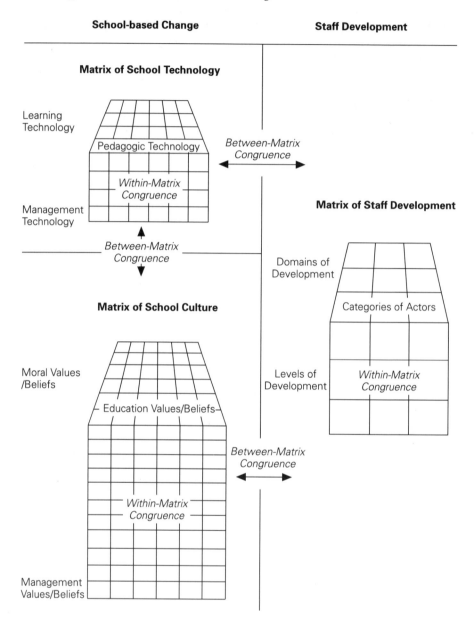

Figure 10.3: School-based change and staff development

school technology (Figure 6.4, see p. 94), within-matrix congruence represents the mutual support and consistency 1) among learning, teaching and management technology and 2) among different components on learning technology (such as learning units, learning organization, learning methods/activities and learning media), teaching technology (such as curriculum arrangement, teaching strategies, teaching methods, instructional media, classroom management and evaluation), or management technology (such as environmental analysis, planning and structuring, staffing and directing, monitoring and evaluating). In the matrix of school culture (Figure 6.5, see p. 98), the within-matrix congruence represents the mutual consistency and reinforcement among the values/beliefs of morality, education, and management and among component values/beliefs on morality (in theoretical, economic, etc., aspects), education (in educational aims, curriculum, pedagogic methods, etc.), or management (in human nature, management, human relationship, relationship to environment, etc.). In the matrix of staff development (Figure 8.1, see p. 134), the within-matrix congruence mainly refers to the mutual consistency and reinforcement among components of actors (administrators, teachers and students) levels (individual, group and school levels), or domains (affective, behavioral and cognitive).

The between-matrix congruence refers to the overall mutual support and consistency between matrices of technology, school culture and staff development. From the concepts of congruence, the following propositions can be made to predict the effectiveness of school-based change and its relationship with staff development:

1   The effectiveness of school-based change is affected by the within-matrix congruence in technological changes and cultural changes:

    1a   *The stronger the within-matrix congruence in technological changes, the higher the effectiveness of school-based change.*

    This proposition suggests that in order to maximize the benefits from any technological changes in learning, we have to consider whether any changes in the existing technologies of teaching and management are needed to support the change of learning technology. On the other hand, if we want to induce any technological changes in management, we have to consider whether this change can facilitate or hinder the improvement of teaching and learning. In general, we encourage mutual support among learning, teaching and management when we plan any technological changes.

    1b   *The stronger the within-matrix congruence in cultural changes, the higher the effectiveness of school-based change.*

    This proposition suggests that in order to maximize the effects of any planned changes or developments in values and beliefs about morality and citizenship in school, we have to determine whether the existing values and beliefs in education process and management are consistent with the changes and whether they are needed to change, too. The inconsistency among these sets of values and beliefs may result in ineffectiveness of school cultural change.

2   The effectiveness of school-based change is affected by the between-matrix congruence in technological changes, cultural changes and staff development:

    2a   *The stronger the congruence between technological changes and cultural changes, the higher the effectiveness of school-based changes.*
It suggests that school changes should be planned to have mutual support between technological and cultural changes in order to achieve long-term effects and maximize change impacts.

    2b   *The stronger the congruence between staff development and technological changes, the higher the effectiveness of school-based changes.*

    2c   *The stronger the congruence between staff development and cultural changes, the higher the effectiveness of school-based changes.*
Technological and cultural changes can be realized only by school members. The within-matrix congruence in technology and culture and the between-matrix congruence between technology and culture can be achieved only through staff development. Therefore, whether the existing practice of staff development meets the needs of the planned technological or cultural changes is a key question in school-based change. Propositions 2a and 2b suggest that in order to maximize the effectiveness of school-based change, the practice of staff development should be designed to facilitate the within-matrix congruence and between-matrix congruence of technological and cultural changes.

3   The effectiveness of staff development is affected by the within-matrix congruence in actors, domains and levels.

    3a   *The higher the congruence across actors, across domains and across levels, the higher the effectiveness of staff development.*

As described in Chapter 8, the congruence in practice of development across administrators, teachers and students, across their affective, behavioral and cognitive domains, and across the individual, group and school levels is critical to the effectiveness of staff development. The degree of within-matrix congruence also reflects whether the school culture is strong or weak, because it reflects the unanimous orientation of school members on behavior, affection and cognition at different levels. As suggested in Chapter 8, development cycles for staff on the different layers should be established to facilitate and manage staff development for effective school-based changes. In the staff development process or the staff development cycles, the force field of change between layers or between cells of the matrix can be reshaped in terms of increasing driving forces and reducing or redirecting restraining forces. From the discussion in Chapter 7, leadership should be taken as the critical driving forces for staff development as well as school-based change (for details of leadership, see Chapter 7).

The theory of congruence proposed in this part can provide a comprehensive framework to understand and manage the complicated nature of school-based change and staff development. To enhance effectiveness of school-based changes, staff development should be designed and implemented to maximize:

- the within-matrix congruence in development across actors, across domains, and across levels;
- the within-matrix congruence in technological and cultural changes;
- the between-matrix congruence between staff development, technological changes, and cultural changes.

Strategies and Techniques of School-based Changes

After introducing the basic concepts of school-based change, we need to discuss the practical side because the success or failure of a school-based change is eventually determined by practical strategies and techniques.

The School-based Management Mechanism

It should be clearly pointed out that the school-based management mechanism proposed in Chapter 6 is the basic mechanism for continuous school development and change. Its self-management at a multi-level system includes stages such as environmental analysis, planning and structuring/affiliating, staffing and directing, implementing, monitoring and evaluating at the school level, the group level and the individual level. This system provides a cyclic process for the whole school, groups and individuals to learn, develop and change (Chapter 5). Within the school-based management mechanism, a school-based change is not something sudden, unnecessary or extra. It is the natural outcome of school development planning or the school self-management process to serve long-term school development and effectiveness. It should be included in the school plan or program plans and aim to support the achievement of school goals. In sum, it should be initiated, planned and managed by the school-based management mechanism.

Analysis of the Force Field of Change

As discussed above, we have to understand and analyze the force field of change in planning a school-based change. Based on the matrix of force field, a table can be designed to facilitate the analysis of driving forces or restraining forces.

As shown in Table 10.2, we list the types of potential major driving forces in an order of its importance to the success of the school-based change. Then, we analyze the nature and source of each major driving force in terms of its involved actors (i.e., principal/administrators, teachers, students), levels (i.e., individual, group and school), and domains (i.e., affective, behavioral and cognitive). Based on the analysis, we identify the possible methods for increasing the strength of each major driving force. To some driving forces, the methods may be identified easily and implemented efficiently. But to some others, there may be no easy and efficient methods to increase their strength. According to the availability of easy and efficient

Table 10.2: Analysis of the driving forces

Type of Potential Driving Force and its Importance	Source			Method for Increasing Driving Force
	Actors	Levels	Domains	
Rank A 1 2 3 4 5 6 7 8				Rank B —— —— —— —— —— —— —— ——

Note: Actors: Administrator/ Teachers / Students Rank A: Importance Rank
Levels: Individual / Group / School Rank B: Method Availability Rank
Domains: Affective / Behavioral / Cognitive

Table 10.3: Analysis of the restraining forces

Type of Potential Restraining Force and its Importance	Source			Methods for Reducing Restraining Force
	Actors	Levels	Domains	
Rank A 1 2 3 4 5 6 7 8				Rank B —— —— —— —— —— —— —— ——

Note: Actors: Administrator/ Teachers / Students Rank A: Importance Rank
Levels: Individual / Group / School Rank B: Method Availability Rank
Domains: Affective / Behavioral / Cognitive

methods for increasing the strength, we can rank the potential driving forces in order. It is often that we have not sufficient resources to increase the strength of all driving forces at the same time. Therefore, from the order of importance and the order of method availability, we can plan the resources and strategies used to increase the strength of driving forces.

Similarly in Table 10.3, we can list the types of potential major restraining forces in the order of its importance to the failure of the school-based change. Then we analyze the nature and characteristics of these restraining forces in terms of its involved actors, levels and domains. Again, based on the analysis, we identify the methods for reducing them or converting their direction into driving forces. According to the availability of easy and efficient methods for reducing or converting restraining forces, we can rank the major restraining forces in order. Then, based

Table 10.4: Stages of a school-based change

Unfreezing Stage	Changing Stage	Refreezing Stage
• Identify, establish, and publicize the need for change • Plan goals and policies for the change through the school-based mechanism • Analyze the force field and develop change strategies • Increase driving forces • Minimize restraining forces • Prepare the necessary psychological (i.e., cognitive and affective) and technical readiness of those involved through staff development • Prepare the necessary resources for the change	• Implement technological changes in management/teaching/learning • Implement cultural changes in values and beliefs about management/education/morality, citizenship • Change the affective, behavioral and cognitive aspects of the involved actors at the individual/group/school levels • Monitor the change process and ensure the progress towards the goals • Clarify the emergent psychological and technical uncertainties and reduce their potential damages to the change • Learn new ideas and techniques and develop new goals	• Identify the overt and hidden advantages of the change • Identify the adverse effects and eliminate them • Estimate all types of costs for the change • Assess the effectiveness of the change • Make recommendations for future actions • Make modifications on the technological changes • Institutionalize the successful technological changes • Internalize the successful cultural changes • Clarify the uncertainties and frustrations due to unsuccessful experiences and encourage continuous learning

on the order of importance and the order of method availability, we can plan the resources and strategies to manage the major restraining forces.

In order to make a decision on whether we should implement a school-based change, we may compare the results of the analysis of driving forces with that of restraining forces. From the comparison, we decide whether we can achieve sufficient driving forces and minimize restraining forces so that the school-based change can be implemented successfully in a reasonable cost-effective way. Sergiovanni (1984, Chapter 7) provides in detail an example of comparing driving forces with restraining forces in a quantitative way. Those interested in quantitative analysis may have a look at it.

Stages of a School-based Change

Based on the model of changing human behavior (e.g., Lewin, 1952; Schermerhorn *et al.*, 1982), the process of a school-based change can be divided into three stages: unfreezing, changing and refreezing, as shown in Table 10.4.

The unfreezing stage. The unfreezing stage aims to prepare a better situation for a school-based change. As discussed previously, due to the increasing pressure from internal and external school environments, a school needs to make changes and adapt to these challenges for its survival and long-term development. But unfortunately, school members are often burdened with daily workload and are used to the existing practice and procedures. They may not be aware of the impacts from these internal and external challenges and they may ignore the need for a school change. Therefore, in the unfreezing stage, the agent of a school-based change should help the school members to identify and understand the need for a change and then establish this need in the school plan or program plans for action. In order to create a better atmosphere for the change, publicizing the need for a school-based change is necessary to all involved members.

The promotion of the awareness of the need change and the planning of goals and policies for a school-based change can be supported by the environmental analysis component and development planning component of the school-based management mechanism (Chapters 5 and 6). The ideas of the matrix of force field can be used to analyze the force field. Based on the analysis, the change agent develops strategies to increase the potential driving forces and minimize the potential restraining forces. At this stage, the agent should help those involved members have the necessary psychological (i.e., cognitive and affective) readiness and technical readiness through staff development activities. In other words, school members should be well prepared to understand the nature and meaning of the change, be willing and committed to it and have the necessary competence to implement it. At the same time, the agent should prepare the necessary resources for the change.

The changing stage. After the unfreezing stage, the planned school-based change is implemented. The implementation of a school change in the changing stage may include the following aspects:

- to implement the planned technological changes in management, teaching and/or learning;
- to implement the planned cultural changes in values and beliefs about management, education, morality and/or citizenship;
- to change the affective, behavioral and cognitive aspects of the involved actors (such as principal/administrators, teachers, students and even parents, if necessary) at the individual level, the group level and the school level;
- to monitor the change process and ensure the progress towards the planned goals;
- to clarify the emergent psychological and technical uncertainties and reduce their potential damages to the change;
- to learn new ideas and techniques and develop new goals in the process, if necessary.

The refreezing stage. After the changing stage, the change agent will try to refreeze the positive outcomes of the change. The purpose of the refreezing stage is to maximize all the advantages gained from the school-based change and perpetuate the positive effects to a longer period. Of course, in this stage, eliminating the potential side effects is also important. In general, this stage may include the following important tasks:

- to identify and confirm all the important, overt and hidden, planned and unintended advantages generated from the school-based change;
- to identify all the important overt and hidden adverse effects on different aspects of the school or members and eliminate them as soon as possible;
- to estimate all types of monetary and non-monetary costs for the change;
- to assess the effectiveness of the change by comparing the achievements with the planned goals and comparing the gained advantages with the disadvantages and the costs;
- to propose recommendations for further actions according to the above evaluation and analysis;
- to make modifications (if necessary) on the technological changes according to the above evaluation and analysis;
- to institutionalize the successful technological changes and the related experiences in order to perpetuate their advantages and benefit more people in future practice;
- to internalize the successful cultural changes among school members through reflecting on the successful experiences, discussing the difficulties and their solutions, providing intrinsic and extrinsic rewards, celebrating the success through ceremony or rituals, providing a vision on the meanings of the change, etc.;
- to clarify the uncertainties and frustrations due to the unsuccessful experiences and encourage continuous learning and development from these experiences.

All three stages are important to the implementation of a school-based change for school effectiveness and development, if we want to maximize and perpetuate the advantages from the change and minimize the adverse effects. Table 10.4 provides a helpful framework to manage these stages of the school-based change process.

Strategies of Change

In order to carry out school changes and innovations effectively, the use of some suitable strategies is necessary and important. Based on the views of Whiteside (1978), Schermerhorn, Hunt, and Osborn (1982) and Bennis, Benne, Chin, and Corey (1969), we can classify strategies of implementing school-based change into three types: the *force–coercive strategy*, the *empirical–rational strategy*, and the *normative–reeducative* strategy. The characteristics of these strategies in terms of power base, human nature assumption, focus of change, managerial behavior and change outcome can be summarized in Table 10.5.

Table 10.5: *The characteristics of different change strategies*

Change Strategy	Power Base	Human Nature Assumption	Focus of Change	Managerial Behavior	Change Outcome	Strengths/ Weaknesses
• Force–coercive	• Reward • Punishment • Legitimacy	• Economic person	• External • Behavioral	• Command • Top-down	• Short-term compliance	• Fast • Less expensive • short-term effect
• Empirical–rational	• Expertise	• Rational person	• Internal • Cognitive	• Rational persuasion • Expert testimony • Demonstration	• Long-term internalization	• Slow • Expensive • Time-consuming • Long-term effect
• Normative–reeducative	• Reference	• Collaborator • Partner	• Internal • Affective	• Participation • Partnership • Group process	• Long-term internalization	• Slow • Time-consuming • Long-term effect

The force–coercive strategy uses legitimacy, reward and punishment as the power base to push a school-based change. It assumes that the human nature of school members is an economic person. The focus of change is on the overt behavior or external structure. The management of change is mainly a top-down approach, depending on the authority or command of the change agent. The effect of change outcome is often short-term and will disappear quickly if the external driving power is decreased or removed. It may be useful for some simple short-term technological changes but not so effective for bringing out long-term cultural changes.

The empirical–rational strategy assumes school members to be rational persons. It uses mainly expert power to push a school-based change and put the focus of change on school members' internal cognitive change. The management of change emphasizes the use of rational persuasion, expert testimony and empirical demonstration to show the functional values of the school change and mobilize people's support. If the change is successful, the effects or outcomes will be internalized and maintained for a long time. This strategy is appropriate for both cultural and technological changes in school.

The normative–reeducative strategy assumes school members to be partners or collaborators in school functioning. The power base used to push the school-based change is mainly the reference power or personal influence of the change agent. The focus of change is on school members' internal affective changes. The group norms, school mission, educational ideal, and shared values and beliefs about the school play an important role to support the change. The management of change encourages participation in making decisions and planning the change. Partnership and group process are important to change implementation. Since the school members are totally involved and committed in the change, the change effects or outcomes can be internalized and perpetuated in a long-term manner. This strategy is particularly appropriate for the cultural changes.

These three strategies have their own strengths and limitations. The force–coercive strategy is appropriate for fast and short-term technological changes but inappropriate for long-term cultural changes. The normative–reeducative strategy is suitable for long-term cultural changes but the process is time-consuming and the effects are very slow. The empirical–rational strategy is appropriate for both technological and cultural changes but the process is time-consuming and expensive. The choice of the change strategy often depends on the purpose and context of the school-based change. It is also possible that different strategies are used in different stages of the change process. If necessary, all the three strategies can be used.

Techniques of Change

The above strategies are some guidelines for school-based change, but when put into practice, different techniques are required. Many scholars have proposed different techniques to implement organizational changes. Dunham and Pierce's (1989: 730–4) seven techniques may be used to support the implementation of school-based change.

Education and communication. When knowledge would help alleviate fears due to inaccurate or sketchy information about the school-based change, this technique is appropriate to use. Its main purpose is to provide the staff with relevant information and help them understand the meanings and advantages of the change; to reduce their misunderstanding and clarify the unnecessary uncertainties and anxiety; and to increase their trust and win their support. In general, school members are often willing to help the implementation of the change after being convinced. The potential drawback of this technique is that it is time-consuming and expensive.

Participation and involvement. When the change agent needs information from other school members to design the school-based change and when the probability of resistance to the change is high, this technique should be appropriate. The technique aims to encourage staff participation and involvement in planning the change, to improve the quality of decision making and to enhance their acceptance and commitment to the change implementation. The limitation of this technique is its heavy time costs.

Facilitative support. This technique aims to provide technical support for staff to face and implement the change, such as skills training, supply of tools and professional opinions. When school members lack the necessary skills or tools to implement the change effectively, this technique is appropriate. It will increase the chance for successful implementation. Of course, it costs time and money for support materials and training programs.

Emotional support. This technique gives those involved members emotional support to reduce their anxiety about the change. It is relatively inexpensive and is a good way to help those with personal adjustment problems. It is not often done systematically, so the results may not be so effective.

Incentives. To the concern of those involved members, the change agent should emphasize the potential personal or general benefits brought by the change, or the compensation for the loss suffered because of the change. When members resist the change unless they can benefit from it, this technique can be useful. It can head off the major restraining forces before they arise. Obviously, it can be very expensive and can encourage more resistance in hopes of gaining more compensation.

Manipulation and co-optation. When a school-based change is absolutely necessary and all other techniques would be ineffective or too costly, this technique may be appropriate. Manipulation refers to systematically controlling and amendment of materials supplied to those involved school members so that they can receive biased information to support the change. Co-optation makes staff feel that they are participating in the decision of the change although the change agent does not really take their opinion seriously. This technique works quite quickly without substantial cost but it is often unethical and can destroy school members' trust on the change agent.

Table 10.6: The choice of strategies and techniques for school-based change

	Changing Stage	Unfreezing Stage	Refreezing Stage
Expected outcomes or goals	1. 2. 3. . . .	1. 2. 3. . . .	1. 2. 3. . . .
Possible difficulties	1. 2. 3. . . .	1. 2. 3. . . .	1. 2. 3. . . .
Required resources	1. 2. 3. . . .	1. 2. 3. . . .	1. 2. 3. . . .
Available resources	1. 2. 3. . . .	1. 2. 3. . . .	1. 2. 3. . . .
Strategies	1. 2. 3.	1. 2. 3.	1. 2. 3.
Techniques	1. 2. 3. 4. 5. 6. 7.	1. 2. 3. 4. 5. 6. 7.	1. 2. 3. 4. 5. 6. 7.

Coercion. Through open declaration, the change agent lets school members know the possible negative results such as losing the job or promotion opportunity due to disobedience or resistance to the planned school change. When the school change must occur quickly and the change agent has significantly more power than the resistors, this technique may be appropriate. It is often the fastest method to suppress resistance and implement the change, but it also decreases the members' satisfaction and increases their resentment.

There are advantages and disadvantages for each technique. Their applicability may vary with the goals and context of school change. It is often that the use of a combination of these techniques is better than the use of only one. The selection and application of these techniques can be considered together with the change strategies and the change stages. In general, the techniques with emphasis on coercion, manipulation and co-optation, incentives are more consistent with the force–coercive strategy. The techniques of facilitative support, education and communication are consistent with the empirical–rational strategy. And the techniques of emotional support, participation, involvement, education and communication are in line with the normative–reeducative strategy.

Table 10.6 provides a simple framework for facilitating consideration of the choice of change techniques and strategies. We can first prioritize our expected outcomes or goals for the school-based change — unfreezing stage, the changing stage and the refreezing stage. Then we list the possible important difficulties, constraints and concerns in an order of importance to the success of achieving the expected goals at each stage of the change. We list the necessary resources and support and at the same time we list those available. Based on the expected goals, possible difficulties and gaps in resource availability, we can design the combination of change strategies and techniques to achieve the expected goals for each stage of the school-based change.

School-based change is necessary for school effectiveness and development. In this chapter, matrix conceptions have been proposed to understand and analyze the complex nature of school-based change. School-based staff development should be the major means to achieve effective school-based changes. The principle of congruence again provides important guidelines to direct the practice of school-based change and staff development. Basically, the school-based management mechanism provides a mechanism to drive continuous school development and change for long-term effectiveness.

The analysis of force field of change is a necessary component for effective management of school change. The matrix of force field proposed in this chapter provide a comprehensive view to conduct the analysis. School change is a dynamic process. Dividing it into the unfreezing stage, change stage, and refreezing stage should be helpful to conceptualize strategies and techniques to manage it. A thorough understanding of the nature and characteristics of different strategies and techniques of change is important to the effective application of them to implement school-based changes.

Chapter 11

Conclusion: The Future of Research on School Effectiveness and School-based Management

The concepts and theories proposed in this book provide a new perspective to understanding the complex nature of school effectiveness and school-based management. Integrating the recent developments in research and practice, the theory of school-based management mechanism provides an alternative comprehensive framework to reconceptualize and manage the internal school process, school development, and school effectiveness in a dynamic way. Implications generated from these ideas for future research on school effectiveness and school-based management should be fruitful. On one hand, the ideas and theories developed in this book create alternative opportunities, conceptions and possibilities for developing research to support the present and future school reforms. On the other hand, research is really needed to further develop these ideas and theories to contribute to our ongoing efforts for school development and education effectiveness and also our knowledge of school effectiveness and school-based management.

School Effectiveness Research

As discussed in Chapter 1, traditional research on school effectiveness is often based on the simplistic conception of school functions, particularly on technical and social functions at the individual or institutional level only. The potential dilemmas from differences in the expectations of different constituencies on school effectiveness are ignored. The assumption about the positive relationship of school effectiveness between types and levels, or between effectiveness and efficiency is problematic. The simplistic conception of school effectiveness sets a great limitation to generating significant implications for effective school development.

In future research, we should pay attention to the multiplicity and complexity of school effectiveness and consider a wider spectrum of school effectiveness with both short-term and long-term time frames. Since there are multi-functions of schools and diverse expectations from constituencies at different levels, dilemmas do exist in efforts for maximizing school effectiveness. The study of these dilemmas should be important in future research. In order to explore the complex nature of school effectiveness, inter-disciplinary efforts should be encouraged. The research focus should include multi-types of effectiveness at multi-levels, relationship between types, relationship between levels, and relationship between effectiveness and efficiency. As suggested in Chapter 1, development of a comprehensive theory is needed to explain the relationship between different categories of school effectiveness. Based on this theory, we may know more about how to ensure congruence between categories of school effectiveness, how to enhance all the five types of school effectiveness at the five levels, and how to solve the dilemmas from the different expectations of various constituencies.

The eight models of school effectiveness in Chapter 2 provide different approaches to explaining, managing and assessing school effectiveness. The contribution of the eight models to different types of school effectiveness at different levels is an important area in future research, if we want to apply these models to manage and maximize school effectiveness. Among them, the organizational learning model and the total quality management may receive more attention because they are more comprehensive and consistent with the dynamic perspective of school effectiveness. The concepts such as model and category congruence as well as the principle of congruence may be used to conceptualize research.

School-based Management Research

Traditionally, school-based management research focuses only on the decentralization of authority to the school level, and assumes that site-level decision making is the critical element for effective school-based management that can produce obvious effect on school effectiveness. This traditional conception of school-based management is simplistic and narrow and usually ignores the multiplicity of self-management in school. Based on such a simplistic conception of school-based management, the outcomes of the implementation are often limited and unsuccessful, if not problematic. It is not surprising that many scholars challenge the ideas of school-based management.

Obviously, there is an urgent need to further develop the theory base for school-based management, that can explain explicitly how it closely relates to school performance and education outcomes. Chapters 5 and 6 give a preliminary theoretical framework for research on school-based management theory. Specifically, the following directions should be important to future research:

- In Chapter 4, the principle of equifinality, principle of decentralization, principle of self-managing system, and principle of human initiative have been proposed as the basic principles for school-based management. In future research, we can test the significance of these principles or use them to observe and assess the design, implementation and outcomes of various types of ongoing school-based management movements in different parts of the world;
- The characteristics of school-based management proposed in Chapter 4 provide a comprehensive profile for directing implementation and facilitating school practice. This profile may be tested and further developed in

empirical studies. The theoretical relationship between different characteristics can be strengthened in future research;
- Multi-level self-management in school is an important concept to the success of school-based management implemented in schools. Ignorance of group self-management and individual self-management may be the major reason explaining why some school-based management reforms fail in improving school performance. The multi-level self-management framework illustrated in Chapter 5 can provide significant research issues to be explored in future studies. The theoretical base for each self-management level can be deepened through interdisciplinary efforts including sociology, psychology, economics and organizational theories. The mutual influence or relationship between school self-management, group self-management and individual self-management is an important area for research. Also the conditions for successful implementation of multi-level self-management are inevitably one of the key research focuses;
- Following the ideas in Chapter 5, the contribution of school-based management, multi-level self-management, strategic management or development planning to school effectiveness in the light of the eight models or the dynamic perspective of school effectiveness, can be further investigated and established in future research.

Research on the School-based Management Mechanism

A number of interesting implications can be generated from the theory of the school-based management mechanism for future research. The concepts of layer management, layer congruence, technological congruence in management, teaching and learning and cultural congruence in education, management, morality and citizenship have brought out alternative ideas to think about research on the relationship between the internal school process and school effectiveness. Specifically, the implications for research on school leadership, staff development, curriculum change and school change are significant.

For the school-based management mechanism, school leadership is completely different from that of the traditional practice. Layer leadership should be one of the important research focuses. The nature of layer leadership in terms of affective, behavioral and cognitive domains at the individual, group and school levels can be further developed with an integration of the recent developments in leadership literature. Its characteristics and performance in the context of school-based management can be empirically investigated. Its contribution to school culture, school development and school effectiveness at different levels and contexts can be studied in future research. In Chapter 7, the meanings of school leadership and school constituencies have been broadened. The relationship or interaction process between the leadership layer and the constituencies matrix is a broad area for research.

Strategic leadership is another important aspect that should receive serious attention in research. The leadership profile of strategic leadership in terms of the structural, human, political, cultural and educational leadership dimensions provides a comprehensive guide to practice as well as a framework to study leadership in school-based management. To different models of school effectiveness, leadership roles may be different. Following the suggestion in Chapter 7, a close investigation of the relationship between school leadership role and model of school effectiveness can benefit the development of effective leadership.

Successful implementation of school-based management needs a new concept of school-based staff development management. The matrix conception proposed in Chapter 8 promises interesting implications for research on staff development. The multi-domains (i.e., affective, behavioral and cognitive) and multi-levels (i.e., individual, group, school) of staff development broadens the perspective and area in research. The principle of congruence for staff development, the staff development cycles on different layers, and the methods for ensuring layer congruence in staff development are important topics for future research.

Traditionally, research on curriculum change often focuses on the technological aspect and ignores the importance of the school organizational context to the success of implementation. Inevitably this type of research suffers from the narrow and simplistic conception and produces very limited findings for practice and theory building.

Based on the school-based management mechanism, the management of school-based curriculum change is quite different from the traditional practice. The multi-level organizational model, the dynamic relationship between curriculum change and staff development, and the integration of school management and curriculum development provide richer ground for future research on the effectiveness and management of curriculum change in the school.

How to implement school change successfully is a topic in current educational reforms and school restructuring movements. Suffering from the poor understanding of the complex nature of school change, many efforts at change experience failure or frustration in many countries. For example, even though school-based management is good for continuous school development and long-term effectiveness, the change of schools from external control management to school-based management is not easy. Research on school change is necessary for understanding the nature of school change and developing strategies of managing it. Currently our knowledge about school change is negligible when compared with the huge scale of ongoing educational reforms in schools.

The ideas in Chapter 10 provide a comprehensive framework to understand school-based change. The matrix conceptions of technological changes and the cultural changes summarize some key elements of school change that should receive attention in research. Furthermore, the proposed matrix of force field should be a powerful tool for understanding change dynamics and analyzing driving and restraining forces in different domains of different change actors at different levels. Particularly, the force field between layers is a key concept in studying school change. The theory developed in Chapter 10 to predict the relationship between the matrixes of technological change, cultural change and staff development can be a fruitful area for future research on school-based change.

Obviously, these implications for future research are only part of the possibility and opportunity generated from the book. As worldwide educational reforms and school restructuring movements are shifting from school improvement to school development, from education quantity to education quality, from school maintenance to school effectiveness, from external control management to school-based management, and from use of simplistic techniques to application of sophisticated technology, I believe numerous opportunities are being created for research and development.

I hope my book can benefit those involved in education reforms or those interested in school-based management, development and effectiveness.

References

ACHILLES, C.M. (1987) 'A vision for better schools', in GREENFIELD, W. (Ed) *Instructional Leadership: Concepts, Issues, and Controversies*, Boston, MA: Allyn & Bacon.

ADVISORY COMMITTEE ON IMPLEMENTATION OF TARGET ORIENTATION CURRICULUM (1994) *Report on the Implementation of TOC*, Hong Kong: The Government Printer.

ALDERFER, C.P. (1972) *Existence, Relatedness, and Growth: Human Needs in Organizational Settings*, New York: Free Press.

ALLPORT, G.W., VERNON, P.E. and LINDZEY, G. (1960) *Study of Values* (3rd ed, Manual and test booklet), Boston, MA: Houghton Mifflin.

ALVESSON, M. (1987) 'Organizations, culture, and ideology', *International Studies of Management and Organizations*, **17**, 3, pp. 4–18.

APPLE, M. (1982) *Cultural and Economic Reproduction in Education*, London: Roultedge and Kegan Paul.

ARENDS, R., HESH, R. and TURNER, T. (1980) *Conditions for Promoting Effective Staff Development*, Washington, DC: Eric Clearinghouse on Teacher Education (SP-015-396).

ARGYRIS, C. (1982) *Reasoning, Learning and Action*, San Francisco, CA: Jossey Bass.

ARGYRIS, C. and SCHÖN, D.A. (1974) *Theory in Practice: Increasing Professional Effectiveness*, San Francisco, CA: Jossey-Bass.

ARGYRIS, C. and SCHÖN, D.A. (1978) *Organizational Learning*, Reading, MA: Addison-Wesley.

ARNOTT, M., BULLOCK, A. and TOMAS, H. (1992) *The Impact of Local Management on Schools: A Source Book*, Birmingham, UK: School of Education, The University of Birmingham.

ATTEWELL, P. (1992) 'Technology diffusion and organization learning: The case of business computing', *Organization Science*, **3**, 1, pp. 1–19.

AVERCH, H.A., CARROLL, S.J., DONALDSON, T.S., KIESLING, H.J. and PINCUS, J. (1974) *How Effective is Schooling? A Critical Review of Research*, Englewood Cliffs, NJ: Educational Technology Publications.

BACHARACH, S.B. (1990) *Education Reform*, Boston, MA: Allyn & Bacon.

BACHMAN, J.D., BOWERS, D.G. and MARCUS, P.M. (1968) 'Bases of supervisory power: A comparative study in five organizational settings', in TANNENBAUM, A.S. (Ed), *Control in Organizations*, New York: McGraw-Hill.

BARTH, R.S. (1988) 'School: A community of leaders', in LIEBERMAN, A. (Ed)

Building a Professional Culture in Schools, New York: Teachers College Press.

BASS, B.M. (1985) *Leadership and Performance Beyond Expectations*, New York: Free Press.

BASS, B.M. (1990) *Bass and Stogdill's Handbook of Leadership: Theory, Research and Managerial Applications*, (3rd ed) New York: Free Press.

BASS, B.M. and AVOLIO, B.J. (1994) *Improving Organizational Effectiveness Through Transformational Leadership*, Thousand Oaks, CA: Sage.

BEARE, H., CALDWELL, B.J. and MILLIKAN, R.H. (1989) *Creating an Excellent School*, London: Routledge & Kegan Paul.

BEARE, H. and SLAUGHTER, R. (1993) *Education for the Twenty-first Century*, London: Routledge.

BENNIS, W. (1984) 'Transformative power and leadership', in SERGIOVANNI, T.J. and CORBALLY, J.E. (Eds) *Leadership and Organizational Culture*, Chicago, IL: University of Illinois Press, pp. 64–71.

BENNIS, W.G., BENNE, K., CHIN, R. and COREY, K. (Eds) (1969) *The Planning of Change*, NY: Holt, Rinehart and Winston.

BERGER, E.H. (1987) *Parents as Partners in Education*, (2nd ed) Columbus, OH: Merrill.

BLACKLEDGE, D. and HUNT, B. (1985) *Sociological Interpretations of Education*, Sydney: Croom Helm.

BLAKE, R.G. and MOUTON, J.S. (1985) *The New Managerial Grid III*, Houston, TX: Gulf Publishing.

BLASE, J. (1989) 'The micropolitics of the school: The everyday political orientation of teachers toward open school principals', *Educational Administration Quarterly*, **25**, 4, pp. 377–407.

BLASE, J. (1991) 'The micropolitics of effective school-based leadership: Teachers' perspectives', Paper presented at the Annual Conference of the American Educational Research Association, San Francisco.

BLOCK, P. (1987) *The Empowered Manager: Positive Political Skills at Work*, San Francisco, CA: Jossey-Bass.

BOLLINGTON, R., HOPKINS, D. and WEST, M. (1990) *An Introduction to Teacher Appraisal*, London, Cassell.

BOLMAN, L.G. and DEAL, T.E. (1991a) *Reframing Organizations*, San Francisco, CA: Jossey-Bass.

BOLMAN, L.G. and DEAL, T.E. (1991b) *Images of Leadership* (Occasional Paper No. 20, pp. 1–21), Cambridge, MA: Harvard University, National Center for Educational Leadership.

BOLMAN, L.G. and DEAL, T.E. (1992) 'Leading and managing: Effects of context, culture, and gender', *Educational Administration Quarterly*, **28**, 3, pp. 314–29.

BOTTERY, M. (1993) *The Ethics of Educational Management*, London: Cassell, pp. 10–17.

BRADLEY, L.H. (1993) *Total Quality Management for Schools*, Lancaster, PA: Technomic.

BRAITHWAITE, V.A. and LAW, H.G. (1985) 'Structure of human values: Testing the adequacy of the Rockeach Value Survey', *Journal of Personality and Social Psychology*, **49**, pp. 250–63.

BROWN, D.J. (1990) *Decentralization and School-based Management*, London: Falmer Press.

BURNS, J.M. (1978) *Leadership*, New York: Harper & Row.

CALDWELL, B.J. (1990) 'Educational reform through school-site management: An international perspective on restructuring in education', in BACHARACH, S.B. (Ed) *Advances in Research and Theories of School Management and Educational Policy*, (**1**), Greenwich, CT: JAI Press, pp. 303–33.

CALDWELL, B.J. and SPINKS, J. (1988) *The Self-managing School*, London: Falmer Press.

CALDWELL, B.J. and SPINKS, J.M. (1992) *Leading the Self-managing School*, London: Falmer Press.

CAMERON, K.S. (1978, December) 'Measuring organizational effectiveness in institutions of higher education', *Administrative Science Quarterly*, **23**, pp. 604–32.

CAMERON, K.S. (1984) 'The effectiveness of ineffectiveness', *Research in Organizational Behavior*, **6**, pp. 235–85.

CAMERON, K.S. and WHETTEN, D.A. (1981) 'Perceptions of organizational effectiveness over organizational life cycles', *Administrative Science Quarterly*, **26**, pp. 524–44.

CAMERON, K.S. and WHETTEN, D.S. (Eds) (1983) *Organizational Effectiveness: A Comparison of Multiple Models*, New York: Academic Press.

CAMMANN, C., FICHMAN, M., JENKINS, G.D., JR. and KLESH, J.R. (1983) 'Assessing the attitudes and perceptions of organizational members', in SEASHORE, S.E. *et al.* (Eds) *Assessing Organization Change*, New York: John Wiley, pp. 71–138.

CHAN, B., CHENG, Y.C. and HAU, K.T. (1991) *A Technical Report on the Study of Principal–Teachers' Relationship in Hong Kong Secondary Schools*, Hong Kong: The Chinese University of Hong Kong.

CHAN, Y.C. and CHENG, Y.C. (1993) 'A study of principals' instructional leadership in secondary schools', *Educational Research Journal*, **8**, pp. 55–67.

CHAPMAN, J.D. (Ed) (1990) *School-based Decision making and Management*, London: Falmer Press.

CARNEGIE TASK FORCE ON TEACHING AS A PROFESSION (1986) *A Nation Prepared: Teacher for the Twenty-first Century*, New York, NY: Carnegie Task Force on Teaching as a Profession.

CHENG, Y.C. (1985) 'Organizational climate in Hong Kong aided secondary schools', *Education Journal*, **13**, 2, pp. 49–55.

CHENG, Y.C. (1986a) 'A framework of curriculum effectiveness' (in Chinese), *Education Journal*, **14**, 1, pp. 30–36.

CHENG, Y.C. (1986b) 'School effectiveness as related to organizational climate and leadership style', *Educational Research Journal*, **1**, pp. 86–94.

CHENG, Y.C. (1987a) 'A study of school organizational environment and teachers' professional behaviours', *Educational Research Journal*, **2**, pp. 13–16.

CHENG, Y.C. (1987b, November) 'Effectiveness of science teaching in contributing to civic education: What teaching strategies', *New Horizons*, **28**, pp. 129–41.

CHENG, Y.C. (1987c) 'School process and effectiveness of civic education' (in Chinese), *Education Journal*, **15**, 2, pp. 11–17.

CHENG, Y.C. (1989) 'Organizational culture: Development of a theoretical framework for organizational research', *Education Journal*, **17**, 2, pp. 128–47.

CHENG, Y.C. (1990a) 'An investigation of antecedents of organizational commitment', *Educational Research Journal*, **5**, pp. 29–42.

CHENG, Y.C. (1990b) 'Conception of school effectiveness and models of school evaluation: A dynamic perspective', *Education Journal*, **18**, 1, pp. 47–61.

CHENG, Y.C. (1990c, September) *The Relationship of Job Attitudes and Organizational Commitment to Different Aspects of Organizational Environment* (Microfiche, 1–45). (ERIC Document Reproduction Service No. ED318-779). Arlington, VA: ERIC.

CHENG, Y.C. (1990d, November) 'Management strategy and school improvement: Looking forward to a new decade' (in Chinese), *New Horizons*, **31**, pp. 62–7.

CHENG, Y.C. (1991a) *Function and Effectiveness of Education* (2nd ed, in Chinese), Hong Kong: Wide Angle.

CHENG, Y.C. (1991b) 'Leadership style of principals and organizational process in Hong Kong secondary schools', *Journal of Educational Administration*, **29**, 2, pp. 25–37.

CHENG, Y.C. (1991c) 'Organizational environment in schools: Commitment, control, disengagement and headless', *Educational Administration Quarterly*, **27**, 4, pp. 481–505.

CHENG, Y.C. (1991d) 'Strategies for conceptualizing school administration research: An effectiveness approach', *Education Journal*, **19**, 1, pp. 69–81.

CHENG, Y.C. (1991e) 'Teachers' job attitudes and school's organizational attributes: A school-level analysis', in HO, W.K. and WONG, R.Y.L. (Eds) *Improving the Quality of the Teaching Profession: An International Perspective*, Arlington, VA: International Council on Education for Teaching, pp. 621–34.

CHENG, Y.C. (1991f) 'The theory of school-based management and external control management' (in Chinese), *Primary Education*, **1**, 1, pp. 3–18.

CHENG, Y.C. (1991g, May) 'The meaning and function of parental involvement in schools' (in Chinese), *ICAC Periodical for Schools*, pp. 1–2.

CHENG, Y.C. (1991h, September) 'School-based management and school management initiative' (in Chinese), *Modern Educational Bulletin*, **19**, pp. 3–9.

CHENG, Y.C. (1992a) 'A preliminary study of school management initiative: Responses to induction and implementation of management reforms', *Educational Research Journal*, **7**, pp. 21–32.

CHENG, Y.C. (1992b) 'A theory of teacher education network' (in Chinese), *Education Journal*, **20**, 1, pp. 17–24.

CHENG, Y.C. (1992c) 'A study of teachers' professionalism in Hong Kong primary schools: Antecedents and consequences' (in Chinese), *Primary Education*, **2**, 2, pp. 11–21.

CHENG, Y.C. (1992d, September) 'An analysis of effectiveness of the recommendations of education commission', Report no. 5 (in Chinese), *Modern Education Bulletin*, **23**, pp. 43–8.

CHENG, Y.C. (1992e, September) 'School improvement and school effectiveness research in Hong Kong', *International Network News*, **2**, 3, pp. 2–3.

CHENG, Y.C. (1993a) 'A mechanism for school-based curriculum change' (in Chinese), *Journal of Primary Education*, **4**, 1, pp. 11–20.

CHENG, Y.C. (1993b) 'A study of principal's leadership in Hong Kong primary schools', *Primary Education*, **3**, 2, pp. 15–26.

CHENG, Y.C. (1993c) *Module 1: Meaning and Principles of SMI and Effective Schools*, (training packages for supervisors, principals, and assistant principals of school management initiative schools). Hong Kong: The Chinese University of Hong Kong.

CHENG, Y.C. (1993d) *Module 2: Planning and Structuring for Development and Effectiveness*, (training packages for supervisors, principals, and assistant principals of school management initiative schools). Hong Kong: The Chinese University of Hong Kong.

CHENG, Y.C. (1993e) *Module 3: Staff Development and Appraisal for Development and Performance*, (training packages for supervisors, principals, and assistant principals of school management initiative schools). Hong Kong: The Chinese University of Hong Kong.

CHENG, Y.C. (1993f) *Module 4: Monitoring School Effectiveness*, (training packages for supervisors, principals, and assistant principals of school management initiative schools). Hong Kong: The Chinese University of Hong Kong.

CHENG, Y.C. (1993g) *Module 5: Leadership and Management of Change*, (training packages for supervisors, principals, and assistant principals of school management initiative schools). Hong Kong: The Chinese University of Hong Kong.

CHENG, Y.C. (1993h) 'Profiles of organizational culture and effective schools', *School Effectiveness and School Improvement: An International Journal of Research, Policy, and Practice*, **4**, 2, pp. 85–110.

CHENG, Y.C. (1993i) 'The theory and characteristics of school-based management', *International Journal of Educational Management*, **7**, 6, pp. 6–17.

CHENG, Y.C. (1993j, April) 'The conceptualization and measurement of school effectiveness: An organizational perspective', Paper presented at the Annual Conference of the American Educational Research Association, Atlanta, USA.

CHENG, Y.C. (1993k, April) 'The strength of principal's leadership: The structural, human, political, symbolic and educational dimensions', (Occasional Paper No. 20), Cambridge, MA: Harvard University, National Center for Educational Leadership, pp. 1–24.

CHENG, Y.C. (1993l, September) 'The characteristics of school-based management: Measurement and profile', Paper presented at the annual conference of the British Educational Research Association, Liverpool, UK.

CHENG, Y.C. (1994a) 'Classroom environment and student affective performance: An effective profile', *Journal of Experimental Education*, **62**, 3, pp. 221–39.

CHENG, Y.C. (1994b) 'Education and development of people and nation: A chain-reaction model proposal', *Proceedings of the Second Academic Research Conference on Modernization of China, The National Institute of Social Science (mainland China) and the Academic Research Foundation of Promoting China Modernization (Taiwan)*, Beijing, pp. 1–24.

CHENG, Y.C. (1994c) 'Effectiveness of curriculum change in school: An organizational perspective', *International Journal of Educational Management*, **8**, 3, pp. 26–34.

CHENG, Y.C. (1994d) 'Principal's leadership as a critical indicator of school performance: Evidence from multi-levels of primary schools', *School Effectiveness and School Improvement: An International Journal of Research, Policy, and Practice*, **5**, 3, pp. 299–317.

CHENG, Y.C. (1994e, December) 'Profile of education quality of primary schools: Multi-levels and multi-indicators', Paper presented at the annual conference of the British Educational Research Association, Oxford, UK.

CHENG, Y.C. (1994f, January) 'School effectiveness and school-based management: A mechanism for education quality and school development', Keynote speech presented at the International Congress for School Effectiveness and Improvement, Melbourne, Australia.

CHENG, Y.C. (1994g) 'Teacher leadership style: A classroom-level study', *Journal of Educational Administration*, **32**, 3, pp. 54–71.

CHENG, Y.C. (1994h) 'Teacher's locus of control as an indicator of teacher's job attitudes and perceived organizational factors', *Journal of Educational Research*, **87**, 3, pp. 180–8.

CHENG, Y.C. (1994i, June) 'A school-based management mechanism for school effectiveness and development in Hong Kong', Keynote speech presented at the Conference on School Effectiveness and Improvement, Hong Kong.

CHENG, Y.C. (1994j, September) 'The effective classrooms: Performance, environment, and family experience', Paper presented at the annual conference of the British Educational Research Association, Oxford, UK.

CHENG, Y.C. (1995a) 'School educational quality: Conceptualization, monitoring, and enhancement', in SIU, P.K. and TAM, T.K.P. (Eds) *Quality in Education: Insights from Different Perspectives*, Hong Kong: Hong Kong Educational Research Association, pp. 123–47.

CHENG, Y.C. (1995b) 'School effectiveness and improvement in Hong Kong, Taiwan, and mainland China', in CREEMERS, B.H.M. and OSINGA, N. (Eds) *ICSEI Country Reports*, Netherlands: Gemeenschappeli jk Centrum voor Onderwijsbegeleiding in Friesland, Leeuwarden, pp. 11–30.

CHENG, Y.C. (in press, a) 'Monitoring educational quality in school' (in Chinese), *Modern Educational Bulletin*, **36**.

CHENG, Y.C. (in press, b) 'School educational quality and school management initiative' (in Chinese), *Modern Educational Bulletin*.

CHENG, Y.C. (in press, c) 'Teachers' professionalism as related to job attitudes, educational outcomes and organizational characteristics', *Journal of Educational Research*.

CHENG, Y.C. (in press, d) 'Management and effectiveness of moral and civic education in school: A framework for research and practice', in LO, L.N.K. and MAN, S.W. (Eds) *Recent Research in Moral and Civic Education*, Hong Kong: Hong Kong Institute of Educational Research, The Chinese University of Hong Kong.

CHENG, Y.C. (in press, e) *The Pursuit of School Effectiveness: Research, Management, and Policy*, Hong Kong: Hong Kong Institute of Educational Research, The Chinese University of Hong Kong.

CHENG, Y.C. and CHAN, B. (1987) ' "Non-intervention" management and school administration' (in Chinese), *The Chinese Journal of Administration*, **42**, pp. 36–45.

CHENG, Y.C. and CHAN, B. (1992) 'The management thought of Lao Tzu: Implications for management of modern organizations' (in Chinese), in the Graduate School of Philosophy of National Central University (Ed), *Articles on Management and Philosophy*, Taipei, Taiwan, pp. 253–73.

CHENG, Y.C. and CHEUNG, W.M. (in press) 'A framework for the analysis of educational policy', *International Journal of Educational Management*.

CHENG, Y.C. and NG, K.H. (1991a) 'School organisational change — Theory, strategy, and technology' (in Chinese), *Education Journal*, **19**, 2, pp. 133–44.

CHENG, Y.C. and NG, K.H. (1991b) 'The characteristics of effective classrooms' (in Chinese), *Primary Education*, **2**, 1, pp. 1–10.

CHENG, Y.C. and NG, K.H. (1992) 'The analysis of the economic aspect of educational policy: A preliminary framework' (in Chinese), *Primary Education*, **3**, 1, pp. 55–64.

CHENG, Y.C. and NG, K.H. (1994) 'School management initiative and strategic management' (in Chinese), *Journal of Primary Education*, **4**, 2, pp. 1–15.

CHENG, Y.C. and TAM, W.M. (1994) 'A theory of school-based staff development: Development matrix' (in Chinese), *Education Journal*, **22**, 2, pp. 221–36.

CHEUNG, W.M. and CHENG, Y.C. (in press) 'A multi-level framework for self-management in school', *International Journal of Educational Management*.

CHILD, J. (1972) 'Organizational structure, environment and performance: The role of strategic choice', *Sociology*, **6**, pp. 1–22.

COHEN, M. (1988) *Restructuring the Education System: Agenda for the 1990s*, Washington, DC: National Governors' Association.

COLLARD, J.L. and CARLIN, P. (1994, January) 'Whole school planning: A strategic mechanism for school improvement and effectiveness', Paper presented at the International Congress for School Effectiveness and Improvement, Melbourne, Australia.

COLLINS, R. (1971) 'Functional and conflict theories of educational stratification', *American Sociological Review*, **36**, pp. 1002–19.

COLLINS, R.A. and HANSON, M.K. (1991) *Summative Evaluation Report School-based Management/Shared Decision making Project 1987–88 through 1989–90*. Miami, FL: Dade County Public Schools.

COMBS, A.W. (1988) 'New assumptions for educational reform', *Educational Leadership*, **45**, pp. 38–40.

CONGER, J.A., KANUNGO, R.N. and ASSOCIATES (1988) *Charismatic Leadership*, San Francisco, CA: Jossey-Bass.

CONLEY, S. and BACHARACH, S. (1990) 'From school-site management to participatory school-site management', *Phi Delta Kappan*, **71**, 7, pp. 539–44.

CORBETT, H.D., FIRESTONE, W.A. and ROSSMAN, G.B. (1987) 'Resistance to planned change and the sacred in school culture', *Educational Administration Quarterly*, **23**, 4, pp. 36–59.

COVEY, S.R. (1989) *The Seven Habits of Highly Effective Leadership*, New York: Simon & Schuster.

CRANDALL, D.P., EISEMAN, J.W. and LOUIS, K.S. (1986) 'Strategic planning issues that bear on the success of school improvement efforts', *Educational Administration Quarterly*, **22**, pp. 21–53.

CREEMERS, B.P.M. (1994) *The Effective Classroom*, London: Cassell.

CROSBY, P.B. (1979) *Quality is Free*, New York: New American Library.

CUTTANCE, P. (1994) 'Monitoring educational quality through performance indicators for school practice', *School Effectiveness and School Improvement*, **5**, 2, pp. 101–26.

CUTTANCE, P. (1995, January) 'Building high performance school systems', Keynote address at the International Congress for School Effectiveness and Improvement, Leeuwarden, the Netherlands.

DAVID, J.L. (1989) 'Synthesis of research on school-based management', *Educational Leadership*, **46**, 8, pp. 45–53.

DEAL, T.E. and CELOTTI, L.D. (1980) 'How much influence do (and can) educational administrators have on classrooms?', *Phi Delta Kappan*, **61**, pp. 471–3.

DEAL, T.E. and KENNEDY, A.A. (1982) *Corporate Cultures: The Rite and Rituals of Corporate Life*, Reading, MA: Addison-Wesley.

DEAL, T.E. and PETERSON, K.D. (1990) *The Principal's Role in Shaping School Culture*, Washington, DC: US Government Printing Office.

DEMPSTER, N., SACHS, J., DISTANT, G., LOGAN, L. and TOM, C. (1993, January) 'Planning in primary schools: A national study in Australian schools', Paper presented at the International Congress for School Effectiveness and Improvement, Norrkoping, Sweden.

DIMMOCK, C. (Ed) (1993) *School-based Management and School Effectiveness*, London: Routledge.

DONOVAN, M. (1989) 'Employees who manage themselves', *Journal for Quality and Participation*, **12**, 1, pp. 58–61.

DUNHAM, R.B. and PIERCE, J.L. (1989) *Management*, Glenview, IL: Scott, Foresman.

DYER, W.G. (1987) *Team Building: Issues and Alternatives* (2nd ed), MA: Addison-Wesley.

EDUCATION AND MANPOWER BRANCH (1993) *School Education in Hong Kong: A Statement of Aims*, Hong Kong: The Government Printer.

EDUCATION AND MANPOWER BRANCH AND EDUCATION DEPARTMENT (1991) *School Management Initiative: Setting the Framework for Education Quality in Hong Kong Schools*, Hong Kong: The Government Printer.

EDUCATION COMMISSION (1984) *Education Commission Report No. 1*, Hong Kong: The Government Printer.

EDUCATION COMMISSION (1986) *Education Commission Report No. 2*, Hong Kong: The Government Printer.

EDUCATION COMMISSION (1988) *Education Commission Report No. 3*, Hong Kong: The Government Printer.

EDUCATION COMMISSION (1990) *Education Commission Report No. 4*, Hong Kong: The Government Printer.

EDUCATION COMMISSION (1992) *Education Commission Report No. 5*, Hong Kong: The Government Printer.

EDUCATION COMMISSION (1993, October 21) *Education Commission Sets up Working Groups* (press release) Hong Kong: The Government Information Office.

EDUCATION COMMISSION (1994) *Working Group Report on Education Standards*, Hong Kong: The Government Printer.

ERAUT, M. (1993) 'The characterisation and development of professional expertise in school management and in teaching', *Educational Management and Administration*, **21**, 4, pp. 223–32.

ETZIONI, A. (1969) 'Two approaches to organizational analysis', in SCHULBERG, H.C. *et al.* (Eds) *Program Evaluation in the Health Fields*, New York: Behavioral Publications.

FARNHAM-DIGGORY, S. (1994) 'Paradigms of knowledge and instruction', *Review of Educational Research*, **64**, 3, pp. 463–77.

FIEDLER, F.E. (1967) *A Theory of Leadership Effectiveness*, New York: McGraw-Hill.

FIEDLER, F.E. (1971) 'Validation and extension of the contingency model of leadership effectiveness: A review of empirical findings', *Psychological Bulletin*, **76**, pp. 128–48.

FIRESTONE, W.A. and CORBETT, H.D. (1988) 'Planned organizational change', in BOYAN, N. (Ed) *Handbook of Research on Educational Administration*, New York: Longman.

FISHER, D.C. (1994) *Measuring up to the Baldrige*, New York: American Management Association.

FRASER, B.J. (1992) 'Developments and changes in the study of learning environments: Looking back, sideways, and forward', in WAXMAN, H.C. and ELLETT, C.D. (Eds) *The Study of Learning Environments* (**5**) Houston, TX: College of Education, University of Houston, pp. 1–20.

FRASER, B.J. and FISHER, D.L. (1990, April) 'Validity and use of the school-level environment questionnaire', Paper presented at the annual meeting of the American Educational Research Association, Chicago, IL.

FRASER, B.J. and WALBERG, H.J. (Eds) (1991) *Educational Environments: Evaluation, Antecedents and Consequences*, Oxford, UK: Pergamon Press.

FRENCH, J.R.P. and RAVEN, B. (1968) 'The bases of social power', in CARTWRIGHT, D. and ZANDER, A. (Eds) *Group Dynamics* (3rd ed), New York: Harper & Row, pp. 259–69.

FULLAN, M. (1991) *The New Meaning of Educational Change* (2nd ed), London: Cassell.

FULLAN, M. (1992) *The New Meaning of Educational Change*, New York: Teachers College Press.

FULLAN, M. and HARGREAVES, A. (Eds) (1992) *Teacher Development and Educational Change*, London: The Falmer Press.

GATTIKER, U.E. (1990) *Technology Management in Organizations*, Thousand Oaks, CA: Sage.

GEORGE, S. (1992) *The Baldrige Quality System*, New York: Wiley.

GIROUX, H. (1981) *Ideology, Culture, and the Process of Schooling*, Lewes, UK: Falmer Press.

GOLDRING, E.B. and RALLIS, S.F. (1993, April) 'Principals as environmental leaders: The external link for facilitating change', Paper presented at the annual meeting of the American Educational Research, Atlanta, GA: USA.

GRAEN, G.B. and UHL-BIEN, M. (1991a) 'The transformation of professionals into self-managing and partially self-designing contributors: Towards a theory of leadership-making', *Journal of Management Systems*, **3**, 3, pp. 25–39.

GRAEN, G.B. and UHL-BIEN, M. (1991b) 'Leadership-making applies equally well to sponsors, competence networks and teammates', *Journal of Management Systems*, **3**, 3, pp. 75–80.

GREENLEY, G.E. (1986) 'Does strategic planning improve company performance?' *Long Range Planning*, **19**, 2, p. 106.

GREENWOOD, M.S. and GAUNT, H.J. (1994) *Total Quality Management for Schools*, London: Cassell.

GREINER, L.E. and SCHEIN, V.E. (1989) *Power and Organization Development: Mobilizing Power to Implement Change*, Reading, MA: Addison-Wesley.

GRIFT, W. VAN DE (1990) 'Educational leadership and academic achievement in elementary education', *School Effectiveness and School Improvement*, **1**, 3, pp. 26–40.

GROSIN, L. (1994, January) 'Do effective schools contribute to greater equity?', Paper presented at the International Congress for School Effectiveness and Improvement, Melbourne, Australia.

HACKMAN, J.R. (1976) 'Group influences on individuals in organizations', in DUNNETTE, M.D. (Ed) *Handbook of Industrial and Organizational Psychology*, Chicago IL: Rand-McNally, pp. 1455–1525.

HACKMAN, J.R. (1985) 'Doing research that makes a difference', in LAWLER, E.E. *et al.* (Eds) *Doing Research that is Useful for Theory and Practice*, San Francisco, CA: Jossey-Bass.

HACKMAN, J.R. (1986) 'The psychology of self-management in organization', in POLLACK, M.S. and PERLOFF, R.O. (Eds) *Psychology and Work: Productivity, Change and Employment*, Washington, DC: American Psychological Association, pp. 85–136.

HACKMAN, J.R. (1987) 'The design of work teams', in LORSCH, J.W. (Ed) *Handbook of Organizational Behavior*, Englewood Cliffs, NJ: Prentice-Hall, pp. 315–42.

HACKMAN, J.R. and OLDMAN, G. (1976) 'Motivation, through the design of work: Test of a theory', *Organizational Behavior and Human Performance*, **16**, 2, pp. 250–79.

HACKMAN, J.R. and WALTON, R.E. (1986) 'Leading groups in organizations', in GOODMAN, P.S. (Ed) *Designing Effective Work Groups*, San Francisco, CA: Jossey-Bass, pp. 72–119.

HAGE, J. and AIKEN, M. (1967) 'Program change and organizational properties: A comparative analysis', *American Journal of Sociology*, **72**, pp. 503–19.

HALL, R.P. (1987) *Organizations: Structures, Processes and Outcomes*, Englewood Cliffs, NJ: Prentice-Hall.

HALLINGER, P. and MURPHY, J.F. (1987) 'Assessing and developing principal instructional leadership', *Educational Leadership*, **45**, 1, pp. 54–61.

HALPIN, A.W. (1966) *Theory and Research in Administration*, New York: Macmillan.

HAMBRICK, D.C. (1989) 'Strategic leadership' [Special issue], *Strategic Management Journal*, **10**(s), pp. 1–172.

HAMPTON, D.R., SUMMER, C.E. and WEBBER, R.A. (1987) *Organizational Behavior and the Practice of Management* (5th ed) Glenview, IL: Scott, Foresman.

HANNAN, M.T. and FREEMAN, J. (1977) 'Obstacles to comparative studies', in GOODMAN, P.S. and PENNINGS, J.M. (Eds), *New Perspectives on Organizational Effectiveness*, San Francisco, CA: Jossey-Bass, pp. 106–31.

HARDING, S. and PHILLIPS, D. (1986) *Contrasting Values in Western Europe: Unity, Diversity, Change*, London: Macmillan.

HARGREAVES, A. (1994) *Changing Teachers, Changing Times*, New York: Teachers College Press.

HARGREAVES, D.H. and HOPKINS, D. (1991) *The Empowered School*, London, Cassell.

HERSEY, P. and BLANCHARD, K.H. (1972) *Management of Organizational Behavior: Utilizing Human Resources* (2nd ed), Englewood Cliffs, NJ: Prentice-Hall.

HERSH, R.H., MILLER, J.P. and FIELDING, G.D. (1980) *Models of Moral Education: An Appraisal*, New York: Longman.

HERZBERG, F. (1966) *Work and Nature of Man*, Cleveland, OH: World Publishing.

HILL, P.T. and BONAN, J. (1991) *Decentralization and Accountability in Public Education*, Washington, DC: Rand.

HINCHLIFFE, K. (1987) 'Education and the labor market', in PSACHAROPOULOS, G. (Ed) *Economics of Education: Research and Studies*, Kidlington, Oxford: Pergamon Press, pp. 315–23.

HOLT, D.H. (1990) *Management: Principles and Practices*, Englewood Cliffs, NJ: Prentice-Hall.

HOUSE, R.J. (1971) 'A path-goal theory of leadership effectiveness', *Administrative Science Quarterly*, **16**, pp. 321–38.

HOUSE, E.R. (1981) 'Three perspectives on educational innovation: Technological, political and cultural', in LEHMING, R. and KANE, M. (Eds) *Improving Schools: Using What We Know*, Beverly Hills, CA: Sage.

HOY, W.K. (1994) 'Foundations of educational administration: Traditional and emerging perspective', *Educational Administration Quarterly*, **30**, 2, pp. 178–98.

HOY, W.K. and MISKEL, C.G. (1991) *Educational Administration* (4th ed), New York: Random House.

HUGHES, P. (Ed) (1988) *The Challenge of Identifying and Marketing Quality in Education*, Sydney, Australia: The Australian Association of Senior Educational Administrators.

HUGHES, B. (1991) '25 stepping stones for self-directed work teams', *Training*, **28**, 12, pp. 44–6.

JENNI, R.W. (1991) 'Application of the school-based management process development model', *School Effectiveness and School Improvement*, **2**, 2, pp. 136–51.

JONES, B. and MALOY, R.W. (1988) *Partnerships for Improving Schools*, New York: Greenwood Press.

JONES, D.C. and MEURS, M. (1991) 'Worker participation and worker self-management in Bulgaria', *Comparative Economic Studies*, **33**, 4, pp. 47–81.

JOYCE, B. (1989) 'Staff development as cultural change', Paper presented at the International Conference on school-based innovation: Looking forward to the 1990s, University of Hong Kong, Hong Kong.

KATZ, D. and KAHN, R.L. (1978) *The Social Psychology of Organizations* (2nd ed), New York: Wiley.

KAZAMIAS, A.M. and SCHWARTZ, K. (1997) 'Intellectual and ideological perspectives in comparative education: An interpretation', *Comparative Educational Review*, **21**, pp. 153–76.

KEELEY, M. (1984) 'Impartiality and participant-interest: Theories of organizational effectiveness', *Administrative Science Quarterly*, **29**, pp. 1–25.

KENZEVICH, S. (1975) *Administration of Public Education* (3rd ed), New York: Harper & Row.

KLUCKHOHN, F.R. and STRODTBECK, F.L. (1961) *Variations in Value Orientations*, Evanston, IL: Row, Peterson. Longman.

LATHAM, G.P. and LOCKE, E.A. (1991) 'Self-regulation through goal setting', *Organizational Behavior and Human Decision Processes*, **50**, 2, pp. 212–47.

LAUGHLIN, R.C. (1991) 'Environmental disturbances and organizational transitions and transformations: Some alternative models', *Organization Studies*, **12**, 2, pp. 209–32.

LEVITT, B. and MARCH, J.G. (1988) 'Organizational learning', *Annual Review of Sociology*, **14**, pp. 319–40.

LEVY, A. (1986) 'Second-order planned change: Definition and conceptualization', *Organizational Dynamics*, **38**, 7, pp. 583–6.

LEWIN, K. (1952) 'Group decision and social change', in SWANSON, G.E. *et al.* (Eds), *Readings in Social Psychology*, New York: Holt, Rinehart and Winston, pp. 459–73.

LIEBERMAN, A. (Ed) (1988) *Building a Professional Culture in Schools*, New York: Teachers College Press, Columbia University.

LIEBERMAN, A., SAZL, E.R. and MILES, M.B. (1988) 'Teacher leadership: Ideology and practice', in LIEBERMAN, A. (Ed) *Building a Professional Culture in Schools*, New York: Teachers College Press.

LIKERT, R. (1961) *New Patterns of Management*, New York: McGraw-Hill.

LIKERT, R. (1967) *The Human Organization*, New York: McGraw-Hill.

LIPHAM, J.A. (1964) 'Leadership and administration', in GRIFFITHS, D. (Ed)

Behavioral Science and Educational Administration, Sixty-third yearbook of the National Society for the Study of Education, Chicago: University of Chicago Press, pp. 119–41.

LITTLE, J.W. (1982) 'Norms of collegiality and experimentation: Workplace conditions of school success', *Educational Research Journal*, **19**, 3, pp. 325–40.

LOCKHEED, M.E. (1988, April) 'The measurement of educational efficiency and effectiveness', Paper presented at the annual meeting of the American Educational Research Association, New Orleans.

LORR, M., SUZIEDELIS, A. and TONESK, X. (1973) 'The structure of values: Conceptions of the desirable', *Journal of Research in Personality*, **7**, pp. 137–47.

LOUIS, K. and MILES, M. (1990) *Improving the Urban High School: What Works and Why*, New York: Teachers College Press.

LOUIS, K.S. (1994) 'Beyond "managed change": Rethinking how school improve', *School Effectiveness and School Improvement*, **5**, 1, pp. 2–24.

LUNDBERG, C. (1989) 'On organizational learning: Implications and opportunities for expanding organizational development', *Research in Organizational Change and Development*, **3**, pp. 61–82.

MACKENZIE, R.A. (1969, November–December) 'The management process in 3-D', *Harvard Business Review*, pp. 80–7.

MCCONKEY, D.D. (1989) 'Are you an administrator, a manager, or a leader?', *Business Horizons*, **32**, 5, pp. 15–21.

MCGREGOR, D. (1960) *The Human Side of Enterprise*, New York: McGraw-Hill.

MCKENNA, B.H. (1973) 'A context for teacher evaluation', *National Elementary Principal*, **52**, 5, pp. 22–31.

MCMAHON, W.W. (1987) 'Consumption and other benefits of education', in PSACHAROPOULOS, G. (Ed) *Economics of Education: Research and Studies*, Kidlington, Oxford: Pergamon Press, pp. 129–33.

MAEROFF, G.I. (1993) *Team Building for School Change*, New York: Teachers College Press, Columbia University.

MALEN, B., OGAWA, R.T. and KRANZ, J. (1990) 'What do we know about school-based management? A case study of the literature — A call for research', in CLUNE, W.H. and WITTE, J.F. (Eds) *Choice and Control in American Education (Vol. 2): The Practice of Choice Decentralization and School Restructuring*, London: Falmer Press, Chapter 8.

MANPOWER AND EDUCATION BRANCH AND EDUCATION DEPARTMENT (1991) *School Management Initiative: Setting the Framework for Education Quality in Hong Kong Schools*, Hong Kong: The Government Printer.

MANZ, C.C. (1983) *The Art of Self-leadership*, Englewood Cliffs, NJ: Prentice-Hall.

MANZ, C.C. (1986) 'Self-leadership: Toward an expanded self-influence processes in organizations', *Academy of Management Review*, **11**, pp. 585–600.

MANZ, C.C. (1991) 'Leading self-managed employees: Some issues and challenges', *Journal of Management Systems*, **3**, 3, pp. 67–73.

MANZ, C.C. and SIMS, H.P. (1987) 'Leading workers to lead themselves: The external leadership of self-managing work teams', *Administrative Science Quarterly*, **32**, pp. 106–28.

MANZ, C.C. and SIMS, H.P. (1990) *Super Leadership*, New York: Berkley Book.

MASLOW, A.H. (1943) 'A theory of human motivation', *Psychological Review*, **50**, pp. 370–96.

MASLOW, A.H. (1970) *Motivation and Personality* (2nd ed), New York: Harper & Row.

MAYO, E. (1945) *The Social Problems of an Industrial Civilization*, Boston, MA: Harvard Graduate School of Business.

MISKEL, G., MCDONALD, D. and BLOOM, S. (1983) 'Structural and expectancy linkages within schools and organizational effectiveness', *Educational Administration Quarterly*, **19**, 1, pp. 49–82.

MITCHELL, D. (1991) 'Monitoring today's schools: A scorecard after eighteen months', *New Zealand Journal of Educational Administration*, **6**, pp. 48–61.

MOHRMAN, S.A., WOHLSTETTER, P. and ASSOCIATES (Eds) (1994) *School-based Management: Organizing for High Performance*, San Francisco, CA: Jossey-Bass.

MOOS, R.H. and TRICKETT, E.J. (1974) *Classroom Environment Scale Manual*, Palo Alto, CA: Consulting Psychologists Press.

MORTIMORE, P. (1993, January) 'School effectiveness and the management of effective learning and teaching', Paper presented at the International Congress for School Effectiveness and Improvement, Norrkoping, Sweden.

MOTT, P.E. (1972) *The Characteristics of Effective Organizations*, New York: Harper & Row.

MURGATROYD, S. and MORGAN, C. (1993) *Total Quality Management and the School*, Buckingham, UK: Open University Press.

NADLER, D.A. and TUSHMAN, M.L. (1983) 'A general diagnostic model for organizational behavior: Applying a congruence perspective', in HACKMAN, R.J. LAWLER III, E.E. and PORTER, L.W. (Eds) *Perspectives on Behavior in Organizations*, New York: McGraw-Hill, pp. 112–26.

NATIONAL EDUCATION GOALS PANEL (1992) *The 1992 National Education Goals Report*, Washington, DC: National Education Goals Panel.

NEWMANN, F.M., RUTTER, R.A. and SMITH, M.S. (1989) 'Organizational factors that affect school sense of efficacy, community and expectations', *Sociology of Education*, **62**, pp. 221–38.

NG, K.H. and CHENG, Y.C. (in press) 'Research on school organizational changes: Approaches and strategies' (in Chinese), *Educational Research Journal*.

NOORI, H. (1990) *Managing the Dynamics of New Technology: Issues in Manufacturing Management*, Englewood Cliffs, NJ: Prentice Hall.

NOVAK, M.A. (1991) 'Toward a model for leading self-managing individuals', *Journal of Management Systems*, **3**, 3, pp. 1–13.

ODIORNE, G.S. (1991) 'The new breed of supervisor: Leaders in self-managed work teams', *Supervision*, **52**, 8, pp. 14–17.

OLDHAM, G.R. and HACKMAN, J.R. (1981) 'Relationships between organizational structure and employees reactions: Comparing alternative frameworks', *Administrative Science Quarterly*, **26**, pp. 66–83.

OLDROYD, D. and HALL, V. (1991) *Managing Staff Development: A Handbook for Secondary Schools*, London: Paul Chapman.

OWENS, R.G. (1991) *Organizational Behavior in Education* (4th ed), Englewood Cliffs, NJ: Prentice-Hall.

PARSONS, T. (1966) *Societies*, Englewood Cliffs, NJ: Prentice-Hall.

PETERS, T.J. and WATERMAN, R.H., JR. (1982) *In Search of Excellence*, New York: Harper and Row.

PRICE, J.L. and MUELLER, C.M. (1986) *Handbook of Organizational Measurement*, London: Pitman Publishing Inc.

PROVENZO, E.F., JR. (1989) 'School-based management and shared-decision making in the Dade County public schools', in ROSOW, J.M. and ZAGER, R. (Eds) *Allies in Educational Reform*, San Francisco, CA: Jossey-Bass, pp. 146–63.

PSACHAROPOLOUS, G. (Ed) (1987) *Economics of Education: Research and Studies*, Oxford, UK: Pergamon Press.

PUCKETT, J.H. (1989) 'Manufacturing excellence: A vision of the future', *Manufacturing Systems*, **7**, 4, pp. 50–1.

QUEENSLAND DEPARTMENT OF EDUCATION (1992) *Collaborative School Development Planning and Review*, Queensland: Publishing Services for Review and Evaluation Directorate.

QUINN, R.E. (1988) *Beyond Rational Management: Mastering the Paradoxes and Competing Demands of High Performance*, San Francisco, CA: Jossey-Bass.

QUINN, R.E. and CAMERON, K. (1983) 'Organizational life cycles and shifting criteria of effectiveness: Some preliminary evidence', *Management Science*, **29**, pp. 33–51.

RENIHAN, F.I. and RENIHAN, P.J. (1984) 'Effective schools, effective administration and effective leadership', *The Canadian Administrator*, **24**, 3, pp. 1–6.

ROBBINS, S. (1993) *Organizational Behavior* (6th ed), Englewood Cliffs, NJ: Prentice-Hall.

ROKEACH, M. (1973) *The Nature of Human Values*, New York: Free Press.

ROSOFF, B.L., WOOLFOLK, A.E. and HOY, W.K. (1991) 'Teacher's beliefs and student's motivation to learn', Paper presented at the annual meeting of the American Educational Research Association, Chicago, IL.

SALEM, M., LAZARUS, H. and CULLEN, J. (1992) 'Developing self-managing teams: Structure and performance', *The Journal of Management Development*, **11**, 3, pp. 24–32.

SANDY, W. (1990) 'Build organizational success around individual success', *Modern Office Technology*, **35**, 11, pp. 10–12.

SANKAR, Y. (1991) *Management of Technological Change*, New York: John Wiley & Sons.

SAUERS, D.A., HUNT, J.B. and BASS, K. (1990) 'Behavioral self-management as a supplement to external sales force controls', *Journal of Personal Selling and Sales Management*, **10**, 3, pp. 17–28.

SCHEERENS, J. (1990) 'School effectiveness research and the development of process indicators of school functioning', *School Effectiveness and School Improvement*, **1**, 1, pp. 61–80.

SCHEERNES, J. (1992) *Effective Schooling*, London: Cassell.

SCHEIN, E.H. (1980) *Organizational Psychology* (3rd ed), Englewood Cliffs, NJ: Prentice-Hall.

SCHEIN, E.H. (1992) *Organizational Culture and Leadership* (2nd ed), San Francisco, CA: Jossey-Bass.

SCHERMERHORN, J.R., JR. HUNT, J.G. and OSBORN, R.N. (1982) *Managing Organizational Behavior*, New York: John Wiley & Sons, Inc.

SCOTTISH EDUCATION DEPARTMENT (1991) *Management of Staff Development and Appraisal, Preliminary Unit. Management Training for Headteachers*, Scotland, UK: Scottish Office Education Department.

SELZNICK, P. (1957) *Leadership in Administration*, New York: Harper & Row.

SERGIOVANNI, T.J. (1984) *Handbook for Effective Department Leadership* (2nd ed), Newton, MA: Allyn and Bacon.

SERGIOVANNI, T.J. (1984) 'Leadership and excellence in schooling', *Educational Leadership*, **41**, 5, pp. 4–13.

SERGIOVANNI, T.J. (1990) *Value-added Leadership: How to Get Extraordinary Performance in Schools*, New York: Harcourt Brace Jovanovich.

SERGIOVANNI, T.J. (1992) *Moral Leadership*, San Francisco, CA: Jossey-Bass.

SERGIOVANNI, T.J., BURLINGAME, M., COOMBS, F.S. and THURSTON, P.W. (1992) *Educational Governance and Administration* (3rd ed), Boston, MA: Allyn & Bacon.

SERGIOVANNI, T.J. and STARRATT, R.J. (1993) *Supervision: A Redefinition* (5th ed), New York: McGraw-Hill.

SHULMAN, L.S. and CAREY, N.B. (1984) 'Psychology and the limitations of individual rationality: Implications for the study of reasoning and civility', *Review of Educational Research*, **54**, 4, pp. 501–24.

SILINS, H.C. (1992) 'Effective leadership for school reform', *The Alberta Journal of Educational Research*, **38**, 4, pp. 317–34.

SILINS, H.C. (1993, April) 'The relationship between school leadership and school improvement outcomes', Paper presented at the annual meeting of the American Education Research Association, Atlanta, GA.

SLATER, R.O. and TEDDLIE, C. (1990/2) 'Towards a theory of school effectiveness and leadership', *School Effectiveness and School Improvement*, **3**, 4, pp. 242–57.

SPARKS, D. and LOUCKS-HORSLEY, S. (1990) 'Models of staff development', in HOUSTON, W.R. *et al.* (Eds) *Handbook of Research on Teacher Education*, New York: Macmillan.

STEERS, R.M. (1977) *Organizational Effectiveness*, Santa Monica, CA: Goodyear.

STERN, G.G. (1970) *People in Context*, New York: Wiley.

STEWART, T.A. (1992) 'The search for the organization of tomorrow', *Fortune*, **125**, 10, pp. 92–8.

STOGDILL, R.M. (1950) 'Leadership, membership, and organization', *Psychological Bulletin*, **47**, pp. 1–14.

STOGDILL, R.M. (1974) *Handbook of Leadership*, New York: Free Press.

STOLL, L. and FINK, D. (1988) 'Educational change: An international perspective', *International Journal of Educational Management*, **23**, pp. 26–31.

STOLL, L. and FINK, D. (1992) 'Effecting school change: The Halton approach', *School Effectiveness and School Improvement*, **3**, 1, pp. 19–41.

STOLL, L. and FINK, D. (1994) 'School effectiveness and school improvement: Voices from the field', *School Effectiveness and School Improvement*, **5**, 2, pp. 149–77.

TAI, W.S. and CHENG, Y.C. (1994) 'The job characteristics of secondary school teachers', *Educational Research Journal*, **9**, 1, pp. 77–86.

TAM, W.M. and CHENG, Y.C. (in press, a) 'A typology of primary school environment: Synergetic, headless, mediocre, and disengaged', *Educational Administration and Management*.

TAM, W.M. and CHENG, Y.C. (in press, b) 'School environment and student performance: A multi-level analysis', *Educational Research Journal*.

TANNENBAUM, A. (1968) *Control in Organizations*, New York: McGraw-Hill.

TANNER, D. and TANNER, L.N. (1980) *Curriculum Development: Theory into Practice* (2nd ed), New York: Macmillan.

TAYLOR, F.W. (1947) *The Principles of Scientific Management*, New York: Harper.

TENNER, A.R. and DETORO, I.J. (1992) *Total Quality Management*, Reading, MA: Addison-Wesley.

THOMAS, R.M. (Ed) (1983) *Politics and Education: Cases from Eleven Nations*, Kidlington, UK: Pergamon.

TICHY, N.M. and ULRICH, D. (1984) 'The leadership challenge: A call for the transformational leader', *Sloan Management Review*, **26**, 1, pp. 59–68.

TJOSVOLD, D. (1992) *The Conflict-positive Organization: Stimulate Diversity and Create Unity*, Addison-Wesley.

TOWNSEND, T. (1994) 'Goals for effective schools: The view from the field', *School Effectiveness and School Improvement*, MA, **5**, 2, pp. 127–48.

URWICK, L. (1947) *Elements of Administration*, London, Sin Isaac: Pitman and Sons.

VALENTINE, J.W. (1992) *Principles and Practices for Effective Teacher Evaluation*, Boston, MA: Allyn & Bacon.

WALTON, R.E. (1985) 'From control to commitment: Transformation of workforce strategies in the United States', in CLARK, K.B., HAYES, R.H. and LORENZ, C. (Eds) *The Uneasy Alliance: Managing the Productivity-technology Dilemma*, Boston, MA: Harvard Business School.

WALTON, R.E. and HACKMAN, J.R. (1986) 'Groups under contrasting management strategies', in GOODMAN, P.S. (Ed) *Designing Effective Work Groups*, San Francisco, CA: Jossey-Bass.

WANG, M.C. and WALBERG, H.J. (1991) 'Teaching and educational effectiveness: Research synthesis and consensus from the field', in WAXMAN, H.C. and WALBERG, H.J. (Eds) *Effective Teaching: Current Research*, San Francisco, CA: McCutchan, pp. 81–104.

WARREN-PIPER, D. and GLATTER, R. (1977) *The Changing University*, Windsor, Ontario: National Foundation for Educational Research.

WEBER, M. (1947) *Theory of Social and Economic Organization*, in PARSONS, T. (Ed) HENDRASON, A.M. and PARSONS, T. (Trans.) New York, NY: Free Press.

WEICK, K.E. (1982) 'Administering education in loosely coupled schools', *Phi Delta Kappan*, **27**, pp. 673–6.

WHITESIDE, T. (1978) *The Sociology of Educational Innovation*, London: Methuen.

YUCHTMAN, E. and SEASHORE, S.E. (1967) 'A system resource approach to organizational effectiveness', *American Sociological Review*, **32**, pp. 891–903.

YUEN, B.Y. and CHENG, Y.C. (1991) 'A contingency study of principal's leadership behavior and teachers' organizational commitment', *Educational Research Journal*, **6**, pp. 53–62.

YUKL, G. (1994) *Leadership in Organizations* (3rd ed), Englewood Cliffs, NJ: Prentice-Hall.

ZALEZNIK, A. (1977) 'Managers and leaders: Are they different?', *Harvard Business Review*, **55**, 5, pp. 67–80.

ZAMMUTO, R.F. (1982) *Assessing Organizational Effectiveness*, Albany, NY: State University of New York Press.

ZAMMUTO, R.F. (1984) 'A comparison of multiple constituency models of organizational effectiveness', *Academy of Management Review*, **9**, 4, pp. 606–16.

Index